LABORATORY MANUAL

PRENTICE HALL

BIOLOGY
THE STUDY OF LIFE

Seventh Edition

LABORATORY MANUAL

BIOLOGY
THE STUDY OF LIFE

Seventh Edition

Warren B. Bjork

William D. Schraer

Ruth D. Horn

Herbert J. Stoltze

PRENTICE HALL
Upper Saddle River, New Jersey
Needham, Massachusetts

Credits

The Authors	Warren B. Bjork
	Ruth D. Horn
	William D. Schraer
	Herbert J. Stoltze

Outside Credits	Editorial Services	Susan G. Wilson
	Computer Consultant	Donald P. Kelley
	Design Services	Helen Reebenacker
	Fourth Edition Illustrations	Boston Graphics, Inc.

ISBN 0-13-435084-7

4 5 6 7 8 9 10   02 01

PRENTICE HALL
Upper Saddle River, New Jersey
Needham, Massachusetts

Contents

Safety in the Biology Laboratory

Laboratory work is an important part of your biology class. The work, however, may require you to handle strong chemicals, sharp instruments, hot materials, or expensive equipment. To prevent accidents, you need to act with care and observe all safety rules at all times.

General Safety Rules

Review these safety rules before starting a lab activity:

1. Know the location of emergency equipment, such as the first-aid kit, fire alarm, or fire extinguisher. Only use the equipment, however, if you are instructed to do so by your teacher.
2. Be familiar with how to leave the laboratory safely in an emergency. Be sure you know a safe exit route in the event of a fire or an explosion.
3. Be prepared for your lab exercise when you arrive in the laboratory. Read the directions for the lab activity beforehand, so that you will know what to do.
4. Do not bring any food or drink into the laboratory. Do not eat or drink out of any lab equipment.

Personal Safety Rules

Each person should follow these additional safety rules:

1. Inform your teacher of any medical problems that may affect your safety in doing lab work. Report allergies, asthma, sensitivity to certain chemicals, epilepsy, or a heart condition.
2. Wear clothing that will not present a safety hazard in the laboratory. Make sure articles of clothing will not interfere with laboratory work or be a fire hazard. Secure or take off a loose tie or jacket. Roll up long sleeves. Remove dangling jewelry.
3. Tie back or cover long hair.
4. Wear regular glasses instead of contact lenses. If you must wear contact lenses, notify your teacher and wear safety goggles to prevent accidents or loss of a contact lens.

Lab Safety Procedures

When working in the lab, follow these safety rules:

1. Understand the correct laboratory procedure to be used and be aware of possible hazards. Perform only those lab activities assigned and explained by your teacher. Listen carefully to your teacher's instructions and follow them exactly.
2. Keep work areas clean and neat at all times. Only textbooks, lab manuals, or notebooks should be in the work area. Allow enough time to clean and dry all work areas before the end of the lab session. Wash your hands thoroughly after the lab is completed and the area cleaned.
3. Report all accidents or unusual occurrences to your teacher immediately.

Safety Symbols

You should recognize the following safety symbols and know what they mean. In the event of an accident or unusual occurrence, remember to report it to your teacher immediately.

Safety Clothing Wear a lab apron or lab coat whenever working with materials that could damage your skin or clothing. For some activities, you may also need protective gloves. Wear safety clothing at all times during a specified laboratory activity.

Safety Goggles Use safety goggles in any lab activity involving chemicals, flames, or the possibility of broken glassware. Wear goggles at all times during these activities. Place them over eyeglasses to protect the sides of the eyes.

Fire Safety Tie hair back, roll up sleeves, and remove or secure loose clothing, such as ties, scarves, or jackets, that may get too close to a flame. Keep all flammable items away from the area of a flame or from an electrical source or appliance. Follow your teacher's instructions on how to light a burner safely. If you use matches, soak them in water before throwing them away. Never use organic solvents, such as ethanol or acetone, in the same room as a burner. Turn burners completely off when you have finished with them. When heating a test tube, point the open end away from yourself and others. Do not heat material in a stoppered test tube. If you do get burned, cool the area with cold water (not ice) and cover with a sterile dressing. If the burn results from chemicals, rinse the burned area under cold running water for 20 minutes. If the burn breaks the skin, if it is on the hands or face, or if it covers a large area, seek medical care immediately. Do not break any blisters that may develop from the burn.

Corrosive Substance Avoid letting any corrosive substance, such as a strong acid or base, touch your skin, eyes, or clothing. Wear protective clothing and goggles. Do not inhale vapors. Use a fume hood if vapors are dangerous. Never smell or taste chemicals in the laboratory. When mixing a strong acid with water, pour the acid into the water to keep it from splattering. Never pour the water into the acid. When labeling the contents of a container, label the empty container before adding the material. Dispose of all hazardous chemicals by putting them into a toxic-waste-disposal container. If a corrosive substance spills on you, immediately rinse the area under cold running water for 20 minutes. Get medical help if needed.

Breakage Handle breakable equipment, such as glassware, carefully. Do not use cracked, chipped, scored, or badly scratched glassware. Always lubricate glassware, such as tubing, with water or glycerin before trying to insert it into a stopper. Wear protective gloves and use a twisting motion when inserting lubricated glassware into a stopper. Do not plunge hot glassware into cold water or let empty glassware get too hot. Never leave any glassware unattended while it is being heated. Place hot glassware on an insulated surface. Remember that glass may remain hot for quite a while after it has been removed from a heat source, even though it may not look hot; handle it with caution. If glassware breaks, clean up the pieces immediately but not with your bare hands. Throw away the pieces in a special container marked "broken glass." If you are cut, rinse the area with soap and water and apply a sterile dressing. Use direct pressure and elevate the injured part to stop the bleeding. If the bleeding cannot be controlled, get medical help.

Hand Safety Dissect specimens in dissecting pans and never while holding the specimen in your hands. Make sure the specimen is pinned down firmly in a dissecting tray before beginning work. Direct sharp-edged instruments away from yourself and others. Use scissors instead of a scalpel whenever possible. Do not use too much force when working with a sharp instrument, such as a scalpel. Cut in a direction away from yourself and others. Do not use chipped or cracked glassware. Use protective gloves when working with hot materials or corrosive substances. If you cut yourself, wash the wound thoroughly with soap and water, control the bleeding, and place a sterile dressing over the wound. If you are burned, cool the burned area with cold water (not ice) and cover with a sterile dressing. If you cannot control the bleeding, or if the burn is large, deep, or on the face or hands, seek medical attention immediately.

Dangerous Vapors Use a fume hood when in the presence of dangerous vapors and avoid inhaling the vapors. When testing an odor, use a wafting motion of your hand to direct the vapor toward your nose. Never directly inhale any laboratory vapors. If you begin to get a headache or feel dizzy or weak, leave the room or open a window to get some fresh air.

Explosion Danger Avoid the danger of explosion by reading laboratory instructions carefully and following them exactly. Never look into the top of a container that is being heated. Do not bring any substance into contact with a flame unless instructed to do so. When heating a substance in a test tube, make sure the mouth of the tube is pointed away from yourself and others.

Poison Do not let a poisonous substance come into contact with your skin, do not swallow any of the substance, and do not breathe any of its vapors. If you accidentally come into contact with a poison, have someone call the local poison control center immediately, and follow their instructions exactly.

Electrical Shock Avoid electrical shock by reading laboratory instructions carefully and following them exactly. Disconnect all electrical equipment when not in use. Do not use any electrical equipment around water, or when the equipment is wet.

Biohazard Assume that any microorganisms, such as bacteria, might be hazardous. Treat microorganisms as directed by your teacher. Do not use preserved specimens showing any signs of decay for any type of lab observation or dissection. Avoid direct contact with a culture of microorganisms, and wash your hands thoroughly with soap and water after working with microorganisms.

Plant Safety Use a reliable field guide when collecting plants and fungi outdoors. Never eat any part of an unknown plant or fungus. Know how to recognize the poisonous plants and fungi in your area and avoid contact with them.

Animal Safety Before handling an animal, get professional advice about how to do so correctly. If you are bitten or scratched, wash the area thoroughly with soap and water, control the bleeding, and place a sterile dressing on the wound. Check with a physician to see whether you need a tetanus booster, especially if you have received a puncture wound. If you think the animal that injured you was poisonous, or if you show signs of an allergic reaction or infection, get medical attention immediately.

Animal Welfare Treat all animals in as humane a way as possible. Handle animals gently to avoid producing undue excitement or trauma. Avoid subjecting animals to stressful conditions, such as exhausting exercise or painful stimuli. Understand the purpose and procedure of an activity involving live animals before you begin work.

Hazardous Waste Disposal Dispose of all potentially hazardous materials in a special way as directed by your teacher. Do not place hazardous materials in the waste basket or wash them down the sink. Do not touch or attempt to clean up any mercury; if you break a thermometer, tell your teacher at once.

Water Safety When conducting experiments near bodies of water, always have a partner. Make sure a life preserver is available at all times. Do not perform these experiments in foul weather.

Humane Treatment of Animals

Some of the most exciting parts of a biology course are those that deal with living animals. Some classrooms have a permanent collection of living animals. Others use living animals only occasionally as part of laboratory activities. It is the moral and ethical responsibility of the teacher and students to give adequate care to all living animals and to treat them humanely. In all your dealings with living animals, you should show a respect for life.

Follow these steps in order to ensure humane treatment of animals in the laboratory or classroom:

1. Be sure that a proper environment can be created and maintained for an animal before it is brought into the classroom. Research the animal's needs and make sure you can meet them.

2. In general, avoid bringing wild animals into the classroom. Most wild animals cannot adapt to a classroom or laboratory setting. Exceptions are small animals, such as earthworms, spiders, insects, fish, and some amphibians. Do not collect any animals that are members of an endangered species. Do not collect animals that are sick or dying. Handle wild animals as infrequently as possible. After a period of observation, return the animals to their natural habitats.

3. Obtain healthy animals from pet stores or biological supply houses.

4. Make sure you know how to treat each kind of animal. Get directions from your teacher before handling a live animal. You need to know how to handle an animal properly in order to prevent injury to it and to yourself. Do not make loud noises, tap on the animals' cages or containers, or otherwise disturb or frighten the animals.

5. Keep records of who is feeding the animals and how much and how often they are fed. Make sure that the animals' nutritional needs are met but not exceeded.

6. Make sure that the areas in which the animals are housed are cleaned regularly.

7. Arrange for the animals to be cared for when school is not in session, as during weekends and vacations.

8. Do not cause any animal pain or injury. Experimenting with live animals should have humane objectives and should be closely supervised by your teacher. Follow your teacher's instructions carefully.

9. Discuss your attitudes and feelings about dissection of preserved animals with your teacher. If you are strongly opposed to dissecting animals, there are alternatives available to you. Your textbook and lab manual lists these alternatives. Some of these are: (1) computer simulations, (2) anatomical models and charts, (3) laser discs, (4) films, (5) filmstrips, (6) transparencies, (7) videotapes, and (8) books.

Laboratory Safety Contract

I,_____, have read
(please print full name)

the "Safety in the Biology Laboratory" section on pages vii–ix of this manual, understand its contents completely, and agree to demonstrate compliance with all safety rules and guidelines that have been established in each of the following categories:

(please check)

☐ General

☐ Handling Chemicals

☐ Handling Glassware

☐ Heating Substances

☐ Handling Dissecting Instruments and Preserved Specimens

☐ Handling Living Specimens

☐ Handling Hazardous Materials

☐ Understanding Safety Symbols

_____
(signature)

Date _____

Using a Compound Microscope

Lab 1

Background

The microscope is an important scientific tool. It enables a person to observe things too small to be seen with the unaided eye. In many of the activities in this lab manual you will use a *compound microscope,* a microscope having two lenses. In this type of microscope, light passes through the specimen, or object being viewed. One lens, the *objective,* causes the light rays coming from the specimen to spread apart, forming an enlarged image of the object. The second lens, the *ocular,* focuses and further enlarges the image.

Working with a compound microscope, you may use specimens that have been prepared in one of two ways. A prepared slide is made to be permanent and can be purchased from a supply house. A wet-mount slide is made for temporary use and can be made and used during a lab period.

Objectives

In this activity you will:

1. Learn the parts and operation of a compound microscope.
2. Learn to prepare and observe a wet mount.

Materials

microscope	water
slides	pipette
cover slips	scissors
lens paper	magazine picture in color
paper towels	hairs of different color
dissecting needle	ruler
sheet of newspaper	pieces of very thin cloth

Procedures and Observations

PART I.   LEARNING ABOUT THE MICROSCOPE _____

1. Obtain your microscope from your teacher. Always carry the microscope in an upright position with one hand holding the arm and the other supporting the base, as shown in Figure 1. Set it down away from the edge of the table. **Note:** *The microscope is an expensive, precision instrument. Handle it carefully.*

2. Compare your microscope with Figure 2 on the next page. Identify each part on your microscope.

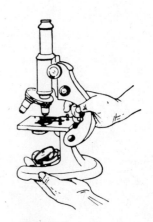

Figure 1

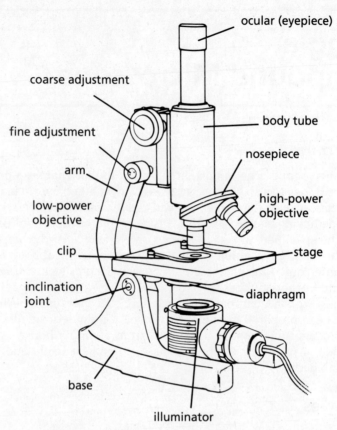

Figure 2

3. Some microscopes have a built-in electric light, or illuminator. Others have a mirror to reflect light onto the specimen. If you have a mirror, note that its angle is adjustable. Practice directing the reflected light upward through the microscope by slanting the face of the mirror. Look through the ocular as you adjust the mirror to obtain the maximum amount of light. **CAUTION:** *Never use direct sunlight as a light source. It can damage your eyes.*

4. Examine the diaphragm. Adjust it to the largest opening so that the most light enters the microscope. You can tell this by looking through the ocular.

5. While looking at your microscope from the side, slowly turn the coarse adjustment one-half turn toward you.

   a. *In which direction does the objective move?*

   _____

   _____

6. Continue to turn the coarse adjustment until the low power objective is about 3 cm from the stage. The low power objective is the shorter, or the shortest, objective.

7. Look at the number followed by an "X" on the side of each objective. This number is the objective's magnifying power. The "X" stands for "times." Thus the number tells how many times an object is magnified by this lens.

Using a Compound Microscope (continued)

b. *What is the magnifying power of the low-power objective?*

_____

8. Locate the high-power objective.

c. *What is its magnifying power?*

_____

9. If the lenses look dirty or smudged, carefully wipe them with lens paper. Use only lens paper because other kinds of paper can damage the lenses.

The ocular lens also has a magnifying power. The total magnifying power of the microscope is easy to calculate. Simply multiply the magnifying power of the ocular by the magnifying power of the objective. For example, if the ocular is 5X and the objective is 10X, the total magnification of the object being viewed is 5X x 10X = 50X.

10. Examine the ocular lens.

d. *What is its magnifying power?*

_____

e. *What is the total magnification produced when the low-power objective is used? Show your calculations.*

_____

f. *What is the total magnification produced when the high-power objective is used? Show your calculations.*

_____

PART II.   PREPARING AND EXAMINING A WET MOUNT _____

1. Find a small letter "e" in a piece of newspaper. Cut a 1-cm square of paper with the "e" near the center.

 2. Place the square in the middle of a clean slide. With a pipette, put 1 drop of water on the square. Drop the water from about 1 cm above the slide. Do not touch the pipette to the paper or the paper will stick to the pipette.

3. Now cover the mount with a clean cover slip. One way to do this is shown in Figure 3-a. Hold the cover slip at about a 45° angle to the slide and move it toward the drop. As the water touches the cover slip, it will spread along the edge. Gently lower the cover slip into place. Another way to put the cover slip into place is to support the cover slip with a dissecting needle, as shown in Figure 3-b. Slowly lower the supported edge and watch as the water fills the space. Use whichever method is easier for you and gives you a good wet mount. Do not press on the cover slip—it should rest on the top of the water. A good wet mount is free of bubbles. If your mount has too many bubbles, take off the cover slip and absorb the water with a paper towel. Then repeat Steps 2 and 3.

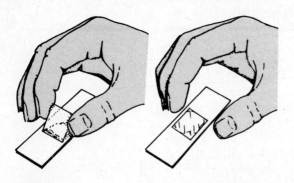

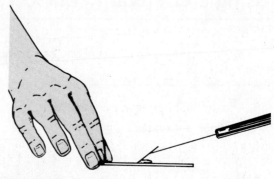

Figure 3-a   **Figure 3-b**

4. Click the low-power objective into place. Make sure you have a good light source and that the diaphragm is at the largest opening. Look through the microscope and adjust the mirror or illuminator to give the brightest light. Remember to never use direct sunlight as a light source.

5. Check to be sure the bottom of the slide is dry before placing it on the stage of the microscope. Set it on the stage so that the "e" is in reading position and over the hole in the stage. Fasten the slide with stage clips.

6. Look at the microscope from the side. Use the coarse adjustment knob to lower the body tube until the objective is about 1/2 to 1 cm above the slide, or until you feel an automatic stop.

7. Look through the ocular, keeping both eyes open. Keeping both eyes open is difficult at first, but it helps to prevent eyestrain. It will become easier with practice. **Note:** *Always look at the microscope from the side while you lower the low-power objective. If you look through the eyepiece you could run the objective into the slide, breaking the slide and damaging the microscope.*

8. Slowly raise the objective by turning the coarse adjustment until the letters come into focus. Use the fine adjustment to sharpen the focus. Observe the letter "e."

   a. *In the space at the left, draw the letter "e" the same size and in exactly the same position as you see it through the microscope.*

9. Move the slide to the left.

   b. *Which way does the image move?*

_____

10. Move the slide to the right.

    c. *Which way does the image move?*

_____

_____

11. Move the slide backward and forward.

    d. *Which ways does the image move?*

_____

_____

Using a Compound Microscope   (continued)

1

12. Observe the wet mount as you change the diaphragm to each of its settings. Adjust it to give good contrast and illumination without glare.

e. *What does the diaphragm control?*

_____

_____

Before using high power, the specimen must be in sharp focus in the center of the low-power field of view. **Note:** *All focusing under high power is done with the fine adjustment knobs.* There is no automatic stop for the high-power objective.

13. Watching from the side, carefully switch to the high-power objective. Make sure that the objective does not hit the slide, but expect it to be very close.

14. Focus on the letter "e." Only a slight turn of the fine adjustment knob will be needed to do this.

f. *In the space at the right, draw the letter "e" exactly as you see it under high power.*

g. *Is the field of view larger under high power or low power?*

_____

h. *Compare the brightness of the field under high power and low power.*

_____

PART III.   RESOLVING POWER AND DEPTH OF FIELD _____

1. Make a wet mount using a 1-cm square of a colored newspaper cartoon or a colored picture from a magazine printed on thin paper. Choose a square that has both light and dark tones, but not black.

a. *Record the colors of the square.*

_____

Resolving power is the ability to distinguish between two separate points that are very close together. Microscopes have a resolving power greater than that of the human eye.

2. Observe the slide under low power. Then switch to high power. Examine the light and dark areas of the square.

b. *How is the color distributed?*

_____

c. What colors do you see?

_____

_____

The *depth of field* is the distance above the slide in which the object is in good focus.

3. Prepare another wet mount, this time using two hairs of different colors. Cross them on the slide, then add a drop of water and the cover slip.

4. View the slide under low power. Focus directly on the point where the hairs cross.

   d. *Are both hairs in focus under low power?*

   _____

5. Switch to high power and observe the hairs.

   e. *Are both hairs in focus under high power? Explain.*

   _____

   _____

6. Prepare some wet mounts of other things, such as pieces of cloth, skin, a fly's wing, or anything that is thin enough for light to pass through it.

   f. *Sketch the things that you observe under the microscope. Label each drawing with its name and the magnification used.*

Using a Compound Microscope (continued)

Analysis and Interpretations

1. Quiz yourself by briefly describing the function of each of the microscope parts listed below.

Part	Function
ocular	
coarse adjustment	
nosepiece	
objectives	
stage	
stage clips	
diaphragm	
mirror or illuminator	
fine adjustment	

2. Why should a wet mount have no bubbles?

_____

3. What did the microscope do to the image of the letter "e"?

_____

4. Why must you center and focus the object in the field of view under low power before switching to high power?

_____

_____

_____

_____

5. Why is only the fine adjustment used for high power?

_____

_____

6. Explain why the color of the magazine picture looked different when you looked at it under the microscope.

_____

_____

7. By using the idea of depth of field, how can you tell which hair was above the other?

_____

_____

8. If you were scanning a slide to find a particular area, which objective would be better to use? Why?

_____

_____

For Further Investigation

1. Use an appropriate resource to investigate the development of the microscope through history. Write a report or make an oral presentation as directed by your teacher.

2. A drop of water will magnify small objects. Put a small object on a slide, add a drop of water, and try to determine its magnifying power.

3. Borrow a microfilm card from a library or other source. Look at it under your microscope. How many pages of information are represented in 1 square centimeter of microfilm?

4. "Working distance" is the distance from the top of the cover slip to the microscope objective. Determine the working distance for both low power and high power.

Living Things in Pond Water

Lab 2

Background

A pond is a small, freshwater lake less than 8 meters deep. In the shallow, quiet water, sunlight penetrates all the way to the bottom. Rooted plants cover most of the bottom. Some live entirely submerged, and some, like the waterlilies, send their leaves and flowers upward to float on the surface of the water. Other plants and tiny, plantlike organisms float about, on or near the surface, thriving on the sunlight they receive. Cattails stand tall along the edges, crowded together and forming hiding places for many birds and other animals. On other parts of the shore, trees and shrubs lean over the water, dropping leaves, pollen, seeds, and fruits in their season. The abundant plant life furnishes food to millions of small animals that live on, in, and near the plants, grazing on them in the same way that cattle graze on land plants. Other animals are present, eating the grazers.

As you study the organisms in pond water, try to find out the source of their food. Notice how their bodies are organized. Observe how they use energy, and respond to changes in their environment.

Objectives

In this activity you will:
1. Try to distinguish nonliving materials from organisms and parts and products of organisms.
2. Use the microscope to observe some of the wide variety of life forms that live in a pond.
3. Study and try to identify organisms collected from different regions of a pond.

Materials

stock cultures of pond water, clearly marked:
    Culture I—collected from the surface or from open water, with
        plants
    Culture II—collected from edges of the pond, with floating
        materials
    Culture III—collected from the bottom of the pond, with twigs and
        decaying materials

culture dishes	slides
glass-marking pencil	cover slips
pipettes	hand lens
small tissues	microscope
paper towels	stereomicroscope (optional)

Procedures and Observations

PART I. PREPARATION AND PRELIMINARY OBSERVATIONS _____

Mark three culture dishes I, II, and III. Obtain the three pond-water cultures from your teacher, making sure to put them in the correct culture dishes. Place each dish on a piece of paper labeled with the appropriate dish number and source of water (surface, edge, bottom).

Observe the materials in each of the three culture dishes and try to distinguish nonliving materials from organisms or materials that were once alive. However, you may not be able to distinguish them until you observe the cultures under the microscope, later in this lab activity.

Put one pipette next to each of the culture dishes, making sure you keep each culture dish and its respective pipette separate. You will be making many wet mounts, looking for different kinds of organisms.

As you prepare the wet mounts, use only two drops of the culture. Use a clean slide and cover slip each time you change samples. Return samples to the culture dishes after observation.

Use a pencil to make sketches of what you see, so that you can erase. If a specimen is large, sketch it under lower power; if it is small, sketch it under high power. Below the drawing, indicate which power was used.

Be prepared to see many organisms that you cannot name.

Sketches of organisms that you might find in pond water are shown in Figure 1.

PART II. THE POND SURFACE AND OPEN WATER _____

The surface of a pond is like a very thin skin. Small plants and animals make use of the surface skin, either resting on it, or hanging from its underside.

Tiny plantlike organisms, the algae, float or swim near the surface, carried about by water currents. Algae in ponds are usually colored green or yellow-green. Other algae, the diatoms, encased in glass shells, are golden-brown in color.

1. Study dish I, pond surface or open water, examining the plants first. Examine organisms and nonliving materials from the regions in dish I, as described in sections 2–6. Make wet mounts and observe them under low and high power.

   a. *As you examine the materials in sections 2–6, draw at least three different types of algae. Use the space provided at the end of Part II. Label the green areas or structures inside the organisms. Also, draw three other organisms that you see. Indicate where they were found.*

2. From dish I, examine organisms and materials from the surface skin of the water.

3. From dish I, make wet mounts of materials or organisms taken from the underside of the surface skin. Snails, various eggs, wormlike animals with breathing tubes, and animals carrying bubbles can be found here.

4. From dish I, make wet mounts of plants or plantlike organisms floating freely in the water. These may be green or yellow-green, threadlike or netlike. Diatoms on surfaces appear as tiny, geometric figures, alone or in groups. Look for animal forms feeding on the algae.

FIGURE 1 Organisms in Pond Water

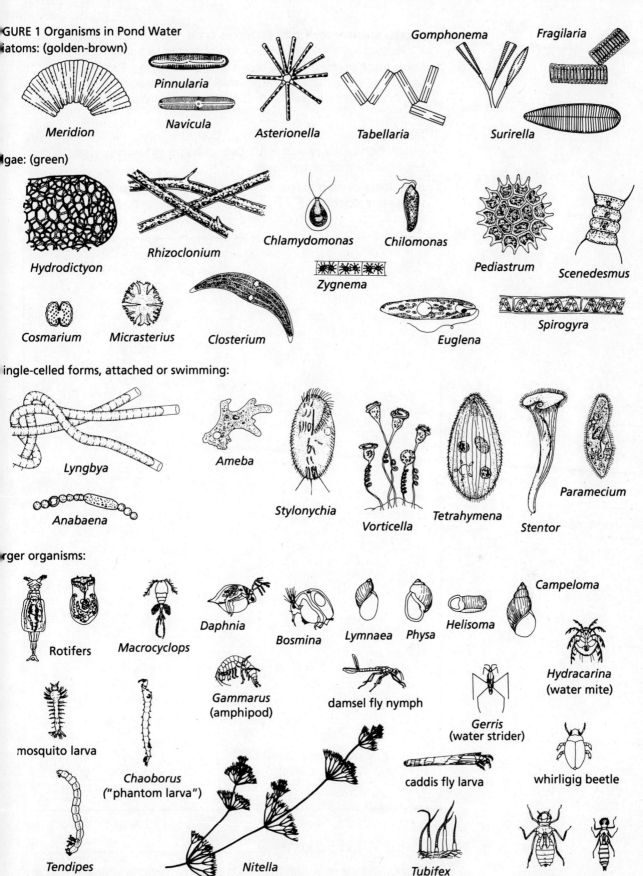

Diatoms: (golden-brown)

Meridion

Pinnularia

Navicula

Asterionella

Tabellaria

Gomphonema

Fragilaria

Surirella

Algae: (green)

Hydrodictyon

Rhizoclonium

Chlamydomonas

Chilomonas

Pediastrum

Scenedesmus

Cosmarium

Micrasterius

Closterium

Zygnema

Euglena

Spirogyra

Single-celled forms, attached or swimming:

Lyngbya

Anabaena

Ameba

Stylonychia

Vorticella

Tetrahymena

Stentor

Paramecium

Larger organisms:

Rotifers

Macrocyclops

Daphnia

Bosmina

Lymnaea

Physa

Helisoma

Campeloma

Hydracarina
(water mite)

Gammarus
(amphipod)

damsel fly nymph

Gerris
(water strider)

mosquito larva

Chaoborus
("phantom larva")

caddis fly larva

whirligig beetle

Tendipes
(blood worm)

Nitella
(green alga)

Tubifex
(red annelid)

dragonfly nymphs

5. Scrape small amounts of materials from the undersides of waterlily leaves onto a slide. Add one drop of water to spread the material. Look for amoebas, which move slowly about by flowing along the surface of the slide; tiny animals with jointed legs; wormlike animals with sectioned bodies; and the immature forms of insects, called larvae.

6. Make wet mounts of water near the algae and plant materials in dish I. Look for organisms that seem to be swimming about. Try to see how they move themselves.

7. Examine a cover slip that was submerged in stock culture I. Obtain it from your teacher.

PART III. THE POND EDGE

1. Examine organisms and materials from the regions in dish II that are described in sections 2–4. Make wet mounts and observe them under low power and high power.

Living Things in Pond Water (continued)

    a. *As you examine the wet mounts from sections 2-4, draw three specimens that you see in the space below. Indicate where they were found.*

2. From dish II, examine the surface of floating materials for organisms. Make wet mounts of any jellylike or egglike patches.

3. From dish II, make wet mounts of floating bits of material. Look for small bits of legs or wings of insects, egg cases, or any structures that have definite form. Pollen grains are often tiny spheres, with points or winglike structures on their surfaces.

4. Look for swimming organisms in wet mounts of water from dish II.

5. Examine a cover slip that was submerged in stock culture II.

PART IV. POND BOTTOMS _____

  1. Search for the following organisms and materials in dish III. Some will be too large to observe in a wet mount. Observe as many as possible with a hand lens or stereomicroscope, if available.

    a. *Examine the wet mounts and materials from sections 2–9. Draw four interesting forms that you find in the space provided on the next page. Include both plant and animal life. Indicate where they were found.*

2. Look for insect larvae, with bodies in sections, and jointed legs. Some are surprisingly large, with prominent eyes. Some also have featherlike gills, or breathing tubes at their posterior ends.

3. Look for insect larvae with cases made from sand grains.

4. Look for animals carrying bubbles.

5. Find wormlike organisms. If they are thrashing about, they are probably roundworms.

6. Look for snails in the culture. They might be carrying a bubble.

7. Try to find euglena in the water. They are slow-moving, bright-green, narrow cells with a red eyespot visible under high power.

8. Examine any rooted plants. There may be animals and diatoms on the leaf surfaces.

9. Search for small, dead animals or plants, or their parts. Leaves often decay so that only their lacy vein patterns remain.

10. Examine a cover slip that was submerged in stock culture III.

Living Things in Pond Water (continued)

Analysis and Interpretations

1. With the help of reference sources and your teacher, try to identify the organisms that you drew. If you are unsure of an identification, write the name with a question mark under the drawing.

2. In studying the pond cultures, why did you keep the samples of the different pond regions separate? Why not mix them?

_____

_____

_____

_____

3. Describe any breathing adaptations that you saw in animal forms.

_____

_____

4. Why might you expect to find animals carrying bubbles both at the surface and at the bottom of a pond?

_____

_____

5. What evidence did you find to suggest that plants and plantlike organisms are plentiful in the pond where the water was collected?

_____

_____

For Further Investigation

1. Continue to study the cultures observed in this lab activity for several more days. If the weather is warm, it may be necessary to refrigerate the cultures overnight. Keep records of the dates that you study the cultures. Sketch the forms that you see each day, and make a note about which forms seem most numerous. Using reference books, try to identify any new organisms.

2. Visit a pond and study the life there. Look for plants and animals larger than those you observed in this lab. Make notes of your observations, recording dates, and conditions of weather, temperature, etc. If possible, collect water samples at different times of the year and keep records of the organisms you find. Record the date, and the region of the pond where you make collections.

Using SI Units of Measure

Lab 3

Background

If you needed to know the length of a room, you might find the distance in feet. The *foot*, along with other terms such as *quart* and *pound*, is a unit in the *English System* of measurement. Scientists, however, use the *International System of Measurement*, or *SI*, the same system used in most countries of the world. SI is a modern adaptation of the metric system. Because SI units are based on multiples of 10, it is easy to change one unit to another. In this activity, you will review SI units for measuring length, volume, and mass. You will practice changing units to larger or smaller units, and you will learn to use some common laboratory measuring equipment.

Objectives

In this activity you will:
1. Identify the SI units of length, volume, and mass.
2. Practice converting one SI unit to another.
3. Measure accurately using the appropriate laboratory equipment.

Materials

meter stick	small beaker
metric ruler	empty can or bottle
graduated cylinder	balance
small test tube	coin
large test tube	rubber stopper

Procedures and Observations

PART I.   REVIEWING SI MEASUREMENTS _____

The basic unit for length in SI is the meter (symbol m). The unit commonly used for measuring volume of solids is the cubic meter (m^3), while the unit commonly used for measuring the volume of liquids or gases is the liter (L); and the gram (g) is the basic unit of mass.

Prefixes are used in SI to form units larger than or smaller than the basic units. All SI units can be formed using these same prefixes. Look at Table 1 to find the meaning of each prefix.

PART II.   CONVERTING SI MEASUREMENTS _____

Anyone who has ever converted inches to yards, or cups to gallons, knows the shortcomings of the English System of measurement: there are various conversion factors. Units of SI are much easier to convert because they are all related to each other by powers of ten. To convert one unit to another, all that is necessary is to move the decimal point.

Table 1

mega-	M	one million	1,000,000
kilo-	k	one thousand	1,000
hecto-	h	one hundred	100
deka-	da	ten	10
deci-	d	one tenth	0.1
centi-	c	one hundredth	0.01
milli-	m	one thousandth	0.001
micro-	μ	one millionth	0.000001

Look at Table 2 to see how different subunits are related to each other. The arrows above the table show the relationship between a unit and the next unit to the right. For example, 1 meter = 10 decimeters. The arrows below the table show the relationship between a unit and the next unit to the left. For example, 1 gram = 0.1 dekagram.

Table 2

		x 1000	x 10	x 10	x 10	x 10	x 10	x 10	x 1000
Length	megameter Mm	kilometer km	hectometer hm	dekameter dam	METER m	decimeter dm	centimeter cm	millimeter mm	micrometer μm
Liquid Volume	megaliter ML	kiloliter kL	hectoliter hL	dekaliter daL	LITER L	deciliter dL	centiliter cL	milliliter mL	microliter μl
Mass	megagram Mg	kilogram kg	hectogram hg	dekagram dag	GRAM g	decigram dg	centigram cg	milligram mg	microgram μg
Multiplication Factors	1,000,000 10^6	1000 10^3	100 10^2	10 10^1	1 10^0	0.1 10^{-1}	0.01 10^{-2}	0.001 10^{-3}	0.000001 10^{-6}
	÷ 1000 or x 0.001	÷ 10 or x 0.1	÷ 10 or x 0.1	÷ 10 or x 0.1	÷ 10 or x 0.1	÷ 10 or x 0.1	÷ 10 or x 0.1	÷ 1000 or x 0.001	

Rule 1: When converting from a <u>large</u> unit to a <u>smaller</u> unit, multiply by the proper multiple of 10 by moving the decimal point to the <u>right</u>.

> ex. 12 cm = __?__ mm
> 12 X 10 =120
> 12 cm = 120 mm

In this case the decimal point in 12 cm was moved to the right one place, resulting in the answer 120 mm.

Rule 2: When converting from a <u>small</u> unit to a <u>larger</u> unit, <u>divide</u> by the proper multiple of 10 by moving the decimal point to the <u>left</u>.

> ex. 250 hg = __?__ kg
> 250 ÷ 10 = 25
> 250 hg = 25 kg

The decimal point in 250 hg was moved to the left one place, resulting in the answer 25 kg.

In the examples above, the decimal point was moved only one place to the right or to the left. When making some conversions, it is necessary to move the decimal point several places.

Using SI Units of Measure (continued)

Example 6 km = _?_ m

In this example the answer can be found two different ways.

1. The decimal point can be moved to the right in three steps to convert kilometers to meters:

    6 km = 60 hm

    60 hm = 600 dam

    600 dam = 6000 m

2. This example can also be computed in one step. Look at the arrows at the top of Table 2. Notice that there are three arrows between the units *kilometer* and *meter*. Each of these arrows indicate that the number of units must be multiplied by 10 to convert it to the next unit. In this case the three arrows are: 10 x 10 x 10, which equals 1000. Thus the number of kilometers multiplied by 1000 will convert kilometers to meters:

    6 km = 6000 m

1. Write the unit of each amount below.

    a. 0.1 gram _____

    b. 0.01 meter _____

    c. 0.000001 liter _____

    d. 100 liters _____

    e. 1,000,000 _____

    f. 10 meters _____

2. Convert the SI units below.

    g. 226 cm = _____ m

    h. 67 mm = _____ μm

    i. 9.4 km = _____ dam

    j. 5400 mL = _____ L

    k. 27.3 hL = _____ dL

    l. 436 mg = _____ g

    m. 32.8 Mg = _____ dag

PART III.   MEASURING LENGTH IN SI UNITS _____

Recall that the basic unit of length in SI is the meter (m). The most common units of length are the kilometer, meter, centimeter, and millimeter.

1. Use a meter stick or metric ruler to measure the items listed below. When possible, measure to the nearest millimeter. Record your measurements in Table 3. (Recall that decimals are used in SI. There should be no fractions in your answers.)

2. Complete the table by converting your measurements to the units given.

Table 3

Item	l/w/h	mm	cm	m
Lab Manual				
	width	210 mm	21.0 cm	0.210 m
	height	276 mm	27.6 cm	0.276 m
Desk or lab table				
	length			
	width			
	height			
Classroom				
	length			
	width			

PART IV.   MEASURING VOLUME WITH SI UNITS

In SI, the volume of a solid is measured in cubic meters (m^3) or cubic decimeters (dm^3). The commonly used basic unit of liquid volume is the liter (L). The units used for solids and for liquids and gases are related in SI: 1 mL = 1 cm^3 (cm^3 is read *cubic centimeter*, and may also be called *cc*). The most common units of volume are the liter and the milliliter.

1. To find the volume of a solid, multiply height, width, and length.

   a. *Find the volume of one of your textbooks. Show your work.*

_____

_____

2. A graduated cylinder, or graduate, is usually used in laboratories to measure the volume of liquids. Very accurate measurements can be made using a graduate. If the graduate you are using is made of glass, handle it carefully.

   b. *Look at the scale on the side of the graduate. What is the maximum volume that can be measured in this graduate?*

_____

   c. *What volume is represented by each single line on the graduate?*

_____

3. Fill a small test tube with water and pour the water into the graduate. Look carefully at the level of the water in the graduate. If the graduate you are using is made of glass, the water will form a meniscus, or curved upper surface. Look at the meniscus shown in Figure 1. The correct volume is found by reading the bottom of the meniscus. To read the volume accurately, the meniscus should be at eye level.

   d. *How much water did the test tube hold? Record this amount in Table 4.*

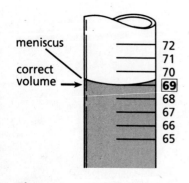

Figure 1

Using SI Units of Measure (continued)

3

Table 4

Item	mL	L
small test tube		
large test tube		
beaker		
empty can or bottle		

4. Measure the volume of each of the items in the table above. Record your measurements. Record the volumes in both milliliters and liters.

PART V.   MEASURING MASS WITH SI UNITS _____

The basic unit of mass in SI is the gram (g). There is a relationship between the SI units of mass and volume: 1 mL of water has a mass of approximately 1 g. The most commonly used units of mass are the milligram, gram, and kilogram.

In the laboratory, a balance is used to find the mass of objects. Balances are sensitive instruments. They must be handled carefully or they will no longer be accurate. Your teacher will show you the proper use of the balance that you will be using.

1. Look at the list of objects in Table 5. Determine the mass of each object as accurately as possible. Record the mass in both grams and kilograms.

Table 5

Item	g	kg
coin		
rubber stopper		
empty can or bottle		
10 mL water		

Analysis and Interpretations

1. List the SI prefixes in order of the smallest unit to the largest unit.

_____

2. Explain how you found the mass of 10 ml water.

_____

_____

_____

3. Why is it easier to convert SI units than English System units?

_____

_____

4. Which SI units would be most useful for expressing the following?

length of an athletic field _____

mass of an aspirin tablet _____

mass of a pencil _____

length of a ruler _____

volume of a swimming pool _____

distance from Earth to Mars _____

length of a car _____

mass of a postage stamp _____

distance between two cities _____

For Further Investigation

1. Find the values for measurements of the items listed in question number 4 above. For some, you may be able to make direct measurements. Use and note outside sources for the remaining items.

2. Find out about the history of SI measurements. Present your findings to the class.

3. Investigate some of the lesser known units of the English System of measurement. What is the origin of the terms, *rod, gill, peck, pennyweight, scruple,* and *league* ?

4. The SI unit of temperature is the Kelvin. The Kelvin scale is related to the Celsius scale, with which you may be familiar. Make a chart showing equivalent temperatures in Kelvin, Celsius, and Fahrenheit scales. On the Celsius scale, what is the significance of 0°C and 100°C? On the Kelvin scale, what is the significance of 0°K?

Measuring with a Microscope

Lab 4

Background

It is interesting and informative to observe specimens under the microscope, but it is often difficult to know the actual size of the object being observed. Magnification causes us to lose the idea of actual size. You cannot hold a ruler up to a paramecium or a plant cell while it is under a microscope. Therefore, size must be measured indirectly—that is, it must be compared with the size of something you already know. The diameter of the microscope field seen through the ocular is a convenient standard to use.

Two metric units are useful when measuring small objects:

1 meter (m) = 1000 *millimeters* (mm)   1 mm = 1000 *micrometers* (μm)

Objectives

In this activity you will:
1. Measure the diameter of the low-power field.
2. Calculate the diameter of the high-power field.
3. Learn how to estimate the sizes of objects under the microscope.

Materials

microscope
transparent metric ruler
prepared slide of paramecium

prepared slide of corn stem,
    cross section

Procedures and Observations

1. Examine the markings on a transparent metric ruler. Determine which marks indicate millimeter lengths. Then place the ruler on the stage so that it covers half of the stage opening as shown in Figure 1.

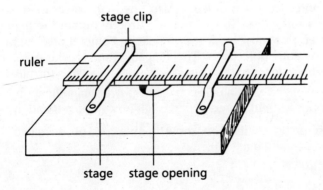

Figure 1

2. Prepare your microscope for low-power observation of the ruler.

3. Look through the ocular. Focus on the edge of the ruler, using the coarse adjustment. Adjust the position of the ruler so that the view in the low-power field is similar to Figure 2.

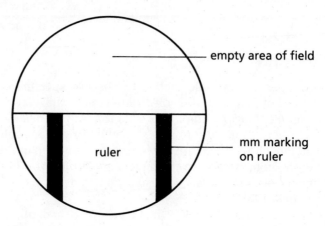

Figure 2

4. Place the center of one mark at the left side of the field of view. Make sure that the edge of the ruler is exactly across the center of the field. If the ruler sticks to your fingers, use the eraser end of a pencil to arrange it.

5. Note that 1 millimeter is the distance from the middle of one mark to the middle of the next mark. The diameter of the low-power field measures 1 millimeter plus a fraction of another.

   a. *Record the measurement of the low-power field diameter in millimeters, expressing the length to the nearest tenth of a millimeter.*

---

6. Convert the measurement in millimeters to micrometers by multiplying by 1000.

   b. *Record the measurement of the low-power field diameter in micrometers.*

You cannot measure the diameter of the high-power field using the process you have just completed. Viewing a ruler under high power presents light and focusing problems. Also, the high-power field diameter is less than 1 millimeter. But you can indirectly obtain the high-power field diameter. You know the low-power field diameter and the magnifying power of both objectives. The magnification of the objectives is inversely proportional to the field size. You can use this formula:

$$\frac{\text{high-power field diameter}}{\text{low-power field diameter}} = \frac{\text{low-power magnification}}{\text{high-power magnification}}$$

7. Substitute the values you know in this formula to calculate the high-power field diameter.

Measuring with a Microscope (continued)

c. *Record the high-power field diameter in micrometers. Show your calculations.*

The measurements of the low-power and high-power field diameters can be used to measure other things indirectly.

8. Under low power, focus on a prepared cross section of corn stem.

The center of a corn stem is filled with large, thin-walled cells. These are *pith cells.*

9. Observe the pith cells.

d. *How many pith cells fit across the diameter of the low-power field?*

_____

10. To calculate the diameter of a pith cell, divide the diameter of the low-power field by the number of cells given for Question d.

e. *Record the diameter of a pith cell in micrometers.*

_____

_____

11. Switch to high power and focus with the fine adjustment.

f. *How many pith cells would fit across the diameter of the high-power field?*

_____

12. To calculate the diameter of a pith cell as seen under high power, divide the diameter of the high-power field by the number of cells given for Question f.

g. *Record the diameter of a pith cell in micrometers, as measured under high power.*

_____

h. *Compare the measurement of the diameter of a cell under low and high power.*

_____

13. Observe a paramecium on a prepared slide under low power. Estimate its length by comparing it to the diameter of the low-power field.

i. *Record the length of the paramecium in micrometers.*

_____

14. Switch to high power. Estimate the length of the paramecium by comparing it to the diameter of the high-power field.

    j. *Record the length of the paramecium in micrometers as measured under high power.*

Analysis and Interpretations

1. Compare the measurements that you calculated for the pith cells and for the paramecium under low with their measurements under high power. If measurements of the same object are different, what could be the reason?

---

2. Find the diameter of the high-power field of a microscope with an ocular marked 10X, a low-power objective marked 10X, a high-power objective marked 40X, and a low-power field diameter of 1600 micrometers.

3. What approximate fraction of the low-power field *area* would you see if you were to change to the high-power objective, using the microscope in Question 2?

For Further Investigation

1. Make a drawing to represent the low-power and high-power fields of the microscope described in Question 2, above. Use a metric ruler and compass. Label every element in your drawing: the low-power field, the high-power field, the diameters and radii, and the diagram as a whole. Begin with a circle having a 12-cm diameter to represent the field under low power. Draw a second circle of *correct size* in the center of the first circle. Using the formula for the area of a circle ($A = \pi r^2$), calculate the areas of both circles. (Remember: the diameter and the radius are not the same.) What fraction of the low-power field area is included in the high-power field area?

2. If you had begun Investigation 1 with a circle of different diameter, which numbers would be different? Which would be the same? Prove your answer by constructing a second drawing, calculating the two areas, and demonstrating their relationship.

3. If a microscope had an ocular lens of 10X, a low-power objective of 10X, and a high-power objective of 100X, how would their field areas be related?

Classifying Mixtures

Lab 5

Background

Many chemicals exist in living things in the form of mixtures: the individual chemicals are mingled together without undergoing a chemical change.

Solutions are homogeneous mixtures that are usually made up of a liquid solvent plus a dissolved substance called the solute. One example of a solution is sea water: water is the solvent and dissolved salts are the solute. In a solution, the substances do not settle, or separate out, when left standing. For example, salts do not separate out of sea water. In solutions that make up living systems, the solvent is usually water. Blood plasma is an example of a solution in a living system.

Suspensions are mixtures of substances in which neither substance dissolves in the other. Because the substances do not dissolve, a suspension is made up of two phases of matter. Thus suspensions usually appear cloudy. An example of a suspension that often has this cloudy appearance is pineapple juice. Unlike particles in solution, particles in a suspension will settle out when the mixture is left standing. Particles in suspension may be small enough to pass through filter paper. Yet even these tiny particles can settle out. An example of a suspension in a living system is fat droplets in cytoplasm.

Colloidal dispersions, like suspensions, are made up of two phases of matter. Unlike suspensions, however, colloidal dispersions are made up of particles so small that they do not settle out, are not filterable, and may not cause the mixture to appear cloudy. Examples of colloidal dispersions are smoke, which is a mixture of a solid in a gas, and fog, which is a liquid in a gas. Colloidal dispersions can often be identified by the Tyndall Effect in which a bright light produces a visible beam. As a light is shined through a colloidal dispersion, the light is reflected off the tiny dispersed particles and produces a visible beam. You have probably noticed this effect when sunlight passes through dust in the air. An example of a colloidal dispersion in a living system is proteins in cytoplasm.

Objectives

In this activity you will:
1. Observe and test mixtures of unknown substances.
2. Classify unknown substances as solutions, suspensions, or colloidal dispersions.

Materials

test tubes	ring stand
glass-marking pencil	ring clamp
test tube racks	funnel
flashlight	filter paper

Procedures and Observations

PART I.   TESTING FOR THE TYNDALL EFFECT _____

Work in groups throughout this lab activity. Take turns with other groups to complete Part I. Until it is your group's turn, you may proceed with Parts II and III.

1. Your teacher will have set up containers of six different mixtures. Use the mixtures in these containers to test for the Tyndall Effect. After stirring a mixture, shine a bright flashlight beam at the side of the container, through the mixture. Then observe the mixture from above.

2. Repeat the test for the Tyndall Effect on each of the six mixtures.

   a. *Carefully observe each of the six mixtures. Does the mixture exhibit the Tyndall Effect? Record your observations in the spaces provided for each mixture in your data table.*

PART II.   OBSERVING MIXTURES _____

1. Using a glass-marking pencil, label six test tubes 1 through 6 and place them in a test tube rack. Fill each test tube about three-quarters full of the corresponding mixture provided by your teacher. **Note:** *To get a representative sample, stir each stock mixture before you transfer it to your test tube.*

2. Carefully examine each of the six mixtures. Answer the following questions for each mixture, writing the answers in the spaces provided on your data table.

   a. *Does the mixture appear to be homogeneous (uniform) or heterogeneous (not uniform)?*

   b. *Does the mixture separate while it stands in the test tube rack?*

   c. *How would you characterize the mixture, as clear or cloudy?*

   d. *What phases of matter—solid, liquid, or gas—appear to be present in the mixture?*

PART III.   FILTERING MIXTURES _____

1. Label six clean test tubes 1 through 6 and place them in a test-tube rack, just as you did in Part I. Set up a ring stand with a ring clamp as shown in Figure 1. Place a funnel in the ring, inserting the end of the funnel in test tube 1. Fold a piece of filter paper in half, and then in half again, as shown in the figure. Set the filter paper in the funnel.

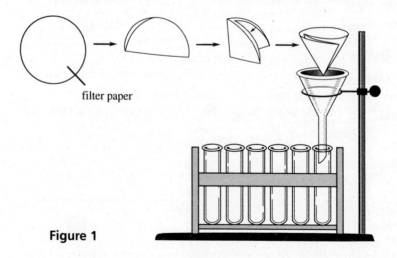

filter paper

Figure 1

28

Classifying Mixtures (continued)

5

2. Test mixture 1 to see if it changes due to filtering. Pour mixture 1 into the funnel and examine the filtered liquid.

   a. *Does filtering change the appearance of the mixture? Record your observations in your data table.*

3. Using fresh pieces of filter paper, repeat Step 2 for each mixture, filtering the mixture into the test tube having the matching number.

Analysis and Interpretations

1. By looking at the information recorded in your data table and studying the background material, classify each of the mixtures as a solution, a suspension, or a colloidal dispersion. Write the answer in the space provided in your data table.

Data Table

	clay/ water	salt/ water	starch/ water	milk/ water	iodine/ alcohol	gelatin/ water
Mixtures	1	2	3	4	5	6
Shows Tyndall Effect?						
Is it homogeneous or heterogeneous?						
Does it separate?						
Is it clear or cloudy?						
What phases of matter?						
Does filtering change it?						
What type of mixture?						

2. Describe each of the three types of mixtures. Tell whether each is homogeneous or heterogeneous, whether or not it separates, whether it is clear or cloudy, the number of phases present, whether or not it exhibits the Tyndall Effect, and whether or not it is changed by filtration.

   Solution: _____

   _____

   Suspension: _____

   _____

   Colloidal Dispersion: _____

   _____

3. Solutions, suspensions, and colloidal dispersions are made up of different-sized particles. Rank the three types of mixtures based on particle size, going from largest to smallest.

_____

4. Using physical science texts and other references as necessary, determine the phases present in each of the following colloidal dispersions:

styrofoam: _____

marshmallow: _____

paint: _____

milk: _____

brass: _____

For Further Investigation

1. Predict the properties of the following mixtures: sugar in water, vinegar and oil salad dressing, food coloring and water, muddy water, alcohol and water. Then test each mixture to check whether your predictions were correct. Record your observations in a table like the one you used in this lab activity.

2. Suggest how the various mixtures mentioned in this lab could be separated. What physical means could be used?

3. With your teacher's supervision, set up a large jar with various layers of insoluble particles of different size, mass, and color. Add water until the jar is three-quarters full and screw the lid on the jar. Carefully but vigorously shake the jar until all the substances are mixed. Then let the jar stand undisturbed for several days. Observe the separation of materials as they settle out of the suspension.

Testing for Nutrients

Lab 6

Background

Substances in food that can be used by an organism for energy or for growth and repair are called nutrients. Nutrients include carbohydrates, proteins, fats, minerals, and vitamins. Cells of all organisms are composed of these nutrients and water. There are several chemical tests that can be used to determine which nutrients, if any, are present in a substance. You will use some of these tests in this activity.

Objectives

In this activity you will:
1. Learn how to test substances for the presence of carbohydrates, proteins, and fats.
2. Perform nutrient tests on several foods to determine which nutrients are present.

Materials

Pyrex test tubes
test tube rack
test tube holder
10-mL graduated cylinders
glass stirring rods
hot plate
5% glucose solution
Benedict's solution
egg albumen solution
biuret reagent in dropper bottle
pieces of potato, bread, carrot,
onion, walnut, apple, and
cheese

scalpel or single-edge razor blade
plastic funnel
glass-marking pencil
paper towels
boiling-water bath
pipettes
dry cornstarch
Lugol's solution in dropper bottle
salad oil
squares of unglazed brown paper
beakers
ruler
water

Procedures and Observations

PART I.   TESTING FOR CARBOHYDRATES _____

Starches and sugars belong to the group of organic compounds called carbohydrates. Starch molecules are composed of many simple sugar molecules linked together. Starch molecules and simple sugar molecules have different chemical behaviors. For this reason, different chemical *reagents,* or testing agents, are used to test for starch and for simple sugars.

A solution of iodine, *Lugol's iodine solution,* is the reagent used to test for the presence of starch. Lugol's solution is yellow-brown. However, it reacts chemically with starch to form a blue-black substance called iodide of starch.

1. With a glass-marking pencil, label one clean test tube *S* for starch. Pour dry cornstarch into the test tube until there is 1 cm of cornstarch in the tube. Then add water to the test tube, to a depth of 3 cm.

2. Mix the starch and water by stirring them carefully with a glass stirring rod. Then set the test tube in a test tube rack.

   a. *What color is the mixture of starch and water?*

   _____

3. Label another clean test tube *C* for control. Pour water into the test tube to a depth of 3 cm. Set it in the test tube rack.

4. Observe the color of Lugol's iodine solution.

   b. *What color is Lugol's iodine solution?*

   _____

5. Add 1 drop of Lugol's solution to the starch and water mixture. Do not stir the mixture. **CAUTION:** *Use care when using Lugol's solution to avoid staining hands and clothing.*

   c. *What color is the mixture around the drop of Lugol's solution?*

   _____

6. Stir the mixture with the stirring rod. Then observe it.

   d. *What color is the mixture after stirring?*

   _____

7. Add 5 more drops of Lugol's solution to the mixture. Then stir it thoroughly. Observe the color.

   e. *What is the color of the mixture?*

   _____

8. Add 1 drop of Lugol's solution to the control test tube. Do not stir it.

   f. *What color is the water around the drop of Lugol's solution?*

   _____

9. Stir the solution with a clean glass stirring rod. Observe it.

   g. *What color is the solution?*

   _____

10. Add 5 more drops of Lugol's solution. Stir it, and then observe it.

    h. *What color is the solution?*

    _____

Benedict's solution, a clear blue solution of sodium and copper salts, is used to test for the presence of simple sugars. In the presence of simple sugars, Benedict's solution changes color to green, yellow, and brick red, depending on the amount of sugar.

11. Label a clean test tube *G* for glucose. Add the initials of a person in your group. Using a graduated cylinder, pour 5 mL of the 5% glucose solution into the test tube. Then set it in the test tube rack.

Testing for Nutrients (continued)

12. Label another clean test tube *C* for control. Add the initials of a person in your group. Using a clean graduated cylinder, pour 5 mL of water into the test tube. Set it in the test tube rack.

13. Use a clean graduated cylinder to add 3 mL of Benedict's solution to each test tube. Mix the contents of each tube by carefully swirling them.

   i. *What color is the solution in tube G?*

   _____

   j. *What color is the solution in tube C?*

   _____

 14. Carefully place both test tubes in a boiling water bath for 3 minutes. During the heating, observe the contents of each tube for any color changes.

15. At the end of 3 minutes, remove your test tubes with a test tube holder and place them in the test tube rack. **CAUTION:** *Avoid getting splashed with hot water. Never touch hot test tubes with your bare hands.* Observe the colors of the solutions.

   k. *Describe what happened to the color of the solution in tube G.*

   _____

   l. *Describe what happened to the color of the solution in tube C.*

   _____

PART II.   TESTING FOR PROTEINS _____

   Biuret reagent, a blue solution, is used to test for the presence of proteins in a substance. In the presence of protein, biuret reagent changes color to pink-purple.

1. Label a clean test tube *P* for protein. Pour 5 mL of egg albumen solution into the test tube. Set it in the test tube rack.

   a. *What color is the egg albumen solution?*

   _____

2. Label another clean test tube *C* for control. Add 5 mL of water to the test tube. Set it in the test tube rack.

3. Observe the color of biuret reagent.

   b. *Record the color of biuret reagent.*

   _____

4. **CAUTION:** *Biuret reagent is caustic and can harm skin and clothing. Handle with care.* Add 1 drop of biuret reagent to tube P. Swirl the contents of the tube to mix them. Then continue to add drops, one at a time, and mix by swirling, until you have added 10 drops. Watch closely for a color change.

c. *Describe what happened to the color of the solution.*

---

5. Add 1 drop of biuret reagent to tube C. Swirl the contents of the tube to mix them. Then continue to add drops, one at a time, and mix by swirling, until you have added 10 drops. Watch for a color change.

   d. *Describe what happened to the color of the solution.*

PART III.   TESTING FOR FATS

   The presence of fats in a substance can be detected by using unglazed *brown paper.* Fats leave an oily, translucent smear when touched to brown paper.

1. Using a pipette, place 1 drop of salad oil on a square of unglazed brown paper. With a pencil, label the spot "oil."
2. Place 1 drop of water on the same piece of brown paper, about 2 cm below the drop of oil. Label the spot "water."
3. Set the piece of paper aside until the water evaporates.
4. When the water has evaporated, observe the brown paper.

   a. *Are the two spots different? If so, describe how.*

---

5. Hold the paper up to light and look at the oil spot.

   b. *Is the oil spot translucent? That is, can you see light through it?*

PART IV.   TESTING FOR FOOD NUTRIENTS

   Keep your food samples on paper towels, numbered according to their positions in Table 1. Wash your hands after handling each sample, to avoid transferring food particles from one food to another.

1. Divide each food sample into the number of parts needed for the tests indicated in Table 1. Note that some foods are not to be tested for all nutrients.

2. Number six depressions in a spot plate 1 to 6. If you do not have a spot plate, number six positions on a paper towel. Then, using a scalpel or single-edge razor blade, chop up one sample of each food to be tested into tiny pieces and put them in the proper place. CAUTION: Use care to avoid cutting yourself.

3. Add a few drops of Lugol's solution to each food sample, in order to test for starch. Observe the samples for any color changes indicating a positive result for starch.

   a. *Record your observations in Table 1. If a food sample shows a positive reaction for starch, place a plus sign (+) in the proper space. If a food sample shows a negative reaction, place a minus sign (–) in the proper space.*

4. Number five Pyrex test tubes 1, 2, 3, 4, and 5. Then add the initials of a person in your group to each. Set them in the test tube rack.

Testing for Nutrients   (continued)

5. Using a scalpel or single-edge razor, scrape, chop up, or crush each food sample to be tested into tiny pieces. Then place each crushed food sample in the proper test tube.

Table 1.   Nutrient Tests

Nutrients Tested for	Foods Tested						
	¹ Carrot	² Bread	³ Potato	⁴ Apple	⁵ Onion	⁶ Walnut	⁷ Cheese
starch							
simple sugars							
proteins							
fats							

6. Add 3 mL of water to each test tube. Then add 3 mL of Benedict's solution to each tube, to test for simple sugars. Swirl the contents to mix them. Place the test tubes in the boiling-water bath for 3 minutes.

7. At the end of 3 minutes, remove your test tubes from the boiling-water bath with test tube holders, and place them in the test tube rack. Observe them for an indication of the presence of simple sugars.

   b. *Record your observations about the presence of simple sugars in each food sample in Table 1.*

8. Number seven test tubes 1 to 7. Place them in the test tube rack.

9. Crush each food sample separately, as in Step 5, and transfer the samples to the proper test tubes. Then add 3 mL of water to each tube and gently swirl the contents to mix them.

10. Add biuret reagent 1 drop a time to each test tube to test for proteins. Watch the samples as you continue to add drops until there is a color change or until you have added 10 drops.

   c. *Record your observations about the presence of proteins in each food sample in Table 1.*

11. Number seven squares of brown paper 1 to 7.

12. Rub each solid food sample on the proper piece of brown paper. When the squares have dried, observe them for the presence of fats.

   d. *Record your observations about the presence of fats in each food sample in Table 1.*

 13. Clean up your work area. **CAUTION:** *Dispose of the biuret reagent solution carefully, according to your teacher's direction.*

Analysis and Interpretations

1. In Parts I, II, III, and IV, why did you apply each test to water?

_____

2. Name the reagent or testing material used to detect the presence of the following:

a. simple sugar _____

b. protein _____

c. starch _____

d. fats _____

3. In each of the chemical tests you performed, how did you know when a positive reaction took place?

_____

_____

_____

_____

4. Did any of the results in this laboratory exercise surprise you? If so, which ones?

_____

For Further Investigation

1. You have learned that nutrients in the foods you eat are used in building cells and supplying energy. In other words, "you are what you eat." keep a list of everything you eat for 3 days. Determine which foods contain what percentage of proteins, carbohydrates, and fats.

2. What are the current recommended amounts of protein, carbohydrates, and fats for a person your age? Recommendations change frequently, as more is learned about the impact of various substances on the body. Obtain the current recommendations of the American Heart Association or the American Cancer Society. Compare your list of foods from Question 1 to the recommended list.

3. Use reference materials to find out what problems are caused by eating a high-fat diet. Summarize your findings in a list. How much fat is in the snacks you usually eat? Using a brownpaper grocery bag, you can easily test for fats at home. Make a list of those foods which contain fat.

Observing Cork Cells and Onion Cells

Lab 7

Background

Over 300 years ago, Robert Hooke, an English scientist, described the appearance of cork under the microscope. He named the tiny, box-like structures he observed *cells*. Cork, which does not contain living tissue, comes from the outer bark of the cork oak tree.

By the early part of the 19th century, it was accepted that all living things are composed of cells. Cells come in a variety of shapes and sizes, and they perform different functions. Although cells are different, they resemble one another because they share certain common structures. The microscope reveals that most plant cells and animal cells have various components including the *nucleus, nucleolus, mitochondria, cytoplasm,* and *cell membrane*. An understanding of the cell is essential to the study of biology.

Objectives

In this activity you will:
1. Observe the structure of dead cork cells.
2. Observe the structure of living onion cells.
3. Apply your knowledge of the operation of a microscope.

Materials

microscope	cork stopper
slides	onion
cover slips	forceps
single-edged razor blade	Lugol's iodine solution in
medicine dropper	dropper bottle
water	paper towels

Procedures and Observations

PART I.   CORK CELLS _____

To observe cork cells under a microscope, you must slice very thin sections of cork.

1. Place the cork on a paper towel or on several sheets of paper. Hold the cork firmly and shave a thin section from the cork with a razor blade. The slice must be paper-thin. This procedure is shown in Figure 1. **CAUTION:** *Razor blades are sharp! To avoid cutting your fingers, slice away from them, not toward them.*

Figure 1

2. When you have cut a slice thin enough for light to pass through it, prepare a wet mount. Place the cork slice in a small drop of water on a slide. Add another drop on top of the cork. Then cover it with a cover slip.

3. Examine the cork under low power. The best place to look is along the thinnest edge of the slice.

   a. *Make a drawing of what you see under low power.*

4. Examine the cork under high power.

   b. *Describe the general shape of cork cells.*

   c. *Draw several cork cells as they appear under high power and label the cell wall.*

d. *What structures do you see within the cell walls? Explain.*

_____

_____

PART II.   ONION EPIDERMAL CELLS _____

1. Cut an onion bulb into quarters.

2. Take an inner layer of the onion and, with a razor blade, cut several 1/2-cm squares through the paper-thin epidermis lining the leaf. Then, with a forceps, remove one of the squares of epidermal tissue. Place it in a drop of water on a slide. Add a cover slip. This procedure is shown in Figure 2.

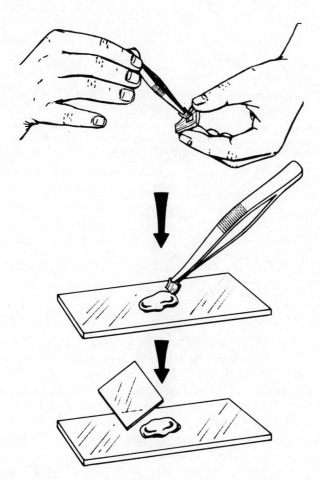

Figure 2

3. Examine the wet mount under low power. Adjust the light to provide the best contrast.

   a. *What is the shape of the cells?*

_____

Every plant cell is surrounded by a nonliving *cell wall* composed chiefly of cellulose. Pressed tightly against the cell wall is the *cell membrane*, which surrounds the granular *cytoplasm*. The central part of the cell consists of the large, fluid-filled *vacuole*. The spherical nucleus appears as a dense body in the cytoplasm near the cell wall. It is surrounded by a *nuclear membrane*. Within the nucleus are *nucleoli*.

b. *Make a diagram of a single cell. Label only the parts you see.*

c. *What structure do you see that indicates these are plant cells?*

_____

4. Carefully focus on the cytoplasm near the cell wall.

d. *Describe the appearance of the cytoplasm and any motion that you observe.*

_____

_____

_____

_____

Stain will enable you to see many cell structures in more detail.

5. Add a drop of Lugol's iodine solution to one side of the cover slip on your onion slide. **CAUTION:** *Stain can damage clothing and discolor skin.* Take a strip of paper towel and touch it to the water at the opposite edge of the cover slip. See Figure 3. This should pull the stain under the cover slip. If more stain is needed, repeat the procedure. Carefully observe the slide under low power, then high power.

e. *How many nuclei are present in each cell?*

_____

f. *What structures do you see in the nucleus? How many are there in each nucleus?*

_____

_____

_____

40

Observing Cork Cells and Onion Cells (continued)

g. *How does the cytoplasm in the stained cell differ in appearance from the cytoplasm in the unstained cell?*

_____

_____

_____

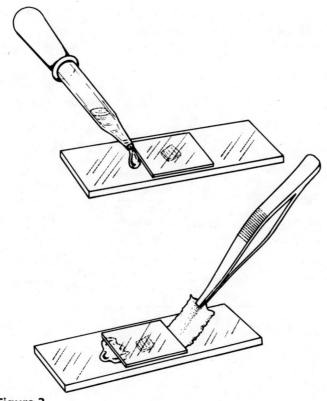

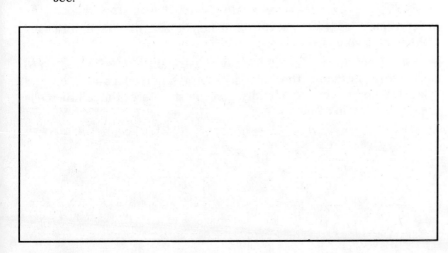

Figure 3

h. *Make a drawing of a stained onion cell. Label the structures you see.*

Analysis and Interpretations

1. How can you tell that cork cells are nonliving?

_____

_____

2. When Robert Hooke examined cork with his microscope, what did he really see?

_____

_____

3. Explain why cork floats on water. (Hint: What do the cork cells contain?)

_____

_____

4. What structures did you see in onion cells that you did not see in cork cells? What structures did you see in both?

_____

_____

5. What is the advantage of using stain?

_____

_____

_____

6. How can you tell that an onion cell has depth?

_____

_____

For Further Investigation

1. Prepare a list of the plant cell parts that you have seen in this lab. Use your text to write about the function of each part.

2. Determine the length, width, and height of an average cork cell. What is its volume?

3. Collect other plant cells (leaves, vegetables, tree bark, etc.) to observe under the microscope. Make drawings of each and label the parts you can identify. List the structures that all the cells seem to have in common.

How Plant and Animal Cells Differ

Lab 8

Background

Although plant and animal cells have many structures in common, they also have basic differences. Plant cells have a rigid cell wall, and if they are green, they also have *chloroplasts*. Animal cells lack both a cell wall and chloroplasts. They also lack the *central vacuole* common to plant cells.

You will observe and compare animal cells and plant cells. You will first examine epithelial cells from the inside of your cheek. Epithelium is a type of tissue that covers the surfaces of many organs and cavities of the body.

You will then examine cells from a leaf of the freshwater plant elodea. Elodea is often used in home fish tanks. The cells of this plant are green because they contain the pigment, *chlorophyll*. Chlorophyll, which is found in chloroplasts within each cell, enables plants to manufacture their own food.

Objectives

In this activity you will:
1. Observe human epithelial cells.
2. Observe elodea cells.
3. Describe the differences between animal cells and plant cells.

Materials

microscope	forceps
slides	Lugol's iodine solution
cover slips	in dropper bottle
toothpick	methylene blue stain
pipette	in dropper bottle
elodea	water

Procedures and Observations

PART I.   HUMAN EPITHELIAL CELLS _____

1. Place a drop of water on a clean slide. Obtain epithelial cells by gently scraping the inside of your cheek with a clean toothpick as shown in Figure 1. **CAUTION**: *Never reuse a toothpick or put anything in your mouth which may not be clean.* Stir the material from the toothpick in the drop of water on the slide. Then immediately break the toothpick in half and throw it away.

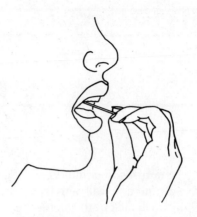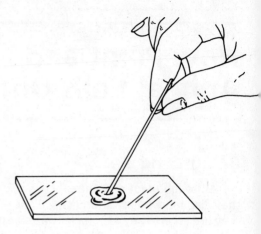

Figure 1

2. Add a small drop of methylene blue stain to the slide. **CAUTION:** *Stain can damage clothing and discolor skin.* Use a clean toothpick to stir the cells on the slide, then immediately break the toothpick and throw it away. Carefully place a cover slip on the slide. Examine the slide under low power. When you find some cells that are separate from each other, examine them under high power. Recall that you may have to adjust the diaphragm to reduce the intensity of the light.

a. *Make a drawing of two or three cells as they appear under high power. Label the nucleus, nuclear membrane, cytoplasm, and cell membrane of one of the cells.*

b. *What is the shape of the cells?*

c. *Describe the appearance of the cytoplasm.*

PART II.   ELODEA LEAF CELLS

1. Break off a small leaf near the tip of an elodea plant. With a forceps place the entire leaf in a drop of water on a clean slide. Add a cover slip. See Figure 2.

How Plant and Animal Cells Differ (continued)

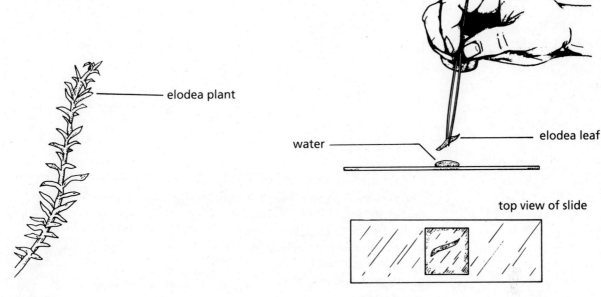

8

Figure 2

2. Examine the leaf under low power.

   a. *What is the shape of the cells?*

   _____

The boundary that you see around each cell is the cell wall. The numerous small, green bodies in the cells are the *chloroplasts*.

3. Look for an area in the leaf where you can see the cells most clearly. Examine these cells under high power, carefully focusing up and down with the fine adjustment.

   b. *Describe the shape and location of the chloroplasts.*

   _____

   _____

4. As you examine the cells, you may see the chloroplasts moving around. If they are not moving, warm the slide in your hand or under a bright lamp for a few minutes. Do not allow the slide to dry out. Then examine again under high power.

   c. *Describe how the chloroplasts move in a cell.*

   _____

   _____

   _____

   d. *Make a drawing of an elodea cell. Label the cell wall, chloroplasts, and any other structures you see.*

The cell membrane is pressed tightly against the inside of the cell wall and is difficult to see. Furthermore, the numerous chloroplasts often make it difficult to observe other cell structures in the elodea leaf cells. In order to see the nucleus, nucleoli, and vacuole more clearly, you are going to use a stain.

5. Break off another elodea leaf and place it in a drop of Lugol's iodine solution on a clean slide. Add a cover slip. Wait a minute or so for the stain to penetrate into the cells. Then examine the stained elodea cells under low and high power.

    e. *Make a drawing of a stained cell. Label the cell wall, cell membrane (if visible), chloroplasts, nucleus, nucleolus, and the large vacuole.*

    f. What structures can you see more clearly after staining?

How Plant and Animal Cells Differ (continued)

Analysis and Interpretations

1. What structures do human epithelial cells have in common with elodea cells?

_____

2. How do human epithelial cells and elodea cells differ?

_____

_____

3. Some of the epithelial cells are folded or wrinkled. What does this tell you about the thickness of the cells?

_____

4. Chloroplasts cannot move on their own. How do you think they move around the cell?

_____

5. What does Lugol's iodine stain do to the activity of the cell?

_____

For Further Investigation

1. What causes cyclosis, and what conditions are needed for it to occur? Design an experiment to increase cyclosis in plant cells.
2. Look at prepared slides of plant and animal tissues selected by your teacher. Write a description of the similarities and differences in the various cells.

Diffusion Through a Membrane

Lab 9

Background

The cell membrane acts as a barrier to some substances while allowing other substances to enter or leave the cell. When a membrane allows a particular substance to pass through it, it is said to be *permeable* to that substance. If a membrane allows the passage of some molecules or ions but blocks others, the membrane is *selectively permeable*. Cell membranes of living organisms are selectively permeable. The cell membrane acts as a selective barrier between the internal and external environments of the cell. The permeability of the cell membrane can change in response to changes in the cell's external and internal environments. Some substances, such as water, oxygen, and carbon dioxide, can pass freely through a cell membrane. Other substances have a more limited access to the cell.

In this activity, a nonliving cellophane membrane will be used as a model for a living cell membrane. Cellophane membranes are selective, but unlike living membranes, their selectivity does not vary. Water and other small molecules can pass through, but large molecules are blocked. The diffusion of molecules through the membrane is caused by random molecular movements and collisions.

Objectives

In this activity you will:
1. Learn simple tests for starch and sugar.
2. Observe the results of diffusion through a cellophane membrane.
3. Determine the permeability of a nonliving membrane for glucose, iodine, and starch.

Materials

cellophane dialysis tubing
starch solution
saturated glucose solution
Lugol's iodine solution
Clinitest tape
25-mL graduated cylinder

300-mL beakers
test tube
glass rod
pipette
string

Procedures and Observations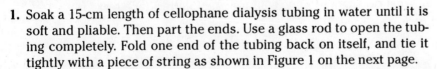

1. Soak a 15-cm length of cellophane dialysis tubing in water until it is soft and pliable. Then part the ends. Use a glass rod to open the tubing completely. Fold one end of the tubing back on itself, and tie it tightly with a piece of string as shown in Figure 1 on the next page.

Fill the tube about half full with starch solution. Then add 10 mL of the glucose solution. Tie the top of the tube tightly with string. Rinse the tubing with running water to remove any spillage from the outside.

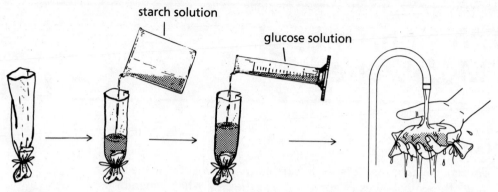

Figure 1

2. Mix 15 mL of Lugol's iodine solution into a 300-mL beaker half filled with tap water. **CAUTION:** *Be careful when using iodine solution to avoid staining hands and clothing.* Place the cellophane dialysis tubing in the beaker, and set it aside for about 20 minutes.

3. Add one pipette-full of glucose solution to a test tube. Rinse the pipette. Add one pipette-full of Lugol's iodine solution to the test tube, and stir. Record any color change you observe in Table 1. If there is no reaction, write "NR." After rinsing the test tube and pipette thoroughly, repeat the procedure twice, testing Lugol's iodine solution with starch and with tap water. Now place one drop of glucose solution on a piece of Clinitest tape, and record the result in Table 1. Repeat the procedure with starch solution and tap water.

4. Observe the colors of the solutions in the cellophane dialysis tubing and in the beaker.

   a. *What color changes do you observe?*

   _____

   _____

5. With a pipette, take several drops of solution from the bottom of the beaker. Apply the drops to a piece of Clinitest tape. Wait for 30 seconds.

   b. *What do you observe?*

   _____

Table 1

	glucose	starch	tap water
Lugol's iodine solution			
Clinitest tape			

Analysis and Interpretations

1. What do Lugol's iodine solution and Clinitest tape test for?

_____

2. What caused the color change observed in Step 4?

_____

_____

Diffusion Through a Membrane (continued)

9

3. Was there any evidence of starch in the solution in the beaker? How could you tell?

_____

_____

4. Given the results in Step 5, what substance was present in the solution in the beaker?

_____

5. Which substances diffused through the cellophane tubing? In which direction?

_____

_____

_____

For Further Investigation

Repeat the activity, substituting different materials for the cellophane dialysis tubing. You can experiment with sausage casings, which are available from butchers, or plastic sandwich bags.

Respiration in Yeast

Lab 10

Background

Yeasts are tiny, unicellular fungi that live on the surfaces of fruits and grains, or wherever sugars are plentiful. Yeasts can carry on either aerobic or anaerobic respiration to produce energy, depending upon conditions.

In the presence of oxygen, yeast carries on *aerobic respiration*. With favorable temperatures (40–45°C), the cells reproduce rapidly as long as oxygen and sugar are present. As sugar molecules are broken down, much ATP energy is released. Carbon dioxide and water are produced as waste products.

In the absence of oxygen, yeast carries on *anaerobic respiration*, also known as *fermentation*. Less energy is released because sugar is only partially broken down. The products of yeast fermentation are carbon dioxide and ethyl alcohol. In bread-making, the bubbles of carbon dioxide produced by fermentation make the dough rise. The ethyl alcohol evaporates rapidly in the heat of the oven. Ethyl alcohol produced by fermentation is used in making alcoholic beverages and in many industrial processes.

Objectives

In this activity you will:
1. Allow common yeast, *Saccharomyces cerevisiae*, to grow under aerobic and anaerobic conditions.
2. Identify the waste products of yeast fermentation.

Materials

250-mL flasks
one-holed stopper fitted with
    a short length of glass tubing
two-holed stopper fitted with
    one long and one short length
    of glass tubing
rubber tubing
glass-marking pencil
10-mL and 50-mL graduated
    cylinders
test tubes

test tube rack
soda straws
limewater
10% glucose solution kept
    at 45–50° C
yeast suspension
Lugol's iodine solution in
    dropper bottle
10% sodium hydroxide solution
    in dropper bottle

Procedures and Observations

PART I.   SETTING UP THE EXPERIMENT _____

Work in a group to assemble the setup and then do the rest of the activity alone.

1. Label one flask *A* and also mark it with the initials of one person in your group.

2. Pour 50 mL of the warm 10% glucose solution into flask A. Add 3 mL of the yeast suspension. Swirl the contents of the flask to mix the yeast thoroughly into the solution. Rinse the graduated cylinder well.

Formation of bubbles indicates that the yeast cells are carrying on aerobic respiration. The bubbles are carbon dioxide gas.

3. Cap the flask with the one-holed stopper fitted with a short glass tube. See Figure 1, flask A. Swirl the contents of the flask again. Set it aside.

   a. *Do you see any bubbles forming?*

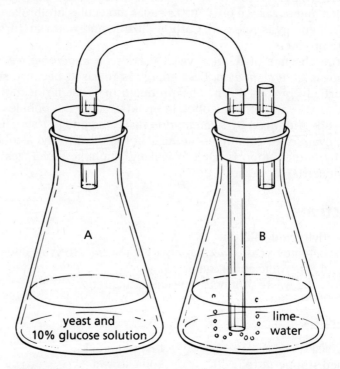

Figure 1

4. Label another flask *B* and mark it with the same initials used before.

Limewater is a clear solution. When it is mixed with carbon dioxide, it turns cloudy.

5. Pour 50 mL of limewater into flask B, using a clean graduated cylinder. Stopper the flask with the two-holed stopper fitted with a long and short glass tube. Make sure that the long glass tube extends well beneath the surface of the limewater as shown in Figure 1, flask B. **CAUTION:** *It is very easy to cut yourself when pushing glass tubing into a rubber stopper. If the glass tubing is not correctly positioned, ask your teacher to help you adjust it.*

6. Watch as your teacher assembles two control setups: (1) a flask containing yeast and warm water connected to a flask containing

Respiration in Yeast   (continued)

limewater; and (2) a flask containing warm 10% glucose solution connected to a flask containing limewater.

7. Using rubber tubing, connect the short glass tube in flask A and the long glass tube in flask B as shown in Figure 1. Make sure the connections are tight. You wish gas to flow from flask A into the limewater in flask B.

8. Carefully swirl the contents of flask A again. Then leave the setup overnight at room temperature.

9. Pour 10 mL of limewater into a test tube. Place a soda straw in the test tube so that its end is in the limewater.

10. Blow gently through the straw so that your breath bubbles into the limewater. **CAUTION:** *Be sure to wear your safety goggles and apron. Be careful not to spatter the limewater.* Continue to blow into the limewater until a change occurs.

   b. *Describe what happened to the limewater after you had blown into it.*

   _____

_____

PART II.   OBSERVATIONS AFTER 24 HOURS _____

1. After 24 hours, observe your group's setup.

   a. *Describe any changes you see in flask A.*

   _____

   b. *Describe any changes you see in flask B.*

   _____

2. Observe the yeast and water control.

   c. *Is there any change in the limewater flask? If so, describe it.*

   _____

3. Observe the glucose control.

   d. *Is there any change in the limewater flask? If so, describe it.*

   _____

4. Leave the setup overnight at room temperature again.

PART III.   OBSERVATIONS AFTER 48 HOURS _____

1. After another 24 hours, observe flask A in your group's setup.

   a. *Do you see any activity in flask A? If so, describe it.*

   _____

2. Observe flask B in your group's setup.

   b. *Describe the appearance of the limewater.*

   _____

_____

3. Disconnect the rubber tubing and unstopper the flasks. Pour 5 mL of the fluid from flask A into a clean test tube. You will test this sample for the presence of ethyl alcohol in the following way.

4. Add 4 drops of 10% sodium hydroxide. **CAUTION:** *Be careful not to spill the sodium hydroxide. If you do get any on yourself, wash the area immediately under cold running water and notify your teacher.*

5. Add 1 drop of Lugol's iodine solution. **CAUTION:** *Lugol's iodine solution can stain hands and clothing.* Gently swirl the contents of the tube. If the color disappears, add another drop of Lugol's solution and swirl again. Stop adding Lugol's solution when the faint yellow color does not disappear when you swirl the contents of the tube.

6. After you have obtained a faint yellow color that does not disappear, let the test tube stand in the rack for 2 minutes.

A layer of light yellow material that settles to the bottom of the test tube indicates the presence of ethyl alcohol.

7. Swirl the contents of the test tube again and set the tube in the rack.

    c. *What do you observe?*

_____

_____

8. Clean up and put away your equipment and materials as directed by your teacher.

Analysis and Interpretations

  1. Why was glucose mixed with the yeast cells?

_____

  2. When the yeast and glucose were first mixed together in flask A, which kind of respiration took place—aerobic or anaerobic? Why?

_____

_____

  3. After the setups were connected, did yeast perform aerobic or anaerobic respiration? Explain.

_____

_____

_____

  4. What solution is used to detect the presence of carbon dioxide?

_____

  5. What was the purpose of breathing into the limewater?

_____

_____

_____

Respiration in Yeast (continued)

6. Did the yeast cells produce carbon dioxide? How do you know?

_____

_____

_____

7. Did the yeast cells produce alcohol? How do you know?

_____

_____

8. Could you see any activity in flask A when you made the observations for Part II? Explain.

_____

_____

9. Why does a flask of yeast and warm water connected to a flask of limewater serve as a control? Why does a flask of glucose solution connected to a flask of limewater serve as a control?

_____

_____

_____

_____

10. Explain the activity you saw in flask A during Part III.

_____

_____

_____

11. How can you reasonably be sure that no oxygen entered flask A once the original oxygen was used up? Why is this important?

_____

_____

_____

_____

12. What was the purpose of the small glass tube in the stopper in flask B?

_____

_____

_____

For Further Investigation

1. Save the controls and test them for the presence of alcohol. Record your results. Using these results and those obtained in your laboratory activity, write a short paragraph telling how the controls help you to verify that yeast cells perform anaerobic respiration.

2. Make bread at home. While it is rising, and while it is first baking, try to detect the odor of alcohol in the vapors coming from the dough.

Classifying Leaves

Lab 11

Background

Over the centuries, people who study the natural world have tried to sort, or classify, organisms into groups whose members show a logical relationship to each other. The science of classification is called *taxonomy*.

One of the products of taxonomy is the development of classification keys. A *classification key* is an organized list of characteristics that can be used to identify organisms. Such keys have been made for almost every group of organisms in the world.

Objectives

In this activity you will:
1. Identify structural characteristics of leaves and find differences between leaves.
2. Construct a classification key based on the characteristics of leaves.

Materials

paper
pencil

Procedures and Observations

PART I. STUDYING LEAF STRUCTURE

In this lab you will observe the leaves of a number of plants, and learn the meanings of some of the terms used to describe leaf characteristics. You will make use of these terms when you construct a key in Part II.

1. Look at Figure 1, which shows a leaf from a willow tree and a leaf from a chestnut oak tree. Compare the shapes of these leaves. Notice that the willow leaf is long and pointed, while the chestnut oak leaf is oval.

2. Compare the edges of the two leaves shown in Figure 1. Notice that the edges of the willow leaf are notched, while the edges of the chestnut oak leaf are wavy. Some other kinds of leaves have edges that are lobed, or deeply indented. Still other leaves have smooth edges.

3. Compare the patterns of the veins of the two leaves shown in Figure 1. As you can see, they are similar: both leaves have a network of small veins that branch off a single, main vein. Compare this pattern of veins, called *pinnate-netted*, to the two other vein patterns shown in Figure 2.

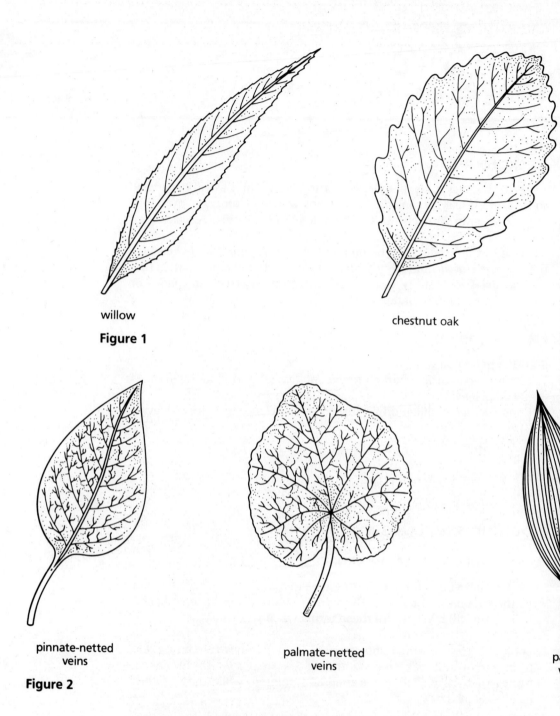

willow

chestnut oak

Figure 1

pinnate-netted
veins

palmate-netted
veins

pa
ve

Figure 2

Notice that the veins in a *palmate* pattern start at the base of the leaf and extend outward, as fingers extend outward from the palm of the hand. The terms palmate and pinnate also refer to other leaf characteristics. Leaves that are lobed show one of two patterns, palmate or pinnate.

4. Compare the leaves of the sweet gum and the post oak, shown in Figure 3. Notice that the sweet gum leaf is palmately lobed, and the post oak is pinnately lobed.

Classifying Leaves (continued)

sweet gum

post oak

Figure 3

So far in this lab activity, you have observed *simple* leaves, or leaves that are in one piece. Sometimes leaves are divided into smaller segments, called *leaflets*. A leaf that is divided in this way is called a *compound* leaf. Compound leaves show one of two patterns, palmate or pinnate.

5. Look at the leaflets of the clover and tick trefoil, shown in Figure 4. Notice that the clover leaf is palmately compound and the tick trefoil leaf is pinnately compound.

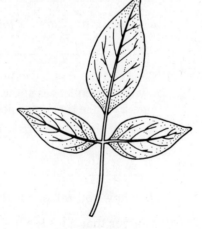

clover

tick trefoil

Figure 4

PART II.   CONSTRUCTING A KEY _____

Classification keys are used in biology to find the classification or the name of a particular organism. By following a series of descriptions, various other organisms are eliminated. At the end of the process, the organism is identified.

A classification key is made up of a series of steps. Each step has two statements that divide the items being classified into two groups. Each statement is then followed by a direction to go to another step or by the name of that group or item.

To make a key, you start with two statements that divide all the items being classified into just two groups. Each of those groups must then be divided into two more groups, continuing to divide groups until all items have been identified. The characteristics used and the order of the steps is chosen by the person constructing the key. Thus there are many possible keys for any group of items.

1. To practice making a key, complete this simple classification key of four items: a pencil, a pen, a shoe, and a glove.

   1a. Used for writing _____......go to Step 2

   1b. Worn on the body _____......go to Step 3

   2a. Contains ink _____......pen

   2b. Contains graphite _____......pencil

   3a. _____......_____

   3b. _____......_____

2. In order to construct a key of leaves, you will need to differentiate between the leaves. Using what you learned in Part I, answer the questions about the leaves shown in Figure 5.

   a. *What is the vein pattern of leaf A?*

   _____

   b. *How are the leaflets arranged in leaf D?*

   _____

   c. *What is the pattern of lobes in leaf F?*

   _____

3. The key that you write should make it possible for someone to identify the seven leaves shown in Figure 5. An outline for the key is provided. Notice that a possible first step has been written for you.

   d. *What leaf characteristic is used in Step 1 for dividing the leaves into two groups?*

   _____

4. Plan how you will divide the group of compound leaves in Step 2.

Remember that all steps will contain two contrasting statements. Use the leaf characteristics you learned in Part I to write the statements for each step. If a statement in any step leads you to more than one leaf, you will need further steps to separate those leaves. For these cases, indicate the number of the next step. If a statement in any step leads you to only one leaf, you have identified that leaf. Write the genus name of the plant. When you have identified and written in the names of all seven plants, you have finished your key.

Classifying Leaves (continued)

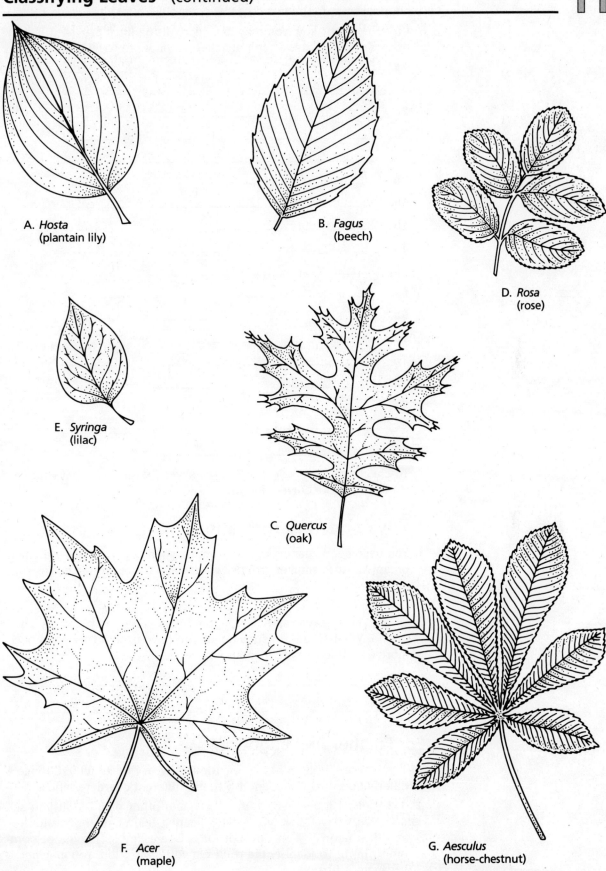

A. *Hosta*
(plantain lily)

B. *Fagus*
(beech)

D. *Rosa*
(rose)

E. *Syringa*
(lilac)

C. *Quercus*
(oak)

F. *Acer*
(maple)

G. *Aesculus*
(horse-chestnut)

Figure 5

5. Write the statements for Step 2 in the blanks provided. This step should separate the two different compound leaves in Figure 5.

6. Complete your key. You may not need all the lines provided. If you need more lines, use a separate sheet of paper to write them.

1a. leaves simple .....go to Step 3

1b. leaves compound .....go to Step 2

2a. _____ ..... _____

2b. _____ ..... _____

3a. _____ ..... _____

3b. _____ ..... _____

4a. _____ ..... _____

4b. _____ ..... _____

5a. _____ ..... _____

5b. _____ ..... _____

6a. _____ ..... _____

6b. _____ ..... _____

7a. _____ ..... _____

7b. _____ ..... _____

8a. _____ ..... _____

8b. _____ ..... _____

9a. _____ ..... _____

9b. _____ ..... _____

7. To check your key, select one of the seven leaves and see if your key leads you to the correct identity.

Analysis and Interpretations

1. You used genus names in constructing your key. If your key divided organisms into smaller groups, what would those groups be?

_____

2. Of the seven leaves shown in Figure 5, only one was pinnately compound. What characteristics might you have used if there had been more than one pinnately compound leaf?

_____

For Further Investigation

1. Try to write a different key for the leaves in this activity. Choose a different starting point, and try to use different characteristics.

2. Collect a few leaves from trees and other plants that you see every day. Before you start collecting, learn to identify, and thus avoid, poison ivy and poison oak. Use a key to leaves of common plants to identify the leaves in your collection. You may find a key in your library.

Nutrition in Paramecia

Lab 12

Background

The paramecium is a freshwater protozoan about 150 micrometers long. You can barely see it with your naked eye. Paramecia live in quiet ponds, swimming about by means of hairlike *cilia* that cover the cell. The cilia are also used for the *ingestion* of food. They sweep bacteria and small organisms into the *oral groove* and *gullet*. The food is then packaged into *food vacuoles* where digestion occurs. You can culture paramecia and then feed them in order to observe the processes of ingestion and digestion. It is possible to feed paramecia, then observe them with the microscope as they ingest the food particles. You can also see evidences of digestion within food vacuoles.

Objectives

In this activity you will:
1. Feed paramecia and watch them ingest food particles.
2. Observe changes inside the food vacuoles as digestion occurs.

Materials

prepared paramecium culture	10% methyl cellulose
grass with seed heads (hay)	Congo red—yeast suspension
culture dish	flat toothpicks
scissors	pipettes
2-L container	slides
hot plate	cover slips
boiled water	paper towels
glass-marking pencil	microscope

Procedures and Observations

Note: *Start Part I one week before you plan to do Part II.*

PART I.   PREPARATION OF PARAMECIUM CULTURE _____

1. With scissors, cut a handful of hay, including the seed heads, into 5-cm pieces. Place the pieces in a 2-L container and cover them with water.

2. Put the container on a hot plate and let the container boil for 10 minutes. Allow the container to cool.

3. With a glass-marking pencil, put the initials of a person in your group on a culture dish.

4. Half fill the culture dish with the boiled hay. Then cover the hay with some of the water in which it was boiled. If there is not enough, use plain boiled water. Keep the water level in the culture dish just above the level of the hay.

5. Set the uncovered culture dish aside at room temperature. Inspect it daily and make sure there is enough water in it. If water must be added, make sure that it has been boiled.

After several days, a scum forms on the surface of the culture. This indicates that bacterial populations are building up.

6. When the scum appears, inoculate your culture with the prepared paramecium culture. First, stir the prepared paramecium culture with a pipette until it is mixed. Then fill the pipette and transfer the culture to the culture dish containing the hay mixture.

The paramecia feed on the bacteria in the hay mixture and reproduce rapidly.

7. Set the culture aside uncovered for 3 days at room temperature. Keep the hay just covered with boiled water.

8. On the fourth day, pick up a drop of thick, cloudy material with a pipette and transfer it to a clean slide. Try to get material from near the hay where it is especially thick. Also, try not to stir up the culture as you do it. Put a cover slip on the slide.

9. Look at the slide in good light, without a microscope. You should see tiny white organisms swimming in the culture.

10. Then examine the slide under low power. Observe the paramecia. If you look closely, you may see some paramecia undergoing binary fission. See Figure 1.

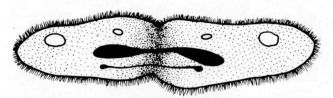

Figure 1

PART II.   INGESTION AND DIGESTION

Methyl cellulose, which is a thick liquid, is used to slow down microscopic organisms on a slide.

1. Place 2 drops of methyl cellulose on a slide. With the flat end of a toothpick, push the methyl cellulose into a ring about the size of a dime in the center of the slide. **CAUTION:** *Be careful not to spill methyl cellulose. It can irritate your hands.*

2. With a pipette, transfer 1 drop of the cloudy paramecium culture to the center of the ring of methyl cellulose. Do not stir up the culture.

3. Carefully place the slide on the microscope stage. Remember that it has no cover slip and can spill easily. Locate a paramecium under low power. Reduce the amount of light reaching the specimen, and observe the cilia.

   a. *Describe the motion of the cilia.*

Nutrition in Paramecia (continued) 12

4. Scoop up a small drop of Congo red—yeast suspension with the flat end of a toothpick. **CAUTION:** *Be careful using the Congo red mixture. It is a dye and can stain hands and clothing.* Without bumping the low-power objective, carefully reach under it and transfer the red yeast cells on the toothpick to the drop of paramecium culture in the center of the methyl cellulose ring. Touch only the tip of the toothpick to the culture.

5. Immediately observe the paramecia under low power. Find the red yeast cells that you added. Try to see the red cells being swept into the oral grooves of the paramecia. Observe 8 or 10 organisms.

   b. *Describe what you observe.*

   _____

   _____

6. Carefully remove the slide from the stage and add a cover slip.

Within the paramecium, the yeast cells are clustered inside food vacuoles. The food vacuoles form one at a time at the base of the gullet. When a vacuole reaches a certain size, it moves away from the gullet and is circulated by the streaming of the cytoplasm. The pathway of a food vacuole in a paramecium is shown in Figure 2.

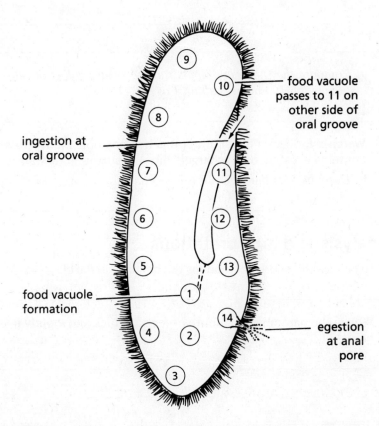

Figure 2

7. Again observe the paramecia under low power. Look for one that has ingested some red yeast cells.

   c. *Describe how the red yeast cells are spread throughout the paramecium.*

   _____

   _____

Congo red is a dye that makes the yeast cells easy to see. It is also a pH indicator. At pH 5 it is red and at pH 3 it is green-blue.

8. Find a paramecium that has been stopped by the methyl cellulose and that contains yeast cells in food vacuoles. Focus on it, then switch to high power.

   d. *Are all the food vacuoles red? If not, what color are they?*

   _____

9. Still under high power, follow the pathway of one red vacuote in the paramecium. Try to see when it turns green-blue.

   e. *At approximately which numbered position does the Congo red indicator turn green-blue?*

   _____

   f. *Compare the size and shape of yeast cells at position 10 and at position 1 or 2.*

   _____

   _____

   g. *Compare the shape and appearance (besides color) of yeast cells at position 10 and at position 1 or 2.*

   _____

10. Watch a food vacuole as it approaches position 14. Try to see its contents egested, or discharged, into the surrounding water.

    h. *Describe how the material is egested.*

    _____

Analysis and Interpretations

1. What was the source of food for the bacteria in Part I?

   _____

2. Why is the paramecium culture especially thick and cloudy near the hay?

   _____

   _____

   _____

   _____

Nutrition in Paramecia (continued)

12

3. By what means does a paramecium ingest food particles?

_____

_____

4. What did the change in color of food vacuoles indicate?

_____

_____

5. What caused the change in pH?

_____

6. Explain why the yeast cells differ in shape and appearance in position 10 from that in positions 1 and 2.

_____

_____

7. If you saw egestion, what happened to the food vacuole afterward?

_____

8. Give two reasons why the cover slip was added before using high power.

_____

_____

Measuring Energy in Foods

Lab 13

Background

Organisms need energy to grow, to respond, and to reproduce. Animals get energy to carry out these life processes by taking in food. To find out how much energy is stored in a food, a device called a calorimeter can be used. In a calorimeter, food is burned, giving off energy in the form of heat. The heat is transferred to a container of water, causing the temperature of the water to rise. The change in water temperature can then be used to calculate how much heat was transferred from the burning material to the water, or how much energy was stored in the food.

Heat energy is measured in units called *calories*. One calorie is the amount of heat needed to raise the temperature of 1 g of water 1°C. The energy in foods is commonly expressed in kilocalories, also called *Calories* (with an uppercase *C*). One Calorie equals 1000 calories, or the amount of heat needed to raise the temperature of 1 kg of water by 1°C. The SI unit of energy is joules. One calorie equals 4.18 joules.

Objectives

In this activity you will:
1. Construct a simple calorimeter.
2. Measure the amount of energy stored in a peanut.
3. Calculate the number of Calories in 100 g of peanut.

Materials

safety goggles	small metal paper clip
apron	cork stopper
ring stand	water
test tube clamp	10-mL graduated cylinder
heat-proof test tube	raw peanuts in shells (not roasted)
balance	2 twist ties (flat plastic-coated wires)
thermometer	matches
metric ruler	table of Calorie yields of foods

Procedures and Observations

PART I. MAKING AND USING A SIMPLE CALORIMETER _____

To obtain the most accurate results possible, follow all directions carefully.

1. First, construct a simple calorimeter, as shown in Figure 1: Attach a test-tube clamp to a ring stand. Fasten a small, heat-proof test tube in the clamp. Make the clamp tight enough to hold the test tube, but loose enough that the test tube can be turned within the clamp. (This will allow the test tube to expand without breaking when it heats.)

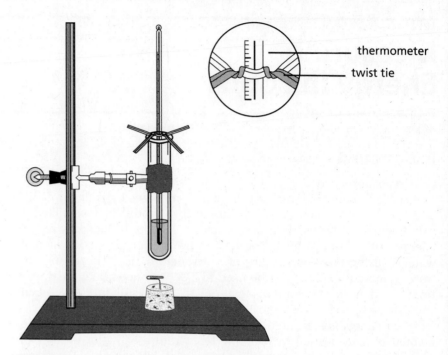

Figure 1

2. Prepare a thermometer for measuring the water temperature in the test tube: Fasten two twist ties to the middle of the thermometer, leaving the ends extended outward on each side, as shown in the figure. The twist ties will suspend the thermometer in the water and prevent it from resting on the bottom of the test tube. Carefully lower the thermometer into the test tube until the bulb is 1 cm from the bottom of the tube, adjusting the twist ties as necessary.

3. Prepare a food platform for the calorimeter: Bend a free end of a small paper clip so that it is at a right angle to the clip. Insert this end into a cork stopper as shown in Figure 2. Set the food platform on the base of the ring stand. Adjust the test-tube clamp so that the bottom of the test tube is 1.5 cm from the top of the food platform.

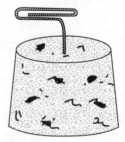

Figure 2

4. Carefully add 10 mL of room-temperature water to the test tube.

   a. *Record the water temperature in your data table.*

5. Shell a raw peanut and separate one seed into halves. Remove the food platform from the calorimeter set up. Set one half of a peanut seed on the food platform. Using the balance, find the combined mass of the peanut and food platform.

Measuring Energy in Foods (continued)

b. *Record the mass of the peanut and food platform in the space on your data table.*

6. Place the food platform near the calorimeter set up. Check that the peanut is well balanced on the platform and that it does not fall off when the platform is moved. Use a match to ignite the peanut. It may take a few seconds for the peanut to begin to flame. Immediately place the food platform under the test tube. **CAUTION:** *Wear your safety goggles. Handle the matches and the burning peanut carefully.*

7. Allow the peanut to burn completely. Immediately check the thermometer.

   c. *Record the water temperature on your data sheet.*

   d. *Calculate and record the change in water temperature.*

8. When the peanut is no longer burning and after you have found the temperature of the water, find the change in mass of the peanut: Use the balance to find the combined mass of the burnt peanut and the food platform. Continue to handle the burnt peanut carefully—it may still be hot.

   e. *Record the mass on your data table.*

   f. *Find the difference in mass of the peanut before and after burning. Record this figure on your data table.*

9. Using another sample of peanut, repeat the calorimetry procedure. Repeat steps 4 through 8, using fresh, room-temperature water in the test tube.

PART II. CALCULATING STORED ENERGY IN FOOD _____

You can now use the data you have collected to calculate the amount of heat released from a food sample. You will use the following formula:

$$\frac{\text{calories in}}{\text{peanut (cal)}} = \frac{\text{mass of water}}{\text{(g)}} \times \frac{\text{change in water}}{\text{temperature (°C)}} \times \frac{\text{specific heat (cal/g°C)}}{\text{of water}}$$

Recall that 1 mL water has a mass of 1 g. The specific heat of water is the number of calories needed to raise the temperature of 1 g of water by 1°C. In the formula, specific heat is expressed as 1 cal/g°C.

1. Use the formula given above to find the energy contained in each of the peanuts used in Part I.

   a. *Show your calculations here.*

   _____

   _____

   b. *On your data table, record the number of calories in each peanut.*

Calorie charts show energy values in Calories, or kilocalories, per 100 g of food. To find the number of calories per gram of food, divide the number of calories you calculated (Step 1-b) by the change in mass of the peanut (recorded on your data table). You will then need to multiply by 100 to find the calories per 100 g of food. To change calories to

Calories (kilocalories), divide by 1000. These calculations are incorporated in the following formula:

$$\text{Cal/100 g} = \left(\frac{\text{calories in}}{\text{peanut (cal)}} \div \frac{\text{change in mass}}{\text{(g)}} \right) \times 100 \times (1 \text{ Cal/1000 cal})$$

2. Use the formula to calculate the Calories of energy per 100 g of peanuts for each of your two tests.

    c. *Show your calculations here.*

_____

_____

    d. *On your data table, fill in the number of Calories found for each 100 g of peanut.*

The values you calculate for the amount of energy in a given food may differ from the values given in published tables. Although the procedure used to generate those values is similar to the procedure you have followed, different equipment, which is not available in a school laboratory, is used.

    e. *How do your two calculations of the number of Calories per 100 g of peanuts, compare to each other? How do these numbers compare to the value given in a table of Calorie yields of foods?*

_____

_____

_____

    f. *Find the average of your two calculations. Record this number on the board. Then find the class average for the number of Calories per 100 g of peanuts.*

      Group Average:

      Class Average:

Data Table

	Trial 1	Trial 2
Starting water temperature (°C)		
Ending water temperature (°C)		
Change in water temperature (°C)		
Mass of peanut and platform before burning (g)		
Mass of peanut and platform after burning (g)		
Change in mass of peanut (g)		
Calories in peanut (cal)		
Kilocalories (Calories) per 100 grams of peanuts (Cal/100 g)		

Measuring Energy in Foods (continued)

13

Analysis and Interpretations

1. Why is it important to prevent the thermometer from resting on the bottom of the test tube?

_____

_____

2. Why do the procedures direct you to quickly place the burning peanut under the water-filled test tube?

_____

_____

3. When you calculated the number of Calories per 100 grams of peanut, did you get the same number for the two samples? If not, explain why.

_____

_____

4. How might the procedure you followed be changed to make more accurate measurement of the heat lost by the peanut?

_____

_____

_____

_____

_____

For Further Investigation

1. Use your calorimeter to find the amount of energy in a different food. In addition to many types of nuts, stale mini marshmallows work well on a calorimeter. Try altering the procedure to get as accurate a measurement as possible. **CAUTION:** *Get permission from your teacher to use the calorimeter. Write down your procedure and check your changes with your teacher to make sure that your experiment will be safe.*

2. Study a Calorie chart. What foods are especially high in Calorie content? What foods are low?

Investigating Pulse Rate

Lab 14

Background

The heart pumps blood through blood vessels to all parts of the body. With each contraction of the heart, blood is forced into the arteries. This surge of pressure is felt in the arteries as the *pulse*. The rhythmic pulse can be felt any place where an artery is close to the surface of the body and can be pressed against some firm tissue.

The pulse rate is exactly equal to the heartbeat rate. Medical personnel use the pulse rate as one indication of how the heart is functioning. Heart rate is influenced by many things, such as age, sex, physiological state, psychological state, and temperature. In this activity you will investigate how several of these factors influence the pulse rate.

Objectives

In this activity, you will:
1. Feel a pulse and determine pulse rates.
2. Determine the effect on pulse rate of standing at attention, holding your breath, breathing into a bag, deep breathing, and exercise.
3. Make a line graph to show the effect of exercise on pulse rate.

Materials

clock or watch with second hand
paper bags

Procedures and Observations

Work in pairs. Throughout this activity you and your partner will take turns being the subject and the experimenter. First you must learn how to take a pulse.
1. Study Figure 1 to see how to locate the pulse in your partner's wrist.

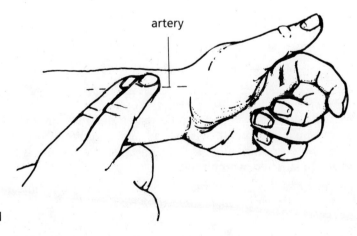

artery

Figure 1

2. After you have sat quietly for 1 minute, have your partner count your pulse for 15 seconds.

    a. *Record this number in Table 1. Determine your pulse rate for 1 minute by multiplying the number by 4. Then record your pulse rate per minute in Table 1.*

Table 1. Determining Resting Pulse Rate

Trial	Pulse rate/15 sec.	Pulse rate/min.
1		
2		
3		

3. Repeat Step 2 two more times. Then switch roles with your partner.

    b. *Record the results in Table 1 and then determine your average resting pulse rate per minute. Record your average resting pulse rate in Table 2 and on the chart on the board according to your sex.*

4. The subject should stand stiffly at attention for 2 minutes. Then, while the subject is still standing at attention, the pulse should be taken by the experimenter for 15 seconds. Switch roles.

    c. *Determine your pulse rate per minute by multiplying this number by 4. Record your at-attention pulse rate in Table 2 and on the board.*

Table 2. Effect of Activity on Pulse Rate

Activity	Your Pulse rate/min.	Average Female Pulse rate/min.	Average Male Pulse rate/min.
resting			
standing at attention			
holding breath			
breathing into paper bag			
breathing deeply			
exercise			
exercise (1 min after)			
exercise (2 min after)			
exercise (3 min after)			
exercise (4 min after)			
exercise (5 min after)			
exercise (6 min after)			

5. While seated, the subject should take a deep breath, exhale part of it, and hold the breath as long as possible. While breath is being held, the subject's pulse should be taken by the experimenter for 15 seconds. Then switch roles.

    d. *Determine your pulse rate per minute by multiplying this number by 4. Record your breath-holding pulse rate in Table 2 and on the board.*

Investigating Pulse Rate (continued)

14

6. While seated, the subject should hold an open paper bag tightly over the mouth. Do not breathe through the nose. The subject should breathe through the mouth from the air in the bag for 2 minutes. Toward the end of the second minute, the pulse of the subject should be taken by the experimenter for 15 seconds. Then switch roles.

   e. *Determine your pulse rate per minute by multiplying this number by 4. Record your breathing-into-bag pulse rate in Table 2 and on the board.*

7. While seated, the subject should take deep breaths regularly for 30 seconds. After the first 15 seconds, the pulse of the subject should be taken by the experimenter for the remaining 15 seconds of deep breathing. Then switch roles.

Note: *If you become lightheaded while taking deep breaths, hold your breath for a few seconds.*

   f. *Determine your pulse rate per minute by multiplying this number by 4. Record your deep-breathing pulse rate in Table 2 and on the board.*

The time needed for your pulse to return to the sitting pulse rate is called recovery time.

8. The subject should step up and down from a sturdy chair, run in place or do jumping jacks for one minute. Immediately after exercise, the subject should sit and the pulse should be taken for 15 seconds. Then it should be taken again after 45 seconds, so that a 15 second pulse is taken every minute for 6 minutes. Switch roles.

   g. *Determine each pulse rate per minute by multiplying the numbers by 4. Record your after-exercise pulse rates in Table 2 and on the board.*

   h. *Determine the class pulse rate averages for males and females in each activity and record them in Table 2.*

Analysis and Interpretations

1. How does your resting pulse rate compare with the average for your sex? What is illustrated by any difference between your resting pulse rate and the average?

_____

_____

2. Why did you take a resting pulse rate?

_____

_____

3. Why do you think that holding your breath or breathing into a bag affects the pulse rate?

_____

_____

4. Which activity increased your pulse rate the most? What does this increase indicate?

_____

_____

5. What do you think is the relationship between physical condition and pulse rate after exercise? Between physical condition and recovery time?

_____

_____

6. Construct a line graph to show what happens to your pulse rate after exercise. Put pulse rate per minute on the vertical axis and time in minutes on the horizontal axis.

7. Why do athletes often have a lower pulse rate than nonathletes?

_____

_____

_____

Computer Activity

In Laboratory Experiment 14, you investigated the effects of physical activity on your resting pulse rate. The computer program called *Cardiovascular Fitness Lab* uses a light probe to automatically monitor your pulse rate during exercise or while at rest.

Identifying Blood

Lab 15

Background

Blood is a complex fluid tissue that transports materials throughout the body. Blood has both liquid and solid parts. The liquid portion of blood, plasma, consists mainly of water and proteins. It transports foods, wastes, salts, and hormones. The solid portion of blood consists of red blood cells, white blood cells, and platelets. Red blood cells carry oxygen to the body cells. White blood cells help the body fight infections. Platelets aid in the clotting of blood.

Karl Landsteiner discovered the ABO blood groups in the early 1900s. This important discovery made blood transfusions safe. In transfusions, the blood types of the donor and the recipient must be carefully matched. Transfusion of the wrong type of blood can result in agglutination, or clumping, of red blood cells. Agglutination is the result of an immune reaction between *antigens* on the red blood cells of the donor and *antibodies* in the blood plasma of the recipient.

Objectives

In this activity you will:
1. Identify blood cells on a prepared slide.
2. Simulate determining blood type using chemical precipitates.

Materials

prepared human blood smear
    (Wright's stain)
microscope
colored pencils
glass-marking pencil
2 depression well slides

6 dropper bottles containing:
    "anti-A serum"
    "anti-B serum"
    simulated blood sample 1
    simulated blood sample 2
    simulated blood sample 3
    simulated blood sample 4

Procedures and Observations

PART I. IDENTIFYING BLOOD CELLS

You will be using a prepared slide of a human blood smear. A blood smear is made by spreading a drop of blood thinly across a microscope slide. The smear is then stained with Wright's stain, which makes white blood cells and platelets more visible. Wright's stain darkly stains the nuclei and cytoplasmic granules of cells.

1. Obtain a prepared slide of a blood smear. Observe the slide under low power on your microscope, then switch to high power. Compare what you see in the microscope to Figure 1.

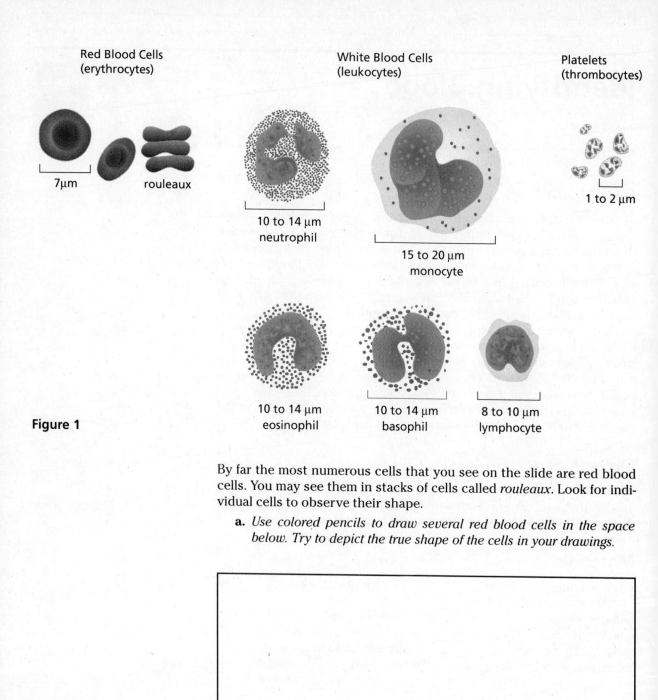

Red Blood Cells
(erythrocytes)

7μm   rouleaux

White Blood Cells
(leukocytes)

10 to 14 μm
neutrophil

15 to 20 μm
monocyte

10 to 14 μm
eosinophil

10 to 14 μm
basophil

8 to 10 μm
lymphocyte

Platelets
(thrombocytes)

1 to 2 μm

Figure 1

By far the most numerous cells that you see on the slide are red blood cells. You may see them in stacks of cells called *rouleaux*. Look for individual cells to observe their shape.

a. *Use colored pencils to draw several red blood cells in the space below. Try to depict the true shape of the cells in your drawings.*

b. *Do the red blood cells appear to have a nucleus? Do they have granules?*

c. *Estimate the number of red blood cells in the high-power field of your microscope.*

Identifying Blood Cells and Blood Types (continued)

Platelets are fragments of larger cells called megakaryocytes, which are found in bone marrow. Platelets are smaller than red blood cells, they are disk-shaped, and they stain a pale-blue color.

2. Locate some platelets in the blood smear.

   d. *In the space provided, draw a few platelets as they appear in the microscope. Keep their size in scale with the red blood cells you drew earlier.*

   e. *Estimate the number of platelets in the high-power field of your microscope.*

   _____

White blood cells are larger and less numerous than red blood cells. There are several types of white blood cells that can be recognized by their size, the shape of their nuclei, and the staining of their cytoplasm.

3. Search the smear for white blood cells. See Figure 1.

   f. *Use colored pencils to draw several different kinds of white blood cells in the space provided. Again, keep the size of your drawings to scale.*

   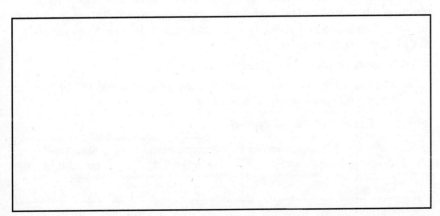

   g. Estimate the number of white blood cells in the high-power field.

   _____

PART II.   SIMULATING BLOOD TYPING

Table 1 shows the four blood types of the ABO system. The table also shows the antigens and antibodies present in each type, and the blood types that can be received safely in a transfusion. Usually the blood given in a transfusion is an exact match between donor and recipient. Other compatible types are transfused only in emergencies.

In this lab activity you will use chemical solutions to simulate the process involved in determining blood type. Keep in mind that the antigen-antibody reactions being simulated here are unique to biological systems and are more complex than the precipitation reactions being used.

Table 1.   Blood Types for Safe Transfusions

Blood Type	Antigen on Red Cells	Antibody in Plasma	Blood Types that Can Be Received in Safe Transfusions
A	A	anti-B	A, O
B	B	anti-A	B, O
AB	A,B	none	A, B, AB, O
O	none	anti-A, anti-B	O

1. Using a glass-marking pencil, mark one depression slide *anti-A*, and the other *anti-B*.
2. Place 1 drop of "anti-A serum" in the well of the slide labeled anti-A. Replace the dropper in its proper bottle.
3. Place 1 drop of "anti-B serum" in the well of the slide labeled anti-B. Replace the dropper in its proper bottle.
4. Add 1 drop of simulated blood sample 1 to each slide. Be careful not to touch the dropper to the "serum." Replace the dropper in its proper bottle.

When blood is tested with typing sera, agglutinated cells appear stuck together in clumps on the slide. An agglutinated blood sample has the appearance of sand grains. If agglutination does not occur, the mixture will remain uniform in consistency. In this simulation, a precipitation reaction will simulate the agglutination of cells. Precipitation is the formation of an insoluble solid. If no precipitation occurs, the mixture on the slide will remain clear.

5. Look for precipitation in the mixture on each slide.
   a. *If precipitation did occur, record in the proper space in Table 2, on which slide precipitation took place.*

Table 2.   Results of Blood Typing

Sample	Precipitation with "anti-A"	Precipitation with "anti-B"	Simulated blood type
1			
2			
3			
4			

Identifying Blood Cells and Blood Types (continued)

6. Carefully wash both slides. Do not wash off the labels *anti-A* and *anti-B*.

7. Repeat Steps 2–6 for simulated blood samples 2–4.

8. Refer to Table 2 to determine the blood types of your samples.

   b. *In the space provided in Table 3, record the blood type of each sample. Verify your findings with your teacher.*

Table 3.   Blood Typing

Results	Blood Type
agglutination on anti-A slide only	
agglutination on anti-B slide only	
agglutination on anti-A and anti-B slides	
no agglutination on either slide	

9. Follow your teacher's instructions for cleaning up and disposing of the chemicals.

Analysis and Interpretations

1. Describe the size, appearance, and relative number of red blood cells in the blood smear.

   _____
   _____
   _____
   _____

2. Describe the size, appearance, and relative abundance of white blood cells in the blood smear.

   _____
   _____
   _____
   _____
   _____

3. Describe the size, appearance, and relative abundance of platelets in the blood smear.

   _____
   _____
   _____
   _____

4. If a blood smear shows a higher than normal number of white blood cells, what might this indicate to a doctor?

_____

_____

_____

_____

5. Explain how you decided on the blood type of your sample.

_____

_____

_____

6. Why should a person with type O blood never be given a transfusion of any other type?

_____

_____

For Further Investigation

Do research on other blood groups, such as Rh. Find out what Rh positive and Rh negative mean, and how blood is tested for the Rh blood group.

Lung Capacity and CO$_2$ Production

Lab 16

Background

The human body obtains energy through *cellular respiration*, a process which uses oxygen and produces waste products of carbon dioxide and water. Cellular respiration is supported by a series of events called *respiration*. Respiration has four phases: breathing; the exchange of carbon dioxide and oxygen in the lungs; the transport of these gases from or to body cells; the exchange of gases between blood and the cells.

In Part I of this experiment, you will study the *capacity* of the lungs, *i.e.*, the volume of air the lungs can inhale and exhale. In Part II, you will measure the different amounts of carbon dioxide produced when you are resting and immediately after you exercise.

Objectives

In this activity you will:
1. Approximate a measurement of the capacity of your lungs.
2. Observe the differences in capacity among females and males, and athletes and nonathletes.
3. Measure the amount of carbon dioxide produced before and after exercise.

Materials

round balloon or spirometer
meter stick
string or yarn
soda straw
glass-marking pencil
graduated pipettes
100-mL graduated cylinder

three 200-mL flasks
stoppers (or plastic wrap or aluminum foil)
1.0% phenolphthalein solution in dropper bottle
0.04% sodium hydroxide solution in dropper bottle

Procedures and Observations

PART I.   VITAL CAPACITY _____

Human lung capacity is influenced by many factors including age, sex, body position, strength of diaphragm and chest muscles, and disease.

Several measurements can be made in the study of lung capacity: (1) *tidal volume*, the amount of air inhaled and exhaled in a normal breath; (2) *inspiratory reserve volume*, the amount of air that can be inhaled after a normal inhalation; (3) *expiratory reserve volume*, the amount of air that can be forcefully exhaled after a normal exhalation; (4) *residual volume*, the amount of air remaining in the lungs after a forceful exhalation; (5) *vital capacity*, the maximum amount of air that can be exhaled (This is the total of the tidal volume, inspiratory reserve volume, and expiratory reserve volume.)

Table 1 gives these values for young adult males. The average volumes for young adult females are usually 20–25% lower. Athletes may have volumes 30–40% greater than average for their sex.

Table 1. Average Lung Capacity for Young Adult Males

Various Types of Measurement	Approximate Volume
Tidal Volume	500 mL
Inspiratory Reserve Volume	3000 mL
Expiratory Reserve Volume	1100 mL
Residual Volume	1200 mL
Vital Capacity	4600 mL

1. Take a few deep breaths. Then exhale deeply once into a balloon. Fill the balloon as much as you can, but only with air from one exhalation.

2. Hold the balloon. Have your partner measure the circumference of the balloon at its widest point with string. Then hold the measured string along a meter stick to determine the circumference of the balloon.

   a. *Record the circumference of the balloon in Table 2.*

3. Repeat Steps 1 and 2 two more times.

   b. *Record the results in Table 2. Then find the average circumference.*

Table 2. Determining Vital Capacity

Trial	Circumference of Balloon
1	
2	
3	

Average circumference:_____

4. Decide whether you are an athlete or nonathlete.

   c. *Enter your average balloon circumference in the appropriate column in Table 3. Record it on the chart on the board also.*

   d. *Write your classmates' data on your chart. Find the average balloon circumference for each column.*

Lung Capacity and CO$_2$ Production (continued)

Table 3. Vital Capacities of Persons in the Class

Male		Female	
Nonathlete	Athlete	Nonathlete	Athlete
Total			
Average			

PART II. CARBON DIOXIDE PRODUCTION _____

Cellular respiration is the process by which nutrient molecules are broken down into smaller molecules, and energy is released. Water and carbon dioxide are waste products of aerobic cellular respiration. In humans, carbon dioxide is carried by the blood to the lungs where it is released through exhalation.

Carbon dioxide (CO_2) reacts chemically with water to form carbonic acid (H_2CO_3). Water will become more acidic as more CO_2 is added to it. An acidic solution can be neutralized with a base such as sodium hydroxide (NaOH). Phenolphthalein is a pH indicator that is pink or red in a basic solution and colorless in an acidic solution. Neutralization of an acidic solution is indicated just at the point when the phenolphthalein in the solution changes from colorless to pink. By knowing the amount of sodium hydroxide needed to neutralize the acid, you can calculate the amount of carbon dioxide in the solution.

1. Label three 200-mL flasks as follows: *#1, #2,* and *control.*

2. Pour 100 mL of tap water, measured with the graduated cylinder, into each of the three flasks. Add 5 drops of phenolphthalein to each flask and swirl to mix. If the water remains colorless, add NaOH drop by drop while swirling, counting the number of drops until the solution stays a pale pink. Add the same number of drops to each flask so that the solutions have the same color.

3. Stopper or tightly cover flask #2 and the control flask.

CAUTION: *Be <u>sure</u> to wear your safety glasses while blowing in the flask in Steps 4 and 6.*

4. To see how much CO_2 is produced before exercising, put on safety glasses and blow gently through a straw into flask #1 for exactly 1 minute. Try to breathe normally, but exhale slowly so that the solution does not splash from the flask.

   a. *What color change do you observe?*

_____

CAUTION: *Use a pipette bulb in the next step. Do not mouth pipette.*

5. Using a graduated pipette, add NaOH 1 mL at a time, swirling and counting the milliliters you add, until the solution is the same pink color as the control flask. The pink color must remain after swirling.

   b. Record in Table 4 the number of milliliters of NaOH added to the solution.

CAUTION: *Recall that you must wear your safety glasses when blowing into the flask in Step 6.*

6. Exercise by running in place for 2 minutes or until you are tired. Immediately blow gently through a straw into flask #2 for exactly 1 minute. .

7. Using flask #2, repeat Step 5 until the solution remains pink.

   c. *Record in Table 4 the number of milliliters of NaOH added to flask #2.*

A micromole is a unit used to measure small amounts of substances.

8. To calculate the number of micromoles of CO_2 in each solution, multiply by 10 the number of milliliters of NaOH added in Steps 5 and 7.

Lung Capacity and CO₂ Production (continued) 16

d. *Record in Table 4 the number of micromoles of CO_2 produced before and after exercise.*

Table 4.   Effects of Exercise on CO_2 Production

	Flask 1 Before Exercise	Flask 2 After Exercise
mL NaOH added		
CO_2 you exhaled (micromoles)		
Class average of CO_2 exhaled (micromoles)		

e. *Record your results on the board, and, after every other student has done the same, calculate the two class averages and record them in Table 4.*

f. *What aspect of respiration is being indirectly measured in Part II of this laboratory?*

_____

_____

9. Follow your teacher's instructions in cleaning up and disposing of the solutions.

Analysis and Interpretations

1. List the groups from Table 3 in order, from greatest vital capacity to smallest. How closely do the results agree with the average given in Table 1?

_____

_____

2. Try to explain the results shown in Table 3. Why do males have greater vital capacities than females? Why do athletes have greater vital capacities than nonathletes?

_____

_____

_____

_____

_____

_____

_____

_____

3. Compare the vital capacities of male athletes and female athletes. Try to explain what you discover.

_____

_____

4. How can vital capacity be increased?

_____

_____

5. Was the control solution in Part II basic or acidic?

_____

6. What did the color change in Step 4 indicate?

_____

7. Did you produce more CO_2 before or after you exercised? How do you know?

_____

_____

8. Which body tissues could account for the change in CO_2 production after exercise?

_____

9. Why did you seal the opening of the control flask?

_____

For Further Investigation

1. Design an experiment to test the effect of smoking on vital capacity. Discuss this with your teacher.
2. Could you adapt Part II of this Lab to measure respiration in other organisms? Explain how this could be done.

Urinalysis

Lab 17

Background

Animals must rid their bodies of the waste products of metabolism. In humans, the kidneys remove waste chemicals from the bloodstream and produce urine. Urine normally contains water, salts, and organic wastes. The amounts of each of these chemicals depends on the person's health, diet, and activity.

From urine tests, doctors can learn much about the general health of an individual. Kidney malfunction, urinary tract infections, liver disease, and diabetes are just some of the problems that can be diagnosed using urinalysis. Urinalysis involves physical, chemical, and visual examination. Color, volume, specific gravity, cloudiness, odor, pH, protein content, sugar content, presence of blood cells, and sediments are some of the characteristics which are tested in medical laboratories.

In this lab activity, you will perform lab tests that are used to analyze urine. However, for safety, you will be working with samples of artificial urine.

Objectives

In this activity you will:
1. Evaluate urine samples for transparency, color, and odor.
2. Test urine samples for the presence of sugar and protein.
3. Measure the pH of urine samples.

Materials

artificial urine samples
test tube rack
glucose test tape
pH paper

test tube holder
Bunsen burner
matches or striker
5% acetic acid

Procedures and Observations

PART I.   PHYSICAL EVALUATION OF URINE _____

One factor to observe in urine is its general appearance. Normal urine is transparent. Old samples of urine may be cloudy due to the presence of bacteria growing in the urine after the sample was collected. Fresh urine samples that are cloudy may be due to urinary tract infections or may indicate the presence of blood cells, pus, or fat.

  1. Obtain the test tube sample marked *control* and set it in a test tube rack. Examine the control sample of artificial urine.

    a. *Evaluate the transparency of the sample. Is the urine sample clear or cloudy? Record your observations in your data table.*

The color of urine depends in part on its concentration. Pale, dilute urine may be the result of drinking large volumes of fluids, but it may also indicate diabetes. Dark, concentrated urine may be the result of dehydration or of fever. A smoky-red to reddish-brown color indicates the presence of red blood cells in the urine. Vegetables and fruits, as well as vitamins and other drugs, can alter the color of urine.

2. Evaluate the color of the sample.

    b. *Record your observations in your data table.*

The normal odor of urine may be altered by several factors. A foul odor in fresh urine can indicate the presence of bacteria. Bacteria may be present as a result of a urinary tract infection. A fruity odor indicates the presence of ketones in the urine. Ketones are a product of the breakdown of fats, which can occur due to diabetes or to starvation.

3. Evaluate the odor of the sample.

    c. *Record your observations on your data table.*

PART II. CHEMICAL EVALUATION OF URINE

The sugar content of urine can be evaluated. Sugar can be present in the urine after eating a meal rich in carbohydrates or during periods of stress. However, a consistent finding of sugar in the urine may indicate diabetes.

1. Test the control sample for its sugar content. Dip the end of one 4-cm strip of glucose test tape into the sample. Follow the directions on the test-tape package and compare your test tape to the color chart on the test-tape dispenser.

    a. *Record the sugar concentration of the sample in your data table.*

Usually urine is slightly acidic, having a pH near 6.0. The normal range, however, may vary from 4.7 to 8.0. Several factors, including food, dieting, stress, drugs, breathing rate, and liquid intake, can affect the pH of urine.

2. Test the control sample for its pH level. Dip the end of one 4-cm strip of pH paper into the sample. Compare the color of the test strip to the color chart on the pH-paper dispenser.

    b. *Record the pH of the sample in your data table.*

Protein in the urine indicates an abnormal condition known as proteinuria. Proteinuria may result from disease or from damage to the glomeruli, Bowman's capsules, or nephron tubules, and is considered very serious.

3. Light your Bunsen burner as directed by your teacher. Hold the test tube containing the control sample with the test tube holder. Carefully heat the top portion of the liquid by passing it through the Bunsen burner flame, as shown in Figure 1. **CAUTION:** *Do not point the mouth of the test tube at anyone.* After a short while, the liquid in the top portion will begin to boil. Watch for cloudiness to appear in this part of the liquid. Remove the test tube from the flame once the cloudiness appears or after a few seconds of boiling. If there is no cloudiness, no protein is present in the urine. If cloudiness does appear after boiling, add three drops of 5% acetic acid to the warm test tube. If the cloudiness disappears, there is no protein present. If the cloudiness remains, protein is present in the urine.

Urinalysis (continued)

    c. *Record the presence or absence of protein in your data table.*

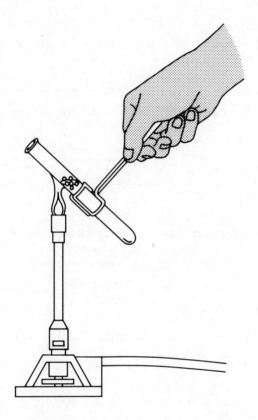

Figure 1

PART III. EVALUATION OF SAMPLES OF UNKNOWNS _____

1. Obtain samples of artificial urine labeled *1* and *2*. Repeat each of the observations and tests, as directed in Parts I and II, on samples 1 and 2.

    a. *Record your observations and results in your data table.*

   2. Discard the leftover samples, as directed by your teacher. Wash the test tubes with detergent and water.·

Data Table

Characteristic	Control	Sample 1	Sample 2
Transparency			
Color			
Odor			
Sugar content			
pH level			
Protein			

Analysis and Interpretations

1. Why should a urine sample be fresh when it is tested?

_____

_____

_____

2. What are two physical changes that occur in urine after it has been acted on by bacteria?

_____

3. What are three observations or tests that could indicate that a person has diabetes?

_____

_____

_____

4. What are two ways that you might recognize blood in urine?

_____

_____

_____

5. What conclusions can you make about urine samples 1 and 2?

_____

_____

_____

_____

6. Why might a urine sample taken early in the morning differ from a sample taken soon after dinner?

_____

_____

7. When a baby wakes up in the morning, his or her diaper may have an odor of ammonia. What causes this odor and why is this odor usually observed only in the morning?

_____

_____

_____

_____

Examining Muscle, Bone, and Cartilage

Lab 18

Background

The tissues involved in the movement and support of vertebrates are muscle, bone, and cartilage. The contraction of muscle cells produces motion. Humans and other vertebrates have three types of muscle: *skeletal muscle, smooth muscle*, and *cardiac muscle*. Each is composed of a distinct type of cell specialized for the type of motion it provides. Contraction of skeletal muscle produces body movements. Smooth muscles are located in the walls of the digestive tract, blood vessels, and other internal organs. They are specialized for slow, prolonged contractions. The heart is made up of cardiac muscle and is specialized to beat rhythmically and continuously.

Bone and *cartilage* are the hardest tissues in the body. Humans and most other vertebrates have internal skeletons composed mainly of bone. The bone supports the body, gives it shape, and protects internal organs. Most skeletons also contain cartilage. In fact, the human skeleton is initially formed of cartilage, which is gradually replaced by bone. Cartilage is found in adult humans between the vertebrae of the spinal column, at the tips of ribs and other bones, and in the nose, ears, and larynx. Some lower vertebrates, such as the shark and the lamprey eel, have skeletons composed entirely of cartilage.

Objectives

In this activity you will:
1. Observe the structure of the three types of muscle.
2. Observe the structure of bone.
3. Observe the structure of cartilage.

Materials

microscope
prepared slides of skeletal muscle, smooth
    muscle, cardiac muscle, bone, and cartilage

Procedures and Observations

PART I. MUSCLE TISSUE

Most muscle cells are long and thin. Skeletal muscle tissue consists of bundles of fused cells called *fibers*. The fibers display a definite pattern of banding. Because of the banding, or *striations*, skeletal muscle is also known as *striated muscle*. The light and dark bands result from an overlapping arrangement of the tiny filaments that make up the muscle tissue. The movement of the filaments causes the muscle to contract.

1. Observe a prepared slide of skeletal muscle under low power.

   a. *Make a drawing of what you see under low power.*

2. Switch to high power. Then examine the skeletal muscle fibers.

   b. *Draw skeletal muscle fibers as seen under high power. Include the striations.*

   c. *Describe the general shape and arrangement of the fibers in skeletal muscle tissue.*

_____

_____

_____

   d. *Where are the nuclei located within the fibers?*

_____

_____

_____

Examining Muscle, Bone, and Cartilage (continued) 18

Smooth muscle tissue does not have the striped appearance of skeletal muscle.

3. Observe a prepared slide of smooth muscle tissue under low power.

　　e. *Make a drawing of what you see under low power.*

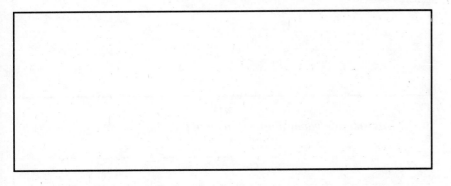

4. Switch to high power. Then examine the smooth muscle cells.

　　f. *Draw several smooth muscle cells as seen under high power.*

　　g. *Describe the general appearance of a smooth muscle cell.*

_____

_____

_____

　　h. *How many nuclei are present in each cell? Where are they located?*

_____

_____

_____

Cardiac muscle tissue appears striated like skeletal muscle, but the cells have connecting branches. The nuclei are located in the center of the cells. Intercalated discs appear between cells.

5. Observe a prepared slide of cardiac muscle tissue under low power.

    i. *Make a drawing of what you see under low power.*

6. Switch to high power. Then examine the cardiac muscle cells.

    j. *Draw cardiac muscle cells as seen under high power.*

    k. *Describe the general appearance of a cardiac muscle cell.*

_____

_____

_____

    l. *How many nuclei are present in each cell? Where are they located?*

_____

_____

PART II.   BONE AND CARTILAGE TISSUE _____

The *matrix,* or intercellular material, of bone is very hard and composed mainly of calcium compounds, including calcium phosphate. The bone cells, called *osteocytes,* are embedded in the matrix in spaces called *lacunae.* A system of canals, the *Haversian canals,* forms passageways through the bone for blood vessels and nerves. Lacunae containing osteocytes are arranged in concentric rings around each Haversian canal. The cells are connected to the Haversian canal and to each other by smaller canals called *canaliculi.*

Examining Muscle, Bone, and Cartilage (continued) 18

1. Observe a prepared slide of bone under low power. Identify the lacunae and the Haversian canals.

   a. *Make a drawing of bone as seen under low power.*

2. Switch to high power. Observe the Haversian canal systems. Note the smaller canals connecting the lacunae and the Haversian canals.

   b. *Draw a Haversian canal system. Label the structures you see.*

Cartilage is more flexible than bone. It can take a great deal of stress. Cartilage cells are called *chondrocytes*. They are found in cavities called *lacunae* within the flexible, elastic matrix. Unlike bone, cartilage has no blood vessels. The cells get needed materials by diffusion from adjacent blood vessels.

3. Observe a prepared slide of cartilage under low power.

 c. *Make a drawing of what you see.*

4. Switch to high power. Then examine the cartilage structure.

 d. *Draw a section of cartilage. Label the structures you see.*

Analysis and Interpretations

1. How do cardiac muscle cells differ in appearance from smooth muscle cells and skeletal muscle fibers?

_____

_____

_____

2. Describe a Haversian canal system in bone.

_____

_____

_____

_____

_____

Observing Responses to Stimuli _____ Lab 19

Background

One characteristic of living things is the ability to react to factors in their environment. A factor that can cause a reaction is called a *stimulus* (pl. stimuli), and the organism's reaction to the stimulus is called a *response*. Some organisms exhibit *taxes* (sing. taxis), unlearned responses in which the organism orients or moves itself toward or away from outside stimuli. There are many kinds of taxes and they are named after the stimuli that cause them. Thus, taxes include *phototaxis*, response to light; *thermotaxis*, response to heat; *geotaxis*, response to gravity; and *chemotaxis*, response to chemicals. A response toward the stimulus is called positive; away from the stimulus is negative. For example, positive phototaxis is a movement toward light.

In this lab activity, you will observe responses of two protists, *Stentor* and *Spirostomum*, which belong to the class Ciliata. You may be more familiar with another ciliated protist, *Paramecium*, which is much smaller and whose responses are therefore more difficult to observe.

Objectives

In this activity you will:
1. Apply stimuli to *Stentor* and *Spirostomum*.
2. Observe responses of the protists.

Materials

bulb pipettes
Syracuse watch glasses
paper towels
white construction paper, cut
    in squares 5 cm on a side
black construction paper, cut
    in squares 5 cm on a side
microscope slides
facial tissues
gooseneck lamp having a
    40-watt or a 60-watt bulb
hand lens
dissecting microscope

aluminum foil
scissors
clock or watch
250-mL beaker
U-shaped glass tube
Syracuse watch glass, labeled,
    containing salt solution and
    pieces of cotton thread
Syracuse watch glass, labeled,
    containing dilute acetic acid and
    pieces of cotton thread
toothpicks
forceps

Procedures and Observations

PART I.   TESTING FOR A RESPONSE TO LIGHT _____

Work in pairs for this lab activity. Select one protist, either *Stentor* or *Spirostomum*, as directed by your teacher. Do the entire activity,

Parts I through III with this protist; then repeat the activity using the other protist. *Stentor* is most easily viewed against a light background; *Spirostomum* is most easily viewed against a dark background. Use the appropriate color of construction paper to view the organism you are working with.

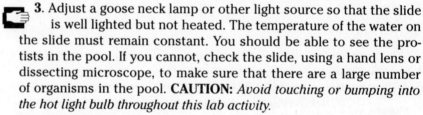

1. Obtain your organism: Your teacher will show you how to recognize the protists in their culture. Use a bulb pipette and a Syracuse watch glass to obtain a supply of the organism. With the bulb of the pipette closed, push the pipette tip into a mass of protists. Keep the tip of the pipette below the surface of the water while you release pressure on the pipette bulb. If you release the pressure while the tip is in the air, the organisms and water will be sucked into the bulb. Add a total of four pipettes of organisms to the watch glass. Add two pipettes of clear culture water, avoiding the dark, plant material.

2. Set up your work station: Label a paper towel with the name of the organism you will first observe. Depending on the organism, place a piece of black or of white construction paper on the paper towel. Place a clean, dry slide on the construction paper. If you should need to position the slide, you can move the entire assembly of towel, construction paper, and slide. To distribute the organisms, use the pipette to gently stir the culture in the watch glass. Then draw up culture into the pipette. Drag the pipette tip along the center of the slide, releasing a pool of water about 1 cm wide by 3 cm long. If you have difficulty making this pool, pour the culture back into the watch glass, dry the slide with a tissue, and try again.

3. Adjust a goose neck lamp or other light source so that the slide is well lighted but not heated. The temperature of the water on the slide must remain constant. You should be able to see the protists in the pool. If you cannot, check the slide, using a hand lens or dissecting microscope, to make sure that there are a large number of organisms in the pool. **CAUTION:** *Avoid touching or bumping into the hot light bulb throughout this lab activity.*

4. Tear or cut a piece of aluminum foil into a strip about 3 cm wide and 5 cm long. Bend the strip into an arch and place the arch over one end of the slide. Position the arch and slide so that half of the pool is shaded and the other half is evenly illuminated.

   a. *Record the current time on your data sheet.*

5. Wait 15 minutes. While you are waiting, you may proceed to Part II.

6. At the end of 15 minutes, carefully remove the aluminum foil without disturbing the slide. With the aid of a hand lens, observe the organisms.

   b. *Record your observations on your data sheet.*

   c. *Why do you think it is important to observe a large number of protists?*

   _____

   _____

   _____

7. Return the culture on the slide to your labeled watch glass. Clean and dry the slide.

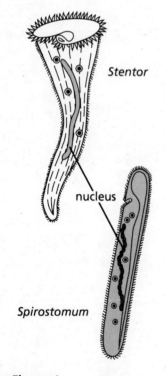

Stentor

nucleus

Spirostomum

Figure 1

Observing Responses to Stimuli (continued) 19

PART II.   TESTING FOR A RESPONSE TO GRAVITY _____

 1. Place a *U*-shaped, glass tube in a 250-mL beaker so that the ends of the *U* point up.

2. Draw up a pipette of organisms and clear culture water, avoiding any dark, plant material. Slowly and gently release the culture into the *U*-shaped tube. Check that there is no plant material in the tube.

3. Make sure that the *U*-shaped tube is upright and evenly lighted, but not heated, by sunlight or another light source.

   a. *Look at the culture in the tube. Where are the organisms?*

   _____

   b. *Record the current time on your data sheet.*

4. Allow the culture to stand undisturbed for 15 minutes. You may proceed to Part III.

5. At the end of 15 minutes, with the aid of a hand lens, examine the culture in the tube. Do not move or disturb the tube or the beaker.

   c. *Are the organisms concentrated in any place within the tube?*

   _____

   _____

   d. *Record your observations on your data sheet.*

6. Allow the tube to stand undisturbed for 24 hours, and examine the culture again.

   e. *Record your observations on your data sheet.*

7. Return your equipment, clean your lab space, and dispose of the organisms as directed by your teacher.

PART III.   TESTING FOR A RESPONSE TO CHEMICALS _____

   Unlike the protist *Paramecium, Stentor* and *Spirostomum* have fibrils which can contract, causing the body to change shape. In *Stentor,* the contracting fibrils cause the body to shorten into an oval shape. The contraction and relaxation of these fibrils in *Spirostomum* can cause thrashing movements and can shorten the cell body to one-fourth its usual length. Try to observe this behavior by looking at individual organisms.

1. Obtain two labeled Syracuse watch glasses containing short pieces of cotton thread. One watch glass should be labeled *Acid,* and contains a dilute acetic acid solution; the second should be labeled *Salt,* and contains a saturated sodium chloride solution. You will also need four toothpicks, two forceps, and two clean slides.

2. Label a paper towel *Acid* and a second paper towel *Salt*. Depending on the organisms you are observing, place a piece of black or of white construction paper on each towel and a clean slide on top of that. Using the pipette, gently stir the organisms in your watch glass and then make a pool of organisms on each slide, as you did in Part I, Step 2. Position the paper towels so that the slides are evenly lighted but not heated.

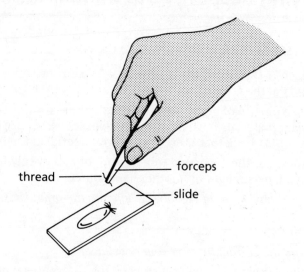

thread —
forceps
slide

Figure 2

a. *How are the organisms distributed in the pool of water?*

_____

_____

3. Using two toothpicks, separate the threads in the acid solution. With forceps, pick up a thread and place it in the culture pool of the *Acid* slide. The thread should be placed just at one edge of the pool so that the acid can slowly diffuse through the water. Add seven more acid-soaked threads on top of, or right next to, the first thread.

    b. *On your data sheet, record the current time and the number of threads added.*

4. Wait 2 minutes; then using a hand lens, observe the organisms on the slide.

    c. *How are the organisms now distributed in the pool of water?*

_____

_____

5. Repeat the procedure in Steps 3 and 4, placing only two salt-soaked threads on the salt-labeled slide. Then immediately proceed to Step 6.

6. Continue to alternate between your two setups. Add two chemical-soaked threads to each slide and observe the organisms every two minutes until you notice a mass movement of the organisms. Continue to record your observations on your data sheet. **Note:** *Too much salt or acid can kill the protists.* If you do not notice any mass movement of organisms, make sure that they are still active and alive. If not, wash and dry the slide and repeat the process.

7. If time permits, repeat Parts I, II, and III, using the second protist.

8. Dispose of your cultures as directed by your teacher. Wash and dry your slides. Return all equipment and supplies, and clean your work area.

Observing Responses to Stimuli (continued)

Data Table

	Stentor	Spirostomum
Response to Light		
Starting time: _____ Observations after 15 min.		
Response to Gravity		
Starting time: _____ Observations after 15 min.		
Observations after 24 hr.		
Response to Chemicals: Acid		
Starting time: _____ No. of threads at starting time: _____ Observations after 2 minutes		
Observations after 2 more minutes and 2 more threads		
Observations after 2 more minutes and 2 more threads		
Observations after 2 more minutes and 2 more threads		
Observations after 2 more minutes and 2 more threads		
Response to Chemicals: Salt		
Starting time: _____ No. of threads at starting time: _____ Observations after 2 minutes		
Observations after 2 more minutes and 2 more threads		
Observations after 2 more minutes and 2 more threads		
Observations after 2 more minutes and 2 more threads		
Observations after 2 more minutes and 2 more threads		

Analysis and Interpretations

1. Which species did you first observe? Did it respond to light, and if so, how? Name the taxis you observed. If you observed both *Spirostomum* and *Stentor*, how did they compare?

_____

_____

_____

_____

2. Did the species you first observed respond to gravity, and if so, how? How did your observations compare to those of other groups? Name the taxis you observed.

_____

_____

_____

_____

3. How did the protists respond to the acid solution? How did they respond to the salt solution? How would you name these responses?

_____

_____

_____

_____

4. What type of response did you observe in individual protists when salt-solution threads were added to their pool?

_____

_____

_____

5. How many threads from each solution, acid and salt, were needed to cause a taxis? How do these numbers compare with those found by other students testing the same organism?

_____

_____

_____

6. Explain why a protist moving toward a food source is an example of positive chemotaxis.

_____

_____

_____

Observing Responses to Stimuli (continued)

7. You observed responses to three different stimuli: light, gravity, and chemicals. Explain how the responses you observed might be adaptive for the species.

_____

_____

_____

_____

_____

_____

For Further Investigation

1. Repeat the procedures in Parts I through III, using the protist, *Paramecium*. Like *Spirostomum, Paramecium* is most easily viewed against a dark background. Because *Paramecium* is quite small, it would be best to set up the apparatus so that the organism can be viewed through a dissecting microscope.

2. Working with the same organisms used in the lab activity, test the effects of different stimuli. You may wish to experiment with different levels of light, various chemicals in different strengths, and different temperatures. For example, you may wish to test a response to a glucose solution or to various strengths of dilute acetic acid. You might also try keeping light constant while varying the temperature of different slides. **CAUTION:** *Check your plans with your teacher to make sure they are safe.*

Testing Reflexes and Reactions

Lab 20

Background

You have probably touched a hot stove or sharp object and pulled your hand away before realizing what had happened. This fast and automatic reaction to a stimulus is a *reflex action*. Some reflexes prevent injury to the body. For example, the withdrawal reflex that allows you to remove your hand from a hot stove before you even feel a sensation of heat helps to prevent a severe burn. Reflexes also control automatic activities in the body, such as the beating of the heart, breathing, gagging, and stomach movements.

In the *reflex arc*, or pathway, of the simple withdrawal reflex described above, a sensory neuron carries impulses from the skin to the spinal cord, where it synapses with an interneuron. The interneuron synapses with a motor neuron. Impulses carried by the motor neuron stimulate the appropriate muscles to withdraw the affected body part. All this happens in a fraction of a second.

In nonreflex responses, impulses must travel to the brain, where they are interpreted and a proper response initiated. The time required for the brain to receive the impulses, interpret them, and initiate a response is much longer than the time required for a reflex arc involving only the spinal cord.

A person's *reaction time* is a measure of how quickly he or she can perceive a stimulus and react to it. Reaction time is important in operating vehicles and machinery, in sports, and in many everyday activities. Reaction time may be increased by fatigue, drugs, and distraction.

Objectives

In this activity you will:
1. Demonstrate some human reflexes.
2. Measure your reaction time.

Materials

clear plastic sheet or plexiglass panel
meter stick
calculator with square root function or a table of square roots

Procedures and Observations

PART 1.   REFLEXES _____

Work in pairs, alternating as subject and experimenter.
1. The subject should sit on a chair with one leg crossed over the other. The top leg must be free to swing. With the side of the hand the experimenter should tap the subject's top knee on the tendon

just below the kneecap. (Not too hard!) It may take several taps before the proper part of the tendon is stimulated.

a. *Describe the response of the leg.*

_____

2. Repeat Step 1, but this time the top leg of the subject should be held out straight.

b. *Describe the response of the leg.*

_____

c. *In which leg position is the response the greatest?*

_____

3. Switch roles and repeat Steps 1 and 2.

4. The subject should close and cover his or her eyes for at least 1 minute. At the end of the minute, the experimenter should watch the subject's pupils as the eyes open.

d. *Describe the response of the iris and its effect on the pupil.*

_____

5. Switch roles and repeat Step 4.

6. The subject should remove a shoe and sock. The experimenter should scratch the bottom of the subject's foot with a fingernail, in one continuous motion from toe to heel.

e. *Describe the response of the toes.*

_____

7. Switch roles and repeat Step 6.

8. The subject should hold a clear plastic sheet in front of his/her face. The experimenter should toss a crumpled sheet of paper at the subject to try to make him/her blink.

f. *Describe the response of the subject's eyes.*

_____

9. Switch roles and repeat Step 8.

PART II.   REACTION TIME

1. The subject should rest his or her elbow on the table, with the arm extending over the side. The experimenter should hold a meter stick in the air, with the 0-cm line between the subject's index finger and thumb. The experimenter then should drop the meter stick and the subject should catch it between the index finger and thumb as quickly as possible. Note the measurement in cm of the meter stick where it was caught (the distance it fell).

a. *Record the distance the meter stick fell before it was caught.*

Trial 1: _____

Testing Reflexes and Reactions (continued)   20

2. Repeat Step 1 four more times.

   b. *Record the distance for each trial.*

   Trial 2: _____   Trial 4: _____

   Trial 3: _____   Trial 5: _____

3. Switch roles and repeat Steps 1 and 2.

4. Determine the average distance the meter stick fell by adding the measurements from the five trials and dividing by 5.

   c. *Record the average distance the meter stick fell.*

   _____

The time it takes for an object to fall a certain distance can be found by the formula.

$$t = \sqrt{\frac{2d}{a}}$$

where t= reaction time (in s)

d= distance the meter stick falls (in cm)

a= acceleration due to gravity= 980 cm/s^2

5. Determine your reaction time by using the above formula. Use the average distance determined in Step 4.

   d. *Use the space below to record your reaction time and show your calculations.*

Analysis and Interpretations

1. How is the iris-pupil response to light a protective reflex?

   _____

   _____

2. How is the blinking response a protective reflex?

   _____

   _____

   _____

3. What is the reaction time of a person who catches the meter stick at the 95-cm mark? Show your calculations.

4. Name three sports and three occupations in which reaction time is important.

_____

_____

5. Give an example of how distraction could slow down reaction time.

_____

_____

_____

For Further Investigation

1. Considering your experiments with reaction time, do you think a subject could catch a dollar bill folded lengthwise and dropped through his/her fingers? Test your prediction.

2. Design an experiment to test the effect of distraction on reaction time. Write down your plan and check with your teacher before trying your experiment.

3. How far will an automobile moving 50 mph (80 kph) travel during your average reaction time? Investigate stopping distance as it relates to reaction time and actual mechanical stopping distance. Construct a graph using your data.

4. Certain poisons act on the nervous system. Use library sources to report on three poisons and how they work.

Computer Activity

In Laboratory Experiment 20 you investigated nervous regulation and control by experimenting with your body's reflexes. *Experiments in Physiology* is a computer program that allows you to *measure* reflexes with a computer.

Investigating Senses: Sight, Touch, and Taste

Lab 21

Background

Your senses provide your brain with information about what is happening both inside and outside your body. When a sense receptor is stimulated, it sends nerve impulses to the brain for interpretation. Various kinds of sense receptors are located throughout the body. They range from tiny nerve endings in the skin to highly specialized organs, such as the eyes and ears. Each type of sense receptor responds only to a certain type of stimulus. Human senses include sight, touch, smell, taste, and hearing.

Objectives

In this activity you will:
1. Investigate your sense of sight.
2. Investigate the distribution of touch receptors in your skin.
3. Investigate your sense of taste.

Materials

eye test chart
toothpicks
blindfold
meter stick
cotton swabs
paper cup filled with
    drinking water

chunks of onion and apple
test tubes containing:
    10% salt solution
    5% sugar solution
    0.1% quinine sulfate solution
    1% acetic acid solution

Procedures and Observations

The sharpness of your sense of sight can be checked by using an eye test chart.

Work in pairs.

1. Obtain an eye test chart from your teacher. Have your partner hold it and stand exactly 6.1 meters (20 feet) away from you. Cover your left eye and read the rows of letters starting at the top. Read down as far as you can.

   a. *Record the number to the right of the row in which sight becomes uncertain.*

   _____

2. Cover your right eye and repeat Step 1.

   b. *Record the number to the right of the row in which sight becomes uncertain.*

   _____

An eye with normal vision can read the bottom row from 20 feet away. This is called 20-20 vision. If, for example, you could read just to the row labeled 30, this means that you would read at 20 feet what a normal eye could read at 30 feet. Your vision would be 20-30.

3. Estimate your vision for your right and left eye.

   c. *Record your estimated vision for each eye.*

   R: _____

   L: _____

Every person has a dominant eye. The dominant eye takes over when focusing on something. In most people, the right eye is dominant.

4. Make a circle with your right thumb and forefinger. With both eyes open, look at an object across the room through the circle. Have your arm extended fully. First close your left eye and look at the object.

   d. *Does the object appear in the center of the circle?*

   _____

5. Next close your right eye and look at the object.

   e. *Does the object appear in the center of the circle?*

   _____

   f. *The dominant eye will be the one for which the object remains in the center of the circle. Which is your dominant eye?*

   _____

   _____

The blind spot is the place on the retina where the optic nerve enters the eye. There are no rods or cones in this area, so no vision occurs at the blind spot. Both right and left eyes have a blind spot.

6. Cover your left eye. Then hold your book about 15 cm away and focus on the star in Figure 1.

Figure 1

7. Continue to look at the star, and slowly move your book away from you.

   g. *What happens to the dot to the right of the star as you move your book away?*

   _____

   _____

   h. *At about what distance from your eye does this occur?*

   _____

8. Repeat Steps 6 and 7, but cover your right eye and stare at the dot with your left.

   i. *What happens to the star as you move the book away? At about what distance?*

   _____

   _____

   _____

Touch receptors are not evenly distributed throughout the skin. They are more heavily concentrated in some areas than in others.

9. Blindfold your partner. Use two toothpicks to gently touch your partner's skin in the areas shown in Table 1. Start with the toothpicks about 1 mm apart. Gradually increase the distance between the toothpicks. Note the distance at which your partner can tell that there are two toothpicks.

   j. *Record the distance at which the subject feels two toothpick points in each area in Table 1.*

Table 1.   Determining Concentration of Touch Receptors in the Skin

Area	Distance Apart (in mm)
back of hand	
palm of hand	
fingertip	
lip	
back of neck	

10. Switch roles and repeat Step 9.

    k. *In which areas listed in Table 1 are touch receptors most concentrated?*

    _____

    _____

    _____

The taste receptors on your tongue can detect four different tastes: salty, bitter, sweet, and sour. The receptors for each taste are located on certain parts of the tongue.

11. Dip a clean cotton swab into the test tube containing 10% salt solution. With the swab, dab the areas of your tongue indicated in Figure 2.

    l. *In Table 2, record a plus (+) if the taste is perceived in that area of the tongue and a minus (-) if it is not.*

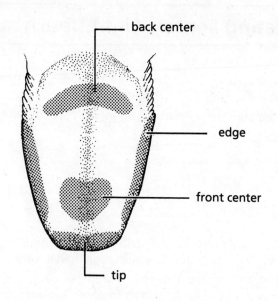

Figure 2

12. Rinse your mouth with water. Using a fresh cotton swab, repeat Step 11 for the other three solutions. Be sure to rinse your mouth each time before switching to a new solution.

  m. *Complete Table 2 for each solution.*

Table 2. Positions and Types of Taste Receptors

Taste	Area of Tongue			
	edge	back center	front center	tip
salty (10% salt solution)				
sweet (5% sugar solution)				
bitter (.1% quinine solution)				
sour (5% acetic acid solution)				

The flavor of food that is perceived by the brain is a combination of taste and smell. Some foods cannot be distinguished by taste alone.

13. Blindfold your partner and have him or her hold his or her nose. Feed your partner either a piece of apple or onion.

  n. *Can your partner identify the food?*

_____

14. Switch roles and repeat Step 13.

Investigating Senses: Sight, Touch, and Taste (continued) 21

Analysis and Interpretations

1. Why do you not notice the blind spot in the course of normal vision? (Hint: Try Steps 6 and 7 again with both eyes open.)

_____

_____

2. Explain why there are differences in the results in Table 1.

_____

_____

3. Can you think of a reason why some body parts should be more sensitive to touch than others?

_____

_____

4. Explain why food is often tasteless to a person with a cold.

_____

_____

_____

For Further Investigation

1. Using your knowledge of the blind spot, try to create an illusion of a headless person!

2. Design an experiment to measure the relative number of receptors in the skin for one of these stimuli: pressure, pain, heat or cold. Write down your procedure and check with your teacher before trying your experiment.

3. Find foods that can be substituted for the apple and the onion in Step 13. Test them to see which foods consistently fool the tasters.

Regulation: Chemical Control

Background

The endocrine system works with the nervous system to regulate and coordinate body functions. While the nervous system works quickly and sends messages directly to specific body parts, the endocrine system takes a longer time to produce a longer-lasting effect. The system operates by releasing chemical messengers called hormones into the bloodstream, which travel throughout the body. Eventually the hormone reaches a target organ or tissue to cause an effect. Growth and development, sexual maturation and reproduction, metabolism and homeostasis are some of the processes regulated by endocrine gland secretions. Endocrine effects can last for hours, days, or even years.

Adrenalin is a hormone secreted by the adrenal glands that helps the body deal with stress. It produces the emergency, or "fight or flight," response and is secreted when a sudden stress such as fear, pain, anger, or extreme physical exertion requires a burst of energy. Adrenalin causes increases in metabolic rate, breathing rate, heart rate, blood pressure, sweating and even blood clotting. It is a convenient hormone to study because its effect is relatively swift.

Objective

In this activity you will study the effect of different concentrations of adrenalin on the heart rate of daphnia, the water flea.

Materials

daphnia culture
medicine dropper
slides
cover slips
toothpick
petroleum jelly
bristles or threads

paper and pencil
paper towels
aquarium water
"recovery" beaker
dropper bottles containing adrenalin
    in various concentrations
microscope

Procedures and Observations

1. With a clean medicine dropper, remove a daphnia from the aquarium. Place it in a small drop of aquarium water on the center of a slide. Add two pieces of bristle or thread to the slide to limit the movement of the animal. With a toothpick, put a speck of petroleum jelly on each corner of a cover slip. Then place the cover slip (jelly side down) over the daphnia. Your setup should look like that in Figure 1.

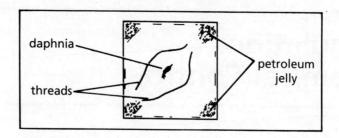

Figure 1

2. With the low-power objective, locate the transparent heart of the daphnia. It is a beating structure found almost midway in the back. See Figure 2. Observe the animal for a few minutes until it calms down.

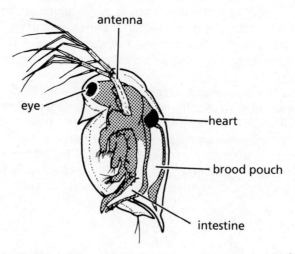

Figure 2

CAUTION: *While not observing the daphnia under the microscope, turn off the illuminator to prevent overheating the daphnia.*

3. Determine the heartbeat rate over a 15-second period. Your partner should tell you when to start and stop counting. If the heart is beating too fast count every other beat and multiply by two. Another method of counting is to tap a pencil on a clean sheet of paper each time the heart beats. After 15 seconds, count the number of pencil marks.

Trial 1

a. *Record the number of heartbeats per 15 seconds in Table 1. Multiply this number by 4 to get the number of heartbeats per minute. Record this number in Table 1.*

4. Repeat Step 3 two more times.

Trials 2 and 3

b. *Record the number of heartbeats per 15 seconds and the number of heartbeats per minute in Table 1. Average the heartbeats per minute and record this number.*

Regulation: Chemical Control (continued)

Table 1.   Effects of Adrenalin on Daphnia Heart Rate

Condition	Trial	Beats/15s	Beats/min	Average Beats/min	Class Average Beats/min
Aquarium Water	1				
	2				
	3				
0.001% Adrenalin	4				
	5				
	6				
0.01% Adrenalin	7				
	8				
	9				
0.1% Adrenalin	10				
	11				
	12				

5. Place a drop of the 0.001% adrenalin solution next to the edge of the cover slip. Touch a piece of paper towel to the other side of the cover slip to draw the solution through. Add a second drop and draw it through in the same manner. Wait about 20 seconds. Count the number of heartbeats in 15 seconds.

   Trial 4

   c. *Record your result in Table 1.*

6. Repeat your count of heartbeats two more times.

   Trials 5 and 6

   d. *Record your results in Table 1. Average the heartbeats per minute and record this number.*

7. Repeat Steps 5 and 6 above using the 0.01% adrenalin solution.

   Trials 7–9

   e. *Record your results in Table 1. Average the heartbeats per minute and record this number.*

8. Repeat Steps 5 and 6 above using the 0.1% adrenalin solution.

   Trials 10–12

   f. *Record your results in Table 1. Average the heartbeats per minute and record this number.*

9. Return your daphnia to the "recovery" beaker designated by your teacher. (Do not return it to the daphnia aquarium.)

   g. *Complete Table 1 by reporting your averages to your teacher for class average determination.*

Analysis and Interpretations

1. How would you expect adrenalin to affect daphnia?

_____

2. At what concentration did the adrenalin seem to take effect (threshold level)?

_____

3. How do your results compare with the class average?

_____

4. How much more concentrated is 0.1% adrenalin than 0.001% adrenalin?

_____

5. Why did you not return your daphnia to the original culture dish (aquarium) after the activity?

_____

_____

For Further Investigation

1. You may have noticed a temperature effect in this lab. Design an experiment to test the effect of temperature on the heart rate of daphnia. Write down your procedure and check with your teacher before trying your experiment.

2. Tadpole development can be influenced by the addition of thyroxin. Design an experiment to test the effect of this hormone and to determine threshold levels. Again, check with your teacher before you conduct your test.

Photosynthesis

Background

Photosynthesis is a process in which organisms containing chlorophyll in chloroplasts synthesize glucose molecules from carbon dioxide and water. Organisms capable of photosynthesis use visible light as a source of energy for the process. Requirements for photosynthesis are (1) an environmental temperature between 5° and 35° Celsius, (2) chlorophyll in chloroplasts, (3) water, (4) carbon dioxide, and (5) light of favorable intensity. In the absence of any of these factors, photosynthesis cannot occur.

Objectives

In this activity you will:
1. Demonstrate that light is necessary for photosynthesis.
2. Demonstrate that chlorophyll is necessary for photosynthesis.

Materials

geranium, begonia, or impatiens plants (leaves entirely green)	250-mL beakers
	100-mL beakers
	tongs
coleus with variegated leaves (green and white)	forceps
	Petri dishes
hot plates and hot-water bath	glass-marking pencil
Lugol's iodine solution in dropper bottles	70% alcohol

Procedures and Observations

PART I. EFFECTS OF LIGHT AND DARK ON STARCH FORMATION ____

The plants used for Part I have leaves that are entirely green. Half of these plants have been exposed to good light during the day. The other half have been kept in the dark for at least 2 days. The plants are labeled *Light* and *Dark*.

1. With a glass-marking pencil, label one 250-mL beaker *light*, and label another 250-mL beaker *dark*. Half-fill the two beakers with water. Place a leaf from a plant exposed to light, and a leaf from a plant kept in the dark, in the appropriately marked beakers. Place the beakers on the hot plate, bring the water to boiling, and boil the leaves 5 minutes.

CAUTION: *Do not use a Bunsen burner or any other type of open flame during this lab activity! An open flame can cause alcohol vapors to burst into flame. Use only an electric hot plate, as directed.*

2. While the leaves are boiling, use another hot plate to prepare a hot-water bath. Label one 100-mL beaker *light* and one *dark*. Half-fill each with 70% alcohol. With a forceps or tongs, remove the boiled leaves from the water and transfer each to the appropriately marked smaller beaker. Place both 100-mL beakers in the boiling water bath. Bring the alcohol to boiling, and boil gently until all the chlorophyll in the leaves has dissolved in the alcohol.

3. While the leaves are boiling, label one Petri dish *light* and another one *dark*. When the leaves have lost their chlorophyll, use the forceps to transfer each to the correctly marked Petri dish.

4. Gently spread out the leaves in the Petri dishes. Add drops of Lugol's iodine solution to each leaf until iodine has come into contact with the entire leaf. **CAUTION:** *Avoid staining hands and clothing with the iodine solution.*

  a. *What color change occurs?*

  _____

  _____

  b. *What do the color changes indicate?*

  _____

  _____

  _____

  _____

5. Wash all glassware thoroughly. Dry the table top with a paper towel.

PART II. EFFECT OF CHLOROPHYLL ON STARCH FORMATION

The plants used in Part II have been exposed to bright light. You will test their leaves for starch, as you did in Part I. One leaf will be all green, and the other will be partly green and partly white (variegated).

1. Repeat Steps 1 through 4 of Part I using one all-green leaf, and one green-and-white leaf. Label the beakers and Petri dishes *G* for the green leaf and *G & W* for the green and white leaf.

  a. *Before boiling the green and white leaf, make a drawing of it, showing the distribution of chlorophyll. Label the drawing "Variegated Leaf."*

Photosynthesis (continued)

    b. *What color changes occur when the Lugol's solution is put on the leaves? What do the color changes indicate?*

_____

_____

_____

    c. *After testing for starch, draw the two leaves and indicate the distribution of starch. Place the correct title under each leaf.*

Analysis and Interpretations

1. In Part I, why did you test leaves that had been exposed to light as well as those that had been in the dark?

_____

_____

2. In Part II, why did you test leaves that were all green as well as leaves that were part green and part white?

_____

_____

3. From the results of Part I, what can you conclude about the relationship between exposure to light and the presence of starch in leaves?

_____

4. From the results of Part II, what can you conclude about the relationship between the presence of chlorophyll and the presence of starch in leaves?

_____

_____

5. Two basic assumptions of the two experiments performed in this activity are (1) that the presence of starch indicates that photosynthesis has occurred, and (2) that the absence of starch indicates that no photosynthesis has occurred. Are these assumptions scientifically valid? State why or why not.

_____

_____

_____

_____

_____

_____

Computer Activity

In Laboratory Experiment 23 you investigated photosynthetic output by comparing starch production in leaves exposed to light with leaves left in the dark. The computer simulation *Solar Food* allows you to measure not only the effects of varied light on sugar production but also the effects of changes in temperature and carbon dioxide on sugar production.

Structure of Roots and Stems

Lab 24

Background

The roots of land plants absorb the water and dissolved minerals used by the plants for food-making and for growth of the plant body. Most roots grow downward, then branch outward from the center of the plant. In this way they anchor the plant firmly in the soil and support the plant body that grows above ground level.

Roots are plant organs that function by means of specialized tissues. Some tissues conduct water and minerals upward to the stem; other tissues conduct food upward or downward. Still other tissues store food for the plant. All the specialized tissues of a root arise from the *apical meristem,* the growth region of a root tip where new cells are produced. Meristem cells are not specialized when they first form, but become specialized as they mature.

The stem of a seed plant is the main axis that supports the leaves, flowers, and fruits. It contains the tissues that conduct water and nutrients between the roots and the upper plant organs. Most stems grow upward, but some creep over the surface of the ground, or grow underground. *Herbaceous stems,* as in corn and buttercup plants, are green and sometimes juicy. *Woody stems,* like the trunks of trees, are strong and hard.

Objectives

In this activity you will:
1. Observe the structure of a root tip.
2. Observe some tissues of roots, including highly specialized absorptive cells, the root hairs.
3. Observe some of the specialized tissues of herbaceous stems.

Materials

prepared slides of:
(1) onion (*Allium*) root tip, longitudinal section,
(2) buttercup (*Ranunculus*) root, cross section,
(3) corn (*Zea mays*) stem (or other monocot stem), cross section,
and (4) buttercup stem (or other dicot stem), cross section

germinated radish seedlings   ruler
    in glass Petri dishes   hand lens
compound microscope   stereomicroscope

Procedures and Observations

PART I. STRUCTURE OF A ROOT TIP _____

Study Figure 1 to become familiar with the zones of growth that are characteristic of the root tips of seed plants. The growth region nearest to the tip of the root is the *meristem,* or *meristematic zone.* This is the region of the root where new cells are produced, when the plant is growing. The *root cap,* the region at the very tip of the root, is pushed through the soil by the growth of the new cells behind it. Although the cells of the root cap are worn away by the soil, they are constantly replaced by new cells from the meristematic zone.

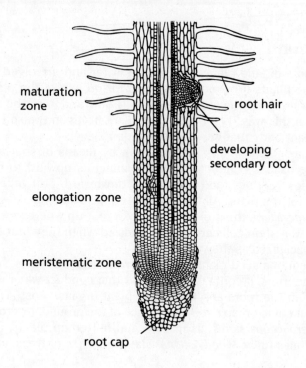

Figure 1

1. Observe a prepared slide of onion root tip (longitudinal section) under low power. Locate the root cap and the root tip meristem.

In the *zone of elongation,* behind the meristem, the young cells undergo enlargement. Behind this zone the cells complete their development, differentiating into specialized cell types, such as root hair cells. The long root hairs greatly increase the area of absorption. The root hair zone is the *zone of maturation.*

2. Locate the zone of elongation and the zone of maturation in the section on your slide.

   a. *Are the cells of the root cap different from the cells in the zone of elongation? If so, how?*

   _____

   _____

   _____

   _____

   b. *Certain cells cause growth in the length of roots. In which zones of the root tip are these cells located?*

   _____

   _____

Structure of Roots and Stems (continued)

PART II.   ROOT TISSUES _____

A cross section of a buttercup root at the zone of maturation reveals the mature tissues of the root. At the inner core of the root is the vascular cylinder. It is bounded by a distinct layer of cells, the *endodermis,* and contains the tissues that conduct water, minerals, and food. In the center of the vascular cylinder, the large diameter cells of the *xylem* are arranged in a star shape. Xylem is the tissue that conducts water and dissolved minerals upward in the root. In the spaces between the "arms" of the xylem are bundles of *phloem* cells. Phloem is the tissue that transports the food made by the plant upward or downward, according to the needs of the plant. Surrounding the xylem and phloem and lying just inside the endodermis is the remaining tissue, the *pericycle.*

1. Observe a prepared slide of buttercup root (cross section) under low power. Locate the endodermis. Everything to its inside is the vascular cylinder. Identify the pericycle, xylem, and phloem. Note the difference in the diameters of the three kinds of cells.

   a. *Draw a cross section of the vascular cylinder, showing the different tissues as they appear in your microscope. Make the drawing 3 centimeters in diameter. Label pericycle, xylem, and phloem. Title the drawing* Vascular Cylinder of Root.

Surrounding the vascular cylinder is the *cortex,* the innermost layer of which is the *endodermis.* Most cortex cells are large and thin-walled, and store starch. In a stained slide, small starch grains can be seen within the cortex cells. These grains are synthesized by the cortex cells from food made in the leaves.

2. Locate the cortex layer, made up of many large, loosely packed cells. Center a few of the cortex cells and switch to high power. Examine the starch grains in a few of the cells.

The *epidermis* of the root is the outer layer of cells. It is made up of large, flat, covering cells and root hair cells. The function of the epidermis layer is to protect the inner tissues of the root and to absorb water and dissolved minerals.

3. Locate the epidermis layer in your cross section. Note that each long root hair is an extension of a single cell.

   b. *Draw one-fourth of a cross-section of a root by drawing the individual cells of the epidermis and the cortex. Make the drawing 3 to 4 centimeters wide at the outer edge. Show the grains of starch within the cortex cells. Indicate only the location of the vascular cylinder, by drawing one-fourth of a circle in the correct position. Label epidermal cell, root hair, cortex cell, grains of starch, endodermis, and vascular cylinder. Title the drawing* Cross Section of Root, Partial Section.

PART III.   ROOT HAIRS

As a root tip grows through the soil, the cells in the zone of maturation become specialized. Many of the epidermal cells develop long, slender projections that greatly increase the surface area of the cell. Such cells are called *root hairs*, and the root hair region of a root tip is highly adapted for absorption of water and minerals.

1. Examine a radish seedling in a covered Petri dish. If water has condensed on the inside of the cover, wipe the cover with a paper towel. Keep the Petri dish closed to prevent the seedling from drying out. Use a hand lens or stereomicroscope to observe the root hairs. Note the long, tiny projections, and recall that each root hair is part of a single cell.

Elongation of most root cells occurs primarily in a region from 1 to 10 millimeters from the end of the root tip. The zone of maturation is behind this zone of elongation.

2. Using a ruler, measure the root hair region, from the first root hairs that you can see, at the beginning of the zone of maturation, to the uppermost layer of root hairs. Record this measurement in millimeters.

Structure of Roots and Stems (continued)

   a. *Record the length of the root hair region.*

_____

3. Refer again to Figure 1, then observe the radish root tip. Estimate the length of the zone of elongation, using the ruler. Record your estimate in millimeters.

   b. *Estimate the length of the zone of elongation.*

_____

PART IV. STRUCTURE OF HERBACEOUS STEMS _____

Herbaceous seed plants occur as monocots and dicots. In monocots, the outermost, protective layer of cells is the *epidermis.* Just under the epidermis is a layer of photosynthetic cells and fiber cells. Within this layer, the stem is composed mainly of *parenchyma,* a tissue made up of large, thin-walled cells. Scattered throughout this tissue are the *vascular bundles,* each made up of the two conducting tissues, xylem and phloem.

1. Observe a prepared slide of a monocot stem. Find the epidermis and the photosynthetic layer. Look for the parenchyma cells that fill the center of the stem and the vascular bundles made up of xylem and phloem.

   a. *Draw a circle about 5 centimeters in diameter, to represent the epidermal layer of the monocot stem. Label the circle* epidermal layer. *Label the parenchyma. Draw the vascular bundles as oval shapes, showing how they are arranged in the monocot stem. Do not try to draw all of the vascular bundles. Draw only enough to demonstrate their arrangement. Label one oval shape* vascular bundle. *Title the drawing* Arrangement of Vascular Bundles, Monocot Stem.

2. Center one vascular bundle at low power. Switch to high power and examine the bundle. The xylem cells are the cells of large diameter. The phloem cells are much smaller in diameter and occur in a mass adjacent to the xylem, but toward the side of the bundle nearest the outer edge of the stem.

b. *Draw the vascular bundle, showing the different sizes, shapes, and diameters of the cells. Label the xylem and phloem. Title the drawing "Vascular Bundle, Monocot Stem."*

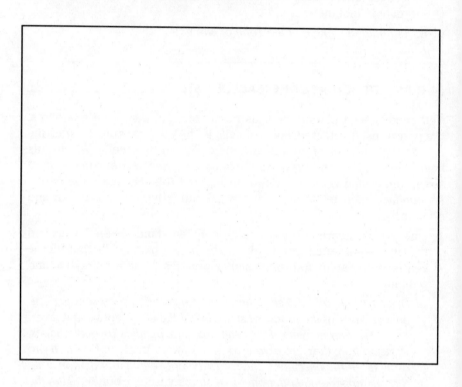

Dicot stems are generally more complex than monocot stems. There are more kinds of tissues, and they are arranged differently. The epidermis is the outside layer, and within it are several layers of cells called the *cortex*. The vascular bundles are made up of xylem and phloem, and in stems that grow in diameter from year to year, there is also a layer of meristematic tissue called the *vascular cambium*. The cambium layer forms a continuous ring of tissue in the stem. Within the bundles it is located between the phloem and xylem. Cells are produced by the cambium to each of its sides—those to the inside differentiate into xylem, and those to the outside differentiate into phloem. Thus, continuous layers of xylem and phloem are produced. The center of the dicot stem is the *pith*.

3. At low power, observe a prepared slide of a herbaceous dicot stem. Find the epidermis and cortex layers around the outside of the stem. Then note the arrangement of the vascular bundles, compared to their arrangement in the monocot stem.

c. *Draw a circle about 5 centimeters in diameter, to represent the outer layers of the herbaceous stem. Label the circle* outer layers of stem. *Draw oval shapes to represent the vascular bundles, showing their arrangement in the dicot stem. Label one oval shape* vascular bundle. *Title the drawing* Arrangement of Vascular Bundles, Dicot Stem.

Structure of Roots and Stems (continued)

[blank boxed drawing area]

4. Center one vascular bundle at low power and switch to high power. The xylem cells are the cells of large diameter. They are in the part of the bundle that is nearest to the center of the stem.

The band of tissue next to the xylem, toward the outside of the stem, is the vascular cambium. Note that the cambium layer extends beyond the boundary of the vascular bundle, on both sides. Returning to the vascular bundle, you will see the mass of phloem cells between the cambium layer and the cortex.

   d. *Draw one vascular bundle at high power. Show the differences in the sizes of the cells. Label* xylem, phloem, *and* vascular cambium. *Title the drawing* Vascular Bundle, Dicot Stem.

[blank boxed drawing area]

5. Return to low power. Find the cambium layer at low power, now that you know where to look for it. Recall that new xylem and phloem cells are produced from this meristem layer.

   e. *Add a circle to your drawing for Step 3-c, to represent the cambium layer in its correct position. Label the circle* vascular cambium.

Analysis and Interpretations

1. Explain how a root increases in length.

_____

_____

2. Where do root cells begin to become specialized and different from each other?

_____

_____

3. In a mature root, where are the xylem and phloem tissues located?

_____

4. According to your measurements in Part III, and your observations of root hairs in the microscope, how would the surface area of the root hair region compare with that of the zone of elongation?

_____

5. Which of the root functions is carried out by the root hairs?

_____

6. Where are the xylem and phloem found in herbaceous stems?

_____

_____

7. How does the arrangement of the vascular bundles differ in monocot and dicot stems?

_____

_____

8. How does the arrangement of the xylem and phloem tissues differ in stems and roots?

_____

_____

_____

9. How does the location of the cambium layer make it possible for stems to grow in diameter?

_____

_____

For Further Investigation

Observe the specialized tissues in a cross section of a woody stem. Using reference materials as an aid, identify the pith, xylem, vascular cambium, phloem, cork, cork cambium, and bark.

Structure of a Leaf

Background

Leaves are the main photosynthetic organs of the plant. The flat part of the leaf is called the *blade*. In some plants the blade is attached directly to the stem; in others, the blade is attached to the main stem by a thin stalk, or *petiole*.

A leaf is composed of three types of tissue: epidermis, mesophyll, and vascular tissue. Leaves have an upper and lower *epidermis*, which protect the internal tissues. Covering the epidermis is a waxy *cuticle*, which helps to conserve water. Most of the photosynthesis of the plant takes place in the *mesophyll*. The *xylem* and *phloem* are found in vascular bundles in the veins of the leaf. They are continuous with the *xylem* and *phloem* of the stem and roots.

Objectives

In this activity you will:
1. Study the tissues that make up the leaves of a plant.
2. Examine the structure of a stomate.

Materials

prepared slide of lilac leaf (cross section)	beaker
	pipette
lettuce leaf	slide
scalpel	cover slip
forceps	microscope

Procedures and Observations

PART I.   LEAF TISSUES

1. Observe a prepared slide of a lilac leaf cross section under low power. Focus first on the upper epidermis, then on the lower epidermis. Switch to high power and examine the epidermal cells.

   a. *Do the epidermal cells contain chloroplasts?*

   _____

Throughout the lower epidermis are tiny openings called *stomates*. Each stomate is surrounded by a pair of *guard cells* that regulate its opening and closing. The stomates allow water vapor, carbon dioxide, and oxygen to pass into and out of the leaf.

2. Switch to low power. Observe the stomates and their guard cells. Note that each stomate opens into an air space.

Most photosynthesis in the leaf occurs in the mesophyll. The mesophyll is made up of two layers. The upper layer, the *palisade mesophyll*, consists of tall, closely packed cells. The lower layer, the *spongy mesophyll*, consists of irregularly shaped, loosely packed cells. The spongy mesophyll layer contains many air spaces.

3. Focus on the mesophyll under low, then high, power. Identify the palisade cells and the cells of the spongy mesophyll.

   b. *Describe the cell layers in the mesophyll.*

_____

_____

   c. *What are the most numerous organelles in the palisade cells?*

_____

   d. *Compare the number of chloroplasts in the cells of the palisade mesophyll with the number in the cells of the spongy mesophyll.*

_____

4. Note the numerous air spaces in the spongy mesophyll.

   e. *Are the air spaces connected to the outside atmosphere? How?*

_____

_____

5. Switch back to low power. Focus on a vascular bundle. Then switch to high power. Observe the xylem cells in the upper part and the phloem cells in the lower part of the bundle. Note that each bundle is surrounded by a layer of thick-walled cells that strengthen the vein.

6. Switch back to low power. Find a section where you can clearly see the epidermis, mesophyll, and vascular tissues of the leaf.

   f. *Make a drawing of the cross section of the leaf. Make it about 5 cm high. Label the* cuticle, upper epidermis, palisade *and* spongy mesophyll layers, vascular bundle, *and* lower epidermis.

Structure of a Leaf (continued)

PART II. STOMATES _____

1. Soak a lettuce leaf in a beaker of water for at least 5 minutes. The leaf will become stiff, or turgid.

2. Remove the leaf from the water when it has become turgid. Crack the leaf midrib as shown in Figure 1. With a forceps, peel off a piece of the lower epidermis.

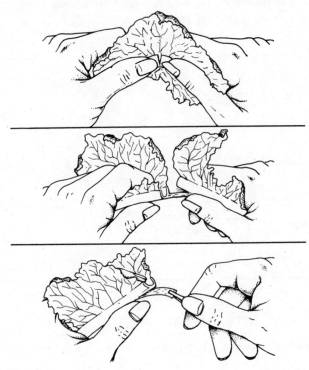

Figure 1

3. Place the epidermis sample on a clean microscope slide. Cut off a small section of it with a scalpel. **CAUTION:** *Handle the scalpel with care.* Place the section in the center of the slide and discard the rest of the epidermis. Add a drop of water and a cover slip.

4. Examine the slide under low power. Adjust the light to provide the best contrast.

   a. *Describe the shape and color of an epidermal cell.*

   _____

5. Focus on a stomate and switch to high power. Observe the stomate and the guard cells surrounding it.

   b. *Describe the appearance of the stomate and the guard cells.*

   _____

   _____

6. Switch back to low power. Count the number of stomates you see in the field of the low-power objective.

    c. *Record the number of stomates in the low-power field.*

_____

7. Estimate the number of stomates you see in a square millimeter of epidermis.

    d. *Record your estimate of the number of stomates/mm^2 of epidermis.*

_____

    e. *Make a drawing of a section of lower epidermis. Label an* epidermal cell, guard cell, *and* stomate.

Analysis and Interpretations

1. How does the shape of a leaf help it to use sunlight efficiently?

_____

2. Explain the function of the cuticle.

_____

_____

3. In which layer of the mesophyll does more photosynthesis occur? How can you determine this?

_____

_____

4. What is the function of the air spaces in the spongy mesophyll?

_____

5. Name the leaf structures that help to conserve water.

_____

Auxins and Tropisms

Lab 26

Background

Plants, like animals, produce hormones, which act as chemical messengers. Plant hormones are produced in definite regions of the plant, and they travel in plant-body fluids to target tissues, where they affect the growth patterns of the tissues. Some plant hormones are produced in regions of rapidly dividing cells, as in the meristem of root tips or stem tips. Some are produced in embryos of seeds. Other types of plant hormones occur in fruits and roots.

Plant hormones, in general, are growth regulators. Some hormones affect the length of cells, and thereby the length of plant parts, such as stems or roots. Other hormones may cause both rapid cell division and elongation of cells.

Because of their sources and effects, plant hormones are grouped into three major groups. The *auxins* are produced in the meristem of root tips and stem tips of complex plants. The *gibberellins* are produced by certain fungi, and by the germinating seedlings of many other species of plants. They stimulate the production of new cells and promote the elongation of cells. The *cytokinins* are produced in seeds after they have germinated; they are also found in the fruits and roots of many species of plants. Cytokinins stimulate cell reproduction, especially in plant embryos, stem tips, and leaves.

The hormones called auxins bring about the responses made by plants to stimuli such as light, gravity, or soil water. Plant responses take the form of turnings of plant parts: turnings of leaves toward light, turning downward into the ground by roots, or turning upward by shoots and stem tips. Such responses of plants to environmental stimuli are called *tropisms*. They are adaptations that contribute to the survival of the plant.

Tropisms are named for the stimulus that causes the response. For example, a response to light is called a *phototropism*, a response to gravity is called a *geotropism*, a response to soil water is called a *hydrotropism*. Tropisms occur because environmental stimuli cause auxins to become unequally distributed in the plant tissues. The tissues of plant organs such as stems and roots then grow at unequal rates, causing turnings in the stems or roots. A tropism may be *positive*, a turning <u>toward</u> the stimulus, or it may be *negative*, a turning <u>away from</u> a stimulus.

Objectives

In this activity you will:
1. Observe tropisms in the developing roots of germinating corn grains, as they respond to the stimulus of gravity.
2. Observe tropisms in the developing shoots of germinating corn grains, as they respond to gravity.
3. Determine the effects of removing the meristem regions of the root-tips of developing corn seedlings.

Materials

soaked corn grains
Petri dishes
white blotting paper or
   No. 1 filter paper
nonabsorbent cotton
glass-marking pencil
masking tape or transparent tape

modeling clay
paper towels
metric ruler
scissors
single-edge razor blade
bulb pipette

Procedures and Observations

PART I. PREPARATION OF SEEDLINGS _____

Work in groups of four. Each group will set up two Petri dishes, two students preparing one dish for the experiment, the remaining two students preparing the other dish as the control.

1. For each Petri dish, cut a circle of white blotting paper or filter paper to fit the bottom of the dish, and set the paper aside.

2. Obtain four soaked corn grains for each dish and examine them. Note that each grain has a pointed end that was once attached to the corncob. Note, also, that both sides of the grain are not alike. On one side of each grain the white, shield-shaped embryo is visible near the pointed end of the grain. The embryo will develop into a seedling plant. The part of the embryo that will become the root is directed toward the pointed end of the grain. The part that will become the shoot is directed toward the wide part of the grain.

3. Place four corn grains in each Petri dish, with the pointed end of each grain pointed toward the center of the dish. If the dish were the face of a clock, put one grain at 12, one at 3, one at 6, and one at 9 o'clock. Place the grains about halfway between the outside edge and the center of the Petri dish. Then turn each grain so that the embryo is "face down" against the dish. When the dish is closed, you must be able to see the embryos through the bottom of the Petri dish.

4. Place the paper from Step 1 on top of the grains, being very careful not to move them. With the bulb pipette, drop water onto the paper until it is completely wet. Do not add excess water.

5. Place a layer of nonabsorbent cotton on top of the paper to hold it in place and prevent the corn grains from moving out of position.

6. Place the cover on the dish and look through the bottom to see if the corn grains are still in place. Try turning the dish at different angles to see if the grains will move. If they move, add more cotton until it holds the grains in place.

7. Dry each dish thoroughly on the outside. The sealing tape will not adhere to a wet dish. Tape the dishes closed by means of four pieces of tape placed between the corn grains. See Figure 1.

8. With the glass-marking pencil, print *TOP* on one side of each dish in line with one of the corn grains. This corn grain will have the embryonic root pointing downward, and the embryonic shoot pointing upward, after you have completed the setup.

Auxins and Tropisms (continued)

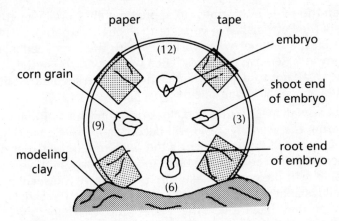

Figure 1

9. After taping and marking, check these points: (1) Are the four corn grains at the correct "clock" points in each dish? (2) Are their pointed ends pointing toward the centers of the dishes? (3) Can you see each corn grain clearly through the bottom of each of the dishes, with no tape or mark obscuring the grains? (4) Can you see the light-colored, shield-shaped embryo clearly in each corn grain? Make any necessary corrections.

10. Place an identifying mark on each dish with the glass-marking pencil. Then set each dish on its side in a lump of modeling clay, so that the side marked TOP points upward. Check the positions of the top corn grains, and compare your setups with Figure 1. When you have checked your setups, set the dishes in the modeling clay in the place indicated by your teacher.

11. Allow the seedlings to germinate and grow until the roots are about 1 cm long. During this first growth, check the appearance of the paper daily to be sure that it has not dried. Open the dish only if it is necessary to add water to the paper.

12. From experience, you might say that the corn grain in the top position (12 o'clock) in the dish is "right side up," and can be expected to grow "normally," the root growing downward and the shoot growing upward. In the spaces below, state your predictions of the direction of growth of the roots and shoots of the other seedlings.

O'clock	Root	Shoot
3		
6		
9		

PART II.   PERFORMING THE EXPERIMENT

Growth of the roots and shoots of seedlings occurs as a result of activity in the cells of the meristem tissues at their tips. Given favorable growing conditions, new cells are produced fairly rapidly. These cells then elongate and mature. The meristem also produces hormones—auxins—that affect the manner of growth of the plant. You will demonstrate the importance of root tips by removing them from seedlings in one dish.

1. When the roots have grown to approximately 1 cm in length, select one of the Petri dishes of your group to be the experiment. Place the dish on the table at your workplace with the corn seedlings facing downward. Remove the tapes. Then remove the top of the dish carefully, so as not to disturb the positions of the seedlings. Lift off the cotton and lay it to one side on a paper towel.

2. Make a small mark at the 12 o'clock position (the TOP) on the paper covering the seedlings. You will need this for reference, later. Very carefully, try to lift the paper off the seedlings. If the paper does not adhere to the seedlings, continue to lift it slowly, remove it, and lay it aside with the cotton. Make sure not to move the seedlings. If the seedlings adhere to the paper, do not try to lift it. Instead, lay the fingers of one hand over the paper and carefully invert paper, seedlings, and dish, all at once. You will now have the paper and seedlings on your hand, with the dish upside down over them. Remove the dish, and gently lay the paper and seedlings on a paper towel. Keep the seedlings in their "clock" places at all times.

3. The seedlings will now be resting on the bottom of the Petri dish, or on the paper. Examine the root of one seedling and try to locate the very dense meristem, close to the root cap. You are going to try to cut off the end of the root that includes the meristem. Using the ruler, measure 4 mm from the tip and judge whether or not all of the meristem is included in that 4 mm. If not, consider 5 mm, etc. When you have determined the amount of root tip that includes the meristem, make a clean cut through the root with the single-edge razor blade. **CAUTION:** *Use care in handling the single-edge razor.*

4. Repeat this process with the other three root tips, moving them as little as possible.

5. Reassemble the dish, placing the seedlings in their original positions. Add a few drops of water to the paper if it has dried. Make sure that you know which seedling was at 12 o'clock, and place it at the mark you made in Step 2, matching it with the marked TOP of the dish. The dish should now be assembled exactly as the control is assembled.

   a. *Why is it important to keep the seedlings in their original positions, even though the root tips have been removed?*

   _____

   _____

   _____

   _____

   _____

6. Set the dish on its side in the modeling clay, as before, TOP up.

7. Allow the seedlings in both dishes to grow for 2 or 3 days, depending upon how fast they grow.

Auxins and Tropisms (continued)

PART III. OBSERVATIONS OF GROWTH PATTERNS _____

Experiments have shown that environmental stimuli may cause unequal distribution of auxins in roots and shoots during the early growth of seedlings. As roots grow out from the seed, the meristem cells in their tips produce auxin, which is pulled toward the center of the earth by gravity. If the root is pointed downward, the auxin remains centered over the tip, and no unequal distribution occurs. If the root grows parallel to the surface of the earth, auxin is pulled to the lower layers of root tissue. The auxin *inhibits* the growth of cells on the underside of the root. Cells on the upper side grow at the normal rate, faster than the cells on the underside. This results in the turning downward by the root, known as a geotropism, a response to gravity.

1. Observe the roots and shoots of the four seedlings in the control dish. Look carefully at each seedling to determine the pattern of its growth.

   a. *Sketch each of the four seedlings in the space provided, showing the direction of the root and shoot growths in relation to the position of the corn grain.*

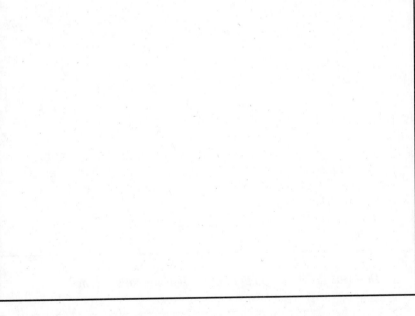

   b. *Did each seedling's root grow in the same direction as its shoot?*

   _____

   c. *Did all of the roots grow in essentially the same direction, or in different directions?*

   _____

   _____

d. *Did all of the shoots grow in essentially the same direction, or in different directions?*

_____

_____

As you examined and sketched the seedlings you noted different responses to gravity in shoots and roots. The meristem tissue of shoots is in the very tip of the shoot. As soon as a seed germinates and the shoot is stimulated to grow, the meristem cells produce auxin, which moves out of the meristem to the adjoining tissues. As in roots, the auxin is pulled downward by gravity. The result is more auxin in the lower layers of cells of the shoot. This unequal distribution of auxin causes unequal growth of the cells of the shoot. *In shoots, the effect of the auxin is different from the effect in roots.* Auxin causes the lower cell layers of the shoot to grow faster than the upper cell layers. Growth of the under side is thus promoted, and the shoot turns upward.

2. Carefully examine the seedlings in the experimental dish and note the growth patterns of their roots and shoots.

    e. *Sketch the four seedlings in their respective positions, showing the growth in relation to the position of each corn grain.*

    f. *Describe the root growth of the experimental seedlings.*

_____

_____

    g. *Describe the shoot growth in the experimental seedlings.*

_____

_____

Auxins and Tropisms (continued)

Analysis and Interpretations

1. Record the patterns of growths of the seedlings in the control dish in the spaces below.

O'clock   Root   *Shoot*

   3   _____   _____

   6   _____   _____

   9   _____   _____

2. Compare the actual growths of the seedlings with your predictions for their growth in Part I, Step 12. How do they compare?

_____

_____

3. Explain the direction of growth of the roots of the seedlings at 3 and 9 o'clock.

_____

_____

_____

_____

_____

_____

_____

4. Explain the growth pattern of the root of the seedling at 6 o'clock.

_____

_____

_____

_____

_____

5. What kind of tropism occurred in the roots of these seedlings? What was the stimulus that caused the tropism? Was this a positive or a negative tropism? Why?

_____

_____

_____

6. What kind of tropism occurred in the shoots of these seedlings? What was the stimulus that caused the tropism? Was this a positive or negative tropism? Why?

_____

_____

7. If auxin was the cause of the tropisms in both the roots and the shoots of the seedlings, what hypotheses might be considered to explain the observed differences in the responses of roots and shoots to gravity? Give at least two hypotheses, A and B, and more if you can.

A. _____

_____

B. _____

_____

8. Suggest an experiment that could test each hypothesis.

_____

_____

_____

_____

_____

_____

_____

For Further Investigation

If the corn seedlings in your control dish are in good condition, let them grow for two more days in a different position. Mark one of the plants "TOP 2" and place it at the top. Record the date and time that you change the position. Also, check to be sure that the paper has not dried. Report to the class what happens as the result of the change, using your control dish as a demonstration. Try to explain the results in terms of the information that you gained in this activity.

Mitosis in Animal Cells

Lab 27

Background

Cell division is essentially the same in unicellular organisms and in multicellular organisms. Two major events occur in a continuous process that produces two new, smaller cells. In the first stage, the nucleus reproduces itself, forming two identical nuclei. In the second stage, the cytoplasm is divided between two new cells in such a way that each nucleus is enclosed in approximately half of the cytoplasm of the parent cell. The new, small cells have the capability of growing.

The nucleus of a cell contains the hereditary material that directs the development of the organism. In the first stage of cell reproduction, the nucleus and its contents undergo orderly changes and activities. The result of these activities is the exact replication of the hereditary material of the parent-cell nucleus, and the formation of two new nuclei. These two nuclei are identical to each other, and to the parent nucleus. The process that produces these identical nuclei is known as *mitosis*.

In the second stage of cell reproduction, the cytoplasm of the parent cell is divided between two new cells. The process of dividing the cytoplasm *(cytokinesis)* is different in cells that have no cell wall, compared with cells that have a cell wall.

Stages of cell reproduction can be observed using stained sections of tissues where there is much cell division activity. Since no movement is visible in prepared slides, it is customary to refer to the activities of the nucleus and cytoplasm as a series of *phases*. In this way, the processes of mitosis and cytokinesis can be conveniently followed and described.

Objectives

In this activity you will:
1. Observe the phases of mitosis in cells of developing animal embryos.
2. Observe the method of cytoplasmic division during cell reproduction in animal cells.

Materials

prepared slides of
    whitefish embryo sections
facial-type tissue

lens paper
microscope

Procedures and Observations

A fertilized whitefish zygote divides into 2, then 4, then 8, then 16 cells, and continues to divide repeatedly until the embryo is in the form of a tiny ball of cells. The tiny ball can be stained and sliced, and the slices mounted on microscope slides. Cells can then be examined to see the phases of mitosis that were occurring when the ball of cells was taken for study.

1. Obtain a prepared slide of whitefish embryo sections from your teacher. If the slide is dirty, carefully hold it by the edges and clean it with a facial tissue. Do not press on the cover slip. Hold the slide up to the light and look at the sections.

   a. *How many sections are there on the slide?*

   _____

   b. *What color are the sections stained?*

   _____

2. Place the slide on the microscope stage and focus on a section under low power.

3. Look for individual cells. Try to count the number of cells in the section.

   c. *How many cells do you count?*

   _____

During interphase, the hereditary material is dispersed throughout the nucleus. This material stains darkly, and in the microscope it looks like dark grains, or tangled threads. At this stage the hereditary material is called *chromatin*.

4. Look for a cell at interphase. See Figure 1. When you find one, center it. Then switch to high power.

interphase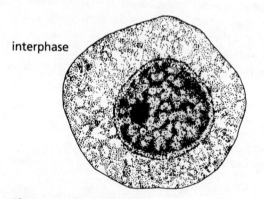

Figure 1

   d. *Describe the structure of a cell at interphase.*

   _____

   _____

   _____

5. Switch back to low power. Look for a cell at early prophase. See Figure 2. If you do not find one in the section you are using, look at other sections on your slide. When you have found one, center it and switch to high power.

Mitosis in Animal Cells (continued)

prophase

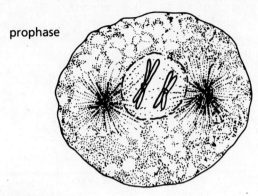

Figure 2

e. *Is a nuclear membrane present?*

_____

f. *Is a nucleolus present?*

_____

_____

The rather large star-shaped structures at the two poles of the cell are the *asters*. The *astral* rays point out from the centrioles and form a *spindle* between the centrioles. *Chromosomes*, now condensed, look like very dark, short threads.

6. Switch back to low power. Look for a cell at metaphase. See Figure 3. When you have found one, center it and switch to high power.

metaphase

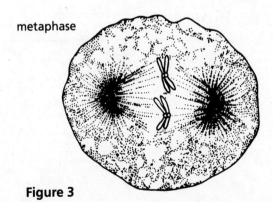

Figure 3

7. Move the fine adjustment knob back and forth a tiny bit in each direction to see the depth of the spindle. Also notice the way the light changes as it passes through the spindle fibers and astral rays.

g. *On the next page, draw a cell at metaphase. Make it about 4 cm across. Lightly sketch in the spindle. Label the* chromosomes, asters, *and* spindle.

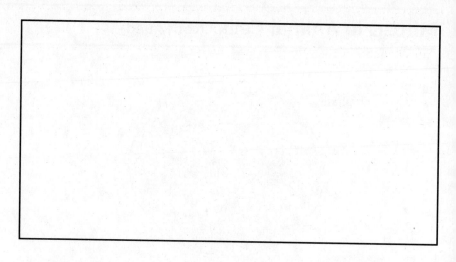

8. Switch back to low power. Look for a cell at anaphase. See Figure 4. When you have found one, center it and switch to high power.

anaphase

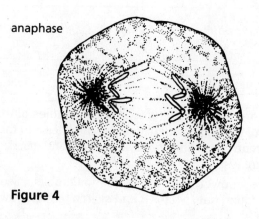

Figure 4

h. *Draw a cell at anaphase. Make it about 4 cm across. Label the structures you see.*

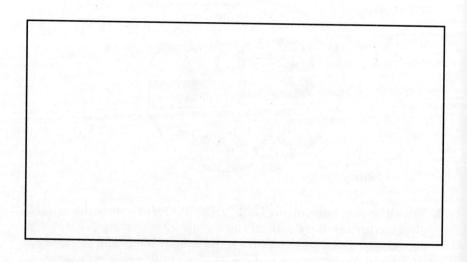

9. Again switch to low power. Look for a cell at telophase. See Figure 5. Examine the cell under high power.

Mitosis in Animal Cells (continued)

telophase

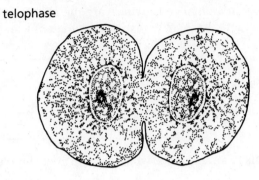

Figure 5

i. *Are the nuclei of the new daughter cells surrounded by a membrane?*

_____

j. *Can you see a nucleolus in the daughter cells?*

_____

k. *Describe what has happened to the cell membrane.*

_____

l. *When the daughter cells mature, how will they compare in size with the parent cell?*

_____

m. *How will the nuclei of the daughter cells compare with the parent cell nucleus?*

_____

_____

_____

Analysis and Interpretations

1. Explain what happens to the nuclear membrane during prophase in animal cells.

_____

_____

2. Explain what happens to the nucleoli of animal cells during prophase.

_____

_____

_____

3. At what phase of mitosis does the spindle appear in animal cells? At what phase does it disappear?

_____

4. During mitosis in animal cells, where are the chromosomes located at the time of metaphase? Where are they at anaphase?

_____

_____

_____

_____

5. During mitosis in animal cells, what is found at each pole of the spindle?

_____

6. Describe how the cytoplasm is divided between the two new cells in animal cells.

_____

_____

_____

7. What happens to the nuclear material in late telophase, in animal cells?

_____

_____

_____

Mitosis in Plant Cells

Lab 28

Background

Cell division, the formation of two new cells from a single parent cell, is a continuous process. Within this process are two major events, or stages. The first stage is *mitosis,* the process that produces two identical nuclei from a single parent nucleus. The second stage is *cytokinesis,* the process that divides the cytoplasm of the parent cell between the two new cells. For ease in understanding, scientists break down and illustrate the processes of mitosis and cytokinesis as a series of *phases.*

Cell division is similar in all organisms. There are, however, differences in the process in plant cells and in animal cells, which can be seen when the phases of mitosis and cytokinesis are studied. In the preceding lab, you observed cell division in animal cells. In this lab activity, you will observe the process in plant cells.

Objectives

In this activity you will:
1. Observe the phases of mitosis in cells of the meristem of onion root tips.
2. Observe the method of cytoplasmic division during cell reproduction in plant cells.

Materials

prepared slides of onion
    root tip, longitudinal
    section

lens paper
microscope
facial-type tissue

Procedures and Observations

Actively reproducing cells in onion root tips can be used for the study of mitosis in plant cells. The meristem, near the root tip, is the tissue where new cells are produced.

1. Obtain a prepared slide of longitudinal sections of onion root tips. If the slide is dirty, hold it by the edges and carefully clean it with a moistened facial tissue. Do not press on the cover slip, for you might crush the root tip sections. Hold the slide up to the light and look at the sections.

   a. *How many sections are there on the slide?*

b. *When you hold the slide so that the label is right-side up, are the pointed ends of the sections pointed upward or downward?*

_____

_____

_____

Recall that the microscope inverts the image. It will be important to locate the root cap, in order to find the meristem tissue.

2. Place the slide on the microscope stage and focus on a section at low power. Move the slide until you can see the root cap clearly. Arrange the slide so that the root cap is pointing toward you.

Just above the root cap is the meristem tissue. See Figure 1. In the meristem region, many of the cells are much smaller than those of the root cap. They are the new cells. They will grow before reproducing. Many of the larger cells of the meristem were in the process of mitosis when the root tip was taken for study. Chromosomes are visible in cells undergoing mitosis because they were stained with a purple stain.

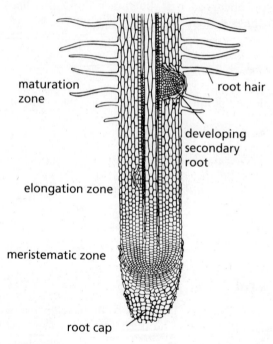

maturation zone

root hair

developing secondary root

elongation zone

meristematic zone

root cap

Figure 1

3. Find the meristem tissue and examine it. Note how it is clearly different from the root cap tissue below it. Move the slide so that you can see the larger cells above the meristem tissue. The differences in the tissues help you to locate the cells of the meristem. Return to the meristem tissue and examine the shape of the cells.

c. *What is the shape of the cells?*

_____

4. Notice that the cells are in rows. In looking for cells in mitosis, you will find it easy to search up one row and down the next. Look at a number of cells at low power to accustom your eye to the size of the cells and their nuclei. Look for cells containing darkly stained chromosomes.

5. Find a cell at early prophase. The nucleus should be round, but darkly stained, because chromosomes were shortening and thickening as mitosis began in that cell. The nuclear membrane may be breaking down, and the nucleoli may be starting to disintegrate. Center the cell in the low power field and switch to high power. If you cannot find the cell you wished to examine, switch again to low power and center the cell more carefully. Examine the nuclei of several cells at high power. Look for darkly staining nucleoli.

   d. *How many nucleoli are present in each nucleus?*

   _____

   _____

   e. *If there are different numbers of nucleoli in the cells you examined, what could be the reason?*

   _____

   _____

One of the ways in which plant cells differ from animal cells is that plant cells lack centrioles, and do not form asters during mitosis. A spindle forms however, and the chromosomes undergo the same kinds of activities as occur in animal cells.

6. Switch back to low power. Look for a cell at metaphase. See Figure 2. When you have found one, center it and switch to high power.

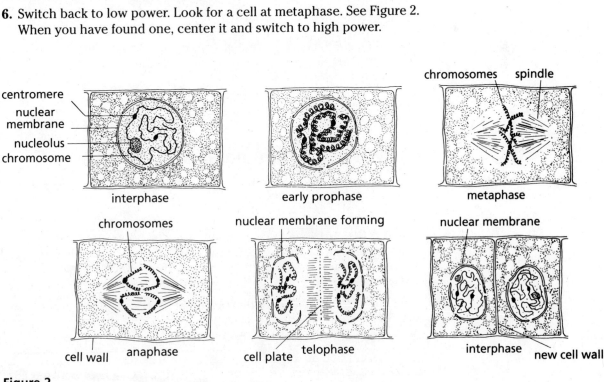

Figure 2

7. Move the fine adjustment knob back and forth a tiny bit in each direction to try to see the depth of the spindle. Also notice the way the light changes as it passes through the spindle fibers.

8. Switch back to low power. Look for a cell at anaphase. See Figure 2. When you have found one, center it and switch to high power.

In the telophase stage of mitosis in plant cells, the cytoplasm is divided by a method different from that in animal cells. A foundation for a new cell wall, called the *cell plate*, is synthesized by the parent cell, across the equator of the spindle. In your microscope, it will look like a line at the equator of the spindle, between the new nuclei. (Recall that a dinner plate looks like a line when you look at it from one edge.) As the new daughter cells develop, a new cell wall is deposited on the cell plate. A new cell membrane is also formed by the new cells, along both sides of the new cell wall. When cell reproduction is complete, each new cell has a nucleus identical to the parent nucleus, each of the new cells is entirely enclosed in a membrane, and the two cells are separated by a new cell wall that they share. The new cells will grow before they undergo mitosis.

9. Again switch to low power. Look for a cell at telophase. See Figure 2. Examine the cell under high power.

   f. *Are the nuclei of the new daughter cells surrounded by a membrane?*

   _____

   g. *Can you see one or more nucleoli in the daughter cells?*

   _____

   h. *How do the daughter cells compare in size with the parent cell?*

   _____

   i. *How will the nuclei of the daughter cells compare in size and content with the parent nucleus? With each other?*

   _____

   _____

Analysis and Interpretations

1. Explain what happens to the nuclear membrane during prophase in plant cells.

   _____

   _____

   _____

2. Explain what happens to the nucleoli of plant cells during prophase.

   _____

   _____

   _____

Mitosis in Plant Cells (continued)

3. At what phase of mitosis does the spindle appear in plant cells? At what phase does it disappear?

_____

4. During mitosis in plant cells, where are the chromosomes located at the time of metaphase? Where are they at anaphase?

_____

_____

_____

_____

5. Describe how the cytoplasm is divided between the two new cells in plant cells.

_____

_____

_____

6. What happens to the nuclear material in late telophase, in plant cells?

_____

_____

_____

Simulating Meiosis

Background

Gametes, the cells which join together during sexual reproduction in animals and begin the formation of a new individual, each contain a single set of chromosomes. When a male and a female gamete unite, forming a *zygote,* the two single sets of chromosomes come together, forming pairs of chromosomes. Thus the cells of the newly formed animal contain pairs of chromosomes, with one member of each pair from the male parent and the other from the female parent. These pairs of chromosomes are called *homologous chromosomes,* meaning that they are similar but not identical.

Somatic cells, or body cells (in general, all cells except gametes), contain pairs of homologous chromosomes. Somatic cells are *diploid*—they have two complete sets of chromosomes. The normal number of chromosomes in a somatic cell is called the *diploid number,* and is abbreviated as *2n.*

When the new individual prepares for sexual reproduction, gametes must be formed once again. Cells with a diploid number of chromosomes must form cells having only one chromosome from each homologous pair. Thus cells having a diploid number of chromosomes give rise to cells having a *haploid number,* or *n* chromosomes. The cell division that forms gametes, halving the number of chromosomes per cell, is called *meiosis.*

Objectives

In this activity you will:
1. Illustrate the movement of chromosomes during meiosis.
2. Demonstrate, by means of a flip book, the separation of homologous chromosomes in meiosis.

Materials

2 handout sheets
lead pencil
2 contrasting-color pencils
scissors
paper punch
paper fasteners

Procedures and Observations

Each species has a characteristic number of chromosomes. For example, a cat has 19 pairs of chromosomes, a mosquito has 3 pairs of chromosomes, and a human has 23 pairs of chromosomes. Thus the diploid number for a cat is 38, 6 for a mosquito, and 46 for a human.

For ease in understanding, this lab activity will use a cell that has only three pairs of chromosomes.

1. Examine Figure 1. Notice that each pair of homologous chromosomes is made up of a dark chromosome and a light chromosome—the dark color represents the chromosome from the male

parent and the light color represents the chromosome from the female parent. The letters on the chromosomes stand for genes. Notice that each pair of chromosomes carries a particular set of genes; that the same genes are found on each chromosome in a pair; and that a full set of genes is contributed by each parent. The centromere of each chromosome is indicated by an asterisk (*). In this figure, and throughout this lab activity, each pair of chromosomes is a different length to make them easily identifiable.

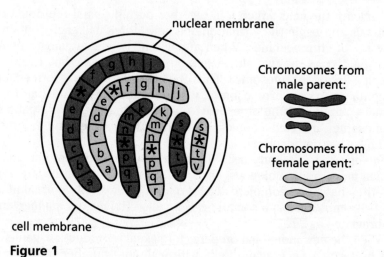

nuclear membrane

Chromosomes from male parent:

Chromosomes from female parent:

cell membrane

Figure 1

    a. *What is the diploid number of the species shown in Figure 1?*

_____

    b. *What is the haploid number of the species?*

_____

  2. Examine the handout pages you will use to make your flip book. Notice that each page contains small rectangles which you will cut apart to form pages of your flip book. In the first rectangle, the title page, write your name in the space provided.

  3. On page 1 of the flip book, the key, color in the chromosomes. Choose two colored pencils of bright, contrasting colors. Use one color for the chromosomes from the male parent, and the other color for the chromosomes from the female parent. You will use the same two colors throughout this lab activity, as you draw the chromosomes in the various stages of meiosis.

Meiosis is made up of two cell divisions—meiosis I and meiosis II. Each of these cell divisions is studied as a series of stages including prophase, metaphase, anaphase, and telophase. The two cell divisions follow a single replication, or copying, of chromosomes which takes place during *interphase,* before the start of meiosis. Thus at the start of meiosis, each chromosome is doubled in the parent cell. Two sister *chromatids,* or chromosome strands, now make up each chromosome. Chromatids are shown in Figure 2.

    4. Figure 3 on the next page shows the positions of the chromosomes at late interphase before meiosis. In the circle on page 2 of your flip book, copy the diagram for late interphase.

replicating chromosome

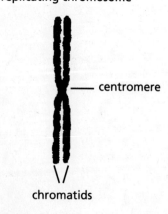

centromere

chromatids

Figure 2

Simulating Meiosis (continued)

c. *How many chromosomes are in the cell at the start of meiosis?*

_____

d. *How many chromatids are in the cell?*

_____

During *prophase I,* the first stage of meiosis, each pair of homologous chromosomes joins together, and is linked at the centromeres. This joining of chromosomes is called *synapsis.* Because each chromosome has already doubled, synapsis results in the forming of *tetrads,* four chromatids joined together. See late prophase I in Figure 4.

5. Skip to page 5 of your flip book. On this page, copy the diagram for late prophase I. Notice that spindle fibers have now formed across the cell.

e. *What structures have the chromosomes formed on page 5?*

_____

f. *What has happened to the nuclear membrane in late prophase I?*

_____

6. Compare the positions of the chromosomes shown in your drawing on pages 2 and 5 of your flip book. Decide how the chromosomes would have to move to get from their positions in late interphase to their positions in late prophase I. On page 3 draw the chromosomes 1/3 of the way between late interphase and late prophase I. Show the early formation of the spindle fibers and the nuclear membrane beginning to break down.

7. On page 4 of your flip book, draw the chromosomes 2/3 of the way between early prophase I and late prophase I. Show the formation of the spindle fibers.

During *metaphase I,* the three pairs of homologous chromosomes line up along the equatorial plane.

8. Skip to page 7 of your flip book. On this page, copy the diagram for metaphase I, shown in Figure 5.

g. *To what part of the chromosomes are the spindle fibers attached?*

_____

9. Compare the positions of the chromosomes shown in your drawings on pages 5 and 7. Decide how the chromosomes would have to move to get from their positions in late prophase I to metaphase I. In the circle on page 6 or your flip book, draw the chromosomes halfway between late prophase I and metaphase I.

During *anaphase I,* the homologous pairs of chromosomes separate and move apart. The chromosome pairs seem to be pulled apart by the spindle fibers.

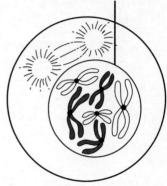

late interphase

Figure 3

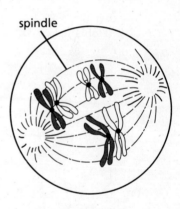

late prophase I

Figure 4

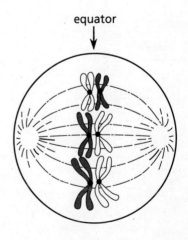

metaphase I

Figure 5

homologous chromosomes

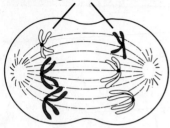

anaphase I

Figure 6

telophase I

Figure 7

prophase II

Figure 8

metaphase II

Figure 9

10. Skip to page 9 of your flip book. On this page, copy the diagram for anaphase I, shown in Figure 6.

   h. *Have sister chromatids separated from each other during anaphase I?*

   _____

11. Compare the positions of the chromosomes shown in your drawings on pages 7 and 9. Decide how the chromosomes would look in early anaphase I. On page 8 or your flip book, draw the chromosomes in early anaphase I.

Telophase I is the last stage of meiosis I. At this point, the chromosomes are divided into two groups. Depending on the species, several things may happen—nuclear membranes may form, the cytoplasm may divide and cell membranes may form between two newly formed cells.

12. On page 10 of your flip book, copy the diagram for telophase I, shown in Figure 7.

   i. *Are spindle fibers present during telophase I?*

   _____

   j. *What is happening to the cell membrane in this cell?*

   _____

Telophase I may be followed immediately by prophase II or it may be followed by a short interphase. Unlike the interphase preceding the start of meiosis, chromosomes are <u>not</u> replicated during this interphase. During *prophase II,* spindle fibers reappear—this time they are in each of the newly formed cells.

13. On page 11 of your flip book, copy the diagram for prophase II, shown in Figure 8.

   k. *How many chromosomes are found in each of the cells during prophase II?*

   _____

   l. *How many chromatids are in each cell?*

   _____

During *metaphase II,* the chromosomes line up at the equator of each of the newly formed cells. Spindle fibers attach to the centromere of each sister chromatid.

14. Skip to page 13 of your flip book. On this page, copy the diagram for metaphase II, shown in Figure 9.

   m. *How is metaphase II different from metaphase I?*

   _____

15. Compare the positions of the chromosomes shown in your drawings on pages 11 and 13. Decide how the chromosomes would have to move to get from their positions in prophase II to metaphase II. On page 12 of your flip book, draw the chromosomes halfway between prophase II and metaphase II.

Simulating Meiosis (continued)

29

During *anaphase II,* the sister chromatids divide and move apart. Because each sister chromatid has formed a separate centromere, the two sister chromatids are now considered separate chromosomes. The single-stranded chromosomes then move to opposite ends of each cell.

16. Skip to page 15 of your flip book. On this page, copy the diagram for anaphase II, shown in Figure 10.

    n. *How does anaphase II differ from anaphase I?*

    _____

    _____

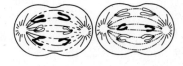

anaphase II

Figure 10

17. Compare the positions of the chromosomes shown in your drawings on pages 13 and 15. Decide how the chromosomes would have to move to get from their positions in metaphase II to anaphase II. Draw the chromosomes in this intermediate position on page 14.

During *telophase II,* the spindle fibers disappear and a nuclear membrane forms around each group of chromosomes. The cytoplasm divides around each newly formed nucleus, resulting in four new haploid cells.

18. On page 16 of your flip book, copy the diagram for telophase II shown in Figure 11.

    o. *How does the number of chromosomes in each newly formed cell compare to the number of chromosomes in the parent cell?*

    _____

    _____

    p. *Are the chromosomes in the newly formed cells diploid or haploid?*

    _____

telophase II

Figure 11

19. Cut apart the pages of your flip book. Stack the pages in order, with all the pages facing the same direction. Using a paper punch, make holes in the two small circles on the left-hand side of the book. Use paper fasteners to clip the pages together.

20. Flip through the pages of your book to see the major movements of chromosomes during meiosis.

Analysis and Interpretations

1. In the process of meiosis, how many nuclei are produced from the nucleus of each parent cell?

   _____

2. In mitosis, replication of chromosomes precedes each cell division. In meiosis, two cell divisions take place without a replication of chromosomes between them. What is the significance of this difference?

   _____

   _____

3. Meiosis is sometimes called reduction division. What does this mean and why is it important to a species?

_____

_____

_____

_____

4. Why is it significant that the four newly formed cells differ in chromosome content?

_____

_____

For Further Investigation

1. Look at your diagram from anaphase I. This diagram shows one of the possible ways the tetrads could be split to form haploid cells. Three other chromosome combinations are possible. Diagram the other possibilities and show the newly formed cells that would result.
2. Add more pages to your flip book by making drawings that show the actions of chromosomes between the stages you have drawn. Adding more pages will smooth out the movements in the flip book.

Development of Chick Embryos

Lab 30

Background

You are familiar with hens' eggs and their contents—the white and the yolk. But how do these materials become a chick? To answer this question, you need more information about an egg. The whole yolk inside an egg is an *ovum*, or egg cell. The ovum was produced in a sac embedded in the surface of the ovary of the hen. The liquid, yellow part of the yolk, inside the yolk membrane, is actually food stored for the chick embryo as the ovum developed. When an ovum matures, it is a full-size yolk. It bursts from its sac on the ovary and enters the funnel of the oviduct. If a rooster has deposited sperm within the hen, many have swum the length of the oviduct and are in the funnel when the ovum arrives. Fertilization takes place almost immediately. As the ovum moves down the oviduct, it is covered with layers of *albumen* (the "white" of the egg). A double *shell membrane* is deposited around the albumen and is filled with water. The hard, but porous, outer shell is formed last. A few hours later, the egg is laid. The egg is produced whether or not fertilization has occurred. If the egg has been fertilized, a chick will develop if the egg is given "nest conditions" for 3 weeks.

Objectives

In this activity you will:
1. Examine the structure of a hen's egg.
2. Observe stages of development of chick embryos on prepared slides.

Materials

prepared slides:
 chick embryos, whole mounts
 series of embryos 16-24 hours
 series of embryos 24-48 hours

hens' eggs
sharp scissors
blunt forceps
pipettes
ruler for measuring

Syracuse dish
paper towels
hand lens
dissecting microscope

Procedures and Observations

PART I. STUDY OF A HEN'S EGG

The egg you will use for study probably has not been fertilized, unless it came from a hen that lives in a flock of chickens (hens and roosters) that rove a barnyard, or live together in a chicken-pen. Eggs that are purchased in cartons at food stores come mostly from poultry farms where eggs are mass-produced.

Research done with birds in the early 1960s revealed that egg laying is related to day length; the longer the day, the more often eggs are laid. On farms where eggs are mass-produced, large hen houses are well lighted 24 hours per day and hens are well fed. The result is a maximum number of eggs for marketing.

1. Place an egg in a Syracuse dish on a crumpled paper towel, as shown in Figure 1. Draw an oval on the egg, 3 cm x 4 cm.

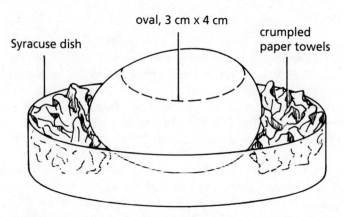

oval, 3 cm x 4 cm

Syracuse dish

crumpled paper towels

Figure 1

2. Using the tip of sharp-pointed scissors, carefully cut out the oval. Try to make shallow cuts just beneath the shell, so that you do not damage any internal structures.

3. Observe the shell membrane lining the shell of the egg. Gases can pass through this membrane and also through the shell.

   a. *Describe the texture of the shell membrane.*

_____

4. Look inside the blunt end of the egg. Note that the shell membrane is double.

   b. *What do you find in the egg's blunt end?*

_____

   c. *Is the shell lined with a membrane in this region? Is the inner egg covered with a membrane in this region?*

_____

_____

The yolk of the egg is suspended in *albumen.* Albumen consists of water, water-soluble proteins, and some minerals.

Chalazae (kuh-LAY-zee), twisted white cords, are attached to opposite sides of the yolk membrane. They hold the yolk in position in the egg.

5. Identify the chalazae. Using the forceps, pull gently on one end of a chalaza.

   d. *What happens to the yolk?*

_____

_____

Development of Chick Embryos   (continued)

The yolks of the eggs (the ova) of birds are some of the largest cells in the world today. On the surface of the yolk is a small disc, the *cytoplasmic disc*, containing the ovum nucleus and some cytoplasm.

Fertilization of the egg, when it occurs, takes place in the nucleus, within the cytoplasmic disc.

6. Examine the top of the yolk. If necessary, carefully remove some of the albumen with a pipette. Locate the small, circular, light-colored cytoplasmic disc. If you cannot see it, pull carefully on one of the chalazae to roll the yolk over.

    e. *Describe the appearance of the disc.*

_____

7. Measure the diameter of the cytoplasmic disc.

    f. *Record (in mm) the diameter of the cytoplasmic disc.*

_____

8. Use Figure 2 to identify all the structures of the hen's egg.

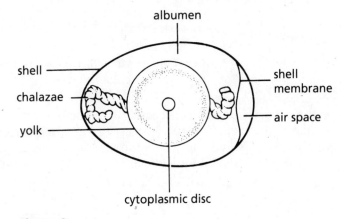

albumen

shell

chalazae

yolk

shell membrane

air space

cytoplasmic disc

Figure 2

PART II.   STUDY OF A 16- TO 24-HOUR EMBRYO _____

An embryo will develop in a fertilized hen's egg if it is incubated either by a hen, or in "nest conditions" in an incubator. In a nest, the hen keeps the eggs at a temperature of 39° to 40°C, the air is moist, and the hen turns the eggs frequently. All these conditions must be maintained in a laboratory incubator in order for an embryo to develop. (Frequent turning of the eggs prevents embryonic membranes from adhering to the shell. Development stops if the eggs are not turned, because materials cannot circulate freely within the egg.)

A series of microscope slides can be prepared showing the early development of a chick from the time an egg is laid, until the developing embryo is too large to mount on a slide. After incubation for a certain number of hours, each egg is opened. The embryo develops in the cytoplasmic disc, which can be seen as a flat disc or oval, lying on the top of the yolk. The flat embryo is removed from the yolk with fine-pointed scissors, treated with several solutions to clear and preserve it, and then mounted as a "whole mount" in a preservative on a slide.

The "age" of each embryo (the approximate time interval of incubation) is recorded on the slide label. You can also judge the approximate age by referring to drawings and diagrams made by scientists who have done extensive research on the development of chick embryos.

1. Obtain a prepared slide of a chick embryo, "whole mount" (w.m.), incubated about 16 hours. Examine the mount and look for a structure that resembles the 16-hour embryo shown in Figure 3. Measure the embryo's length and width.

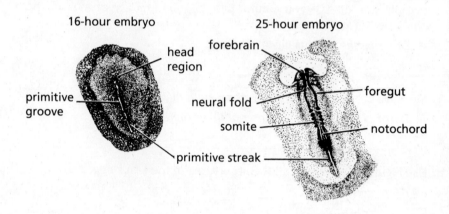

Figure 3

a. *Record the length and width (in mm) of the embryo.*

_____

2. Observe the embryo under a dissecting microscope. Compare it with the stages of development shown in Figure 3. Remember, the "age" given on the label can only be approximate. The embryo you observe may have developed for a longer or shorter period of time.

b. *What is the approximate age (in hours) of the embryo on the slide?*

_____

c. *Make a sketch of the embryo on a separate sheet of paper. Label any structures that you can identify.*

_____

_____

PART III.   STUDY OF 24- TO 48-HOUR EMBRYOS _____

After the first 24 hours of incubation, the embryo has developed sufficiently for the beginnings of the major organ systems to be visible with a microscope. Several slides can be observed in sequence, for example 24-, 36-, and 48-hour embryos, to see the development that takes place in this 24-hour period.

1. Obtain a slide of an embryo close to 24 hours in age. Use a hand lens to observe the embryo before putting it under the microscope. Compare it with the drawings in Figure 3.

Development of Chick Embryos   (continued)

2. Obtain several other slides, if available, in which the embryos were incubated longer than 24 hours, but less than 48 hours. Examine these embryos with the hand lens, and compare them with the drawings in Figure 4. Determine the order of their ages.

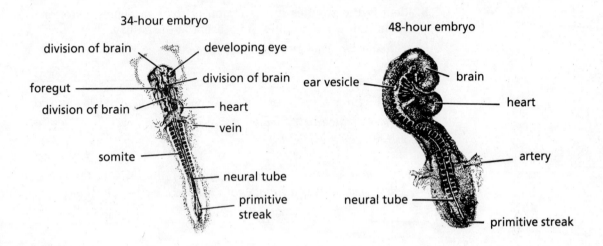

Figure 4

Arrange the slides in sequence on a paper towel. In steps 3 through 9, examine each of them in order with the dissecting microscope, so as to see the development of each organ and organ system.

3. Note the heart. It forms like an enlarged blood vessel, then loops outward to the right of the embryo, becoming larger, thicker, and more curved.

4. Observe the blood vessels. They may look dark if blood had already been formed. In the egg, the blood vessels branched out over the surface of the yolk. It was necessary to cut them when the embryo was removed from the egg for mounting.

5. Locate the bulbous part of the brain, anterior to the heart.

   a. *Has the brain begun to bend to one side?*

   _____

   b. *Does it bend to the embryo's right, or left?*

   _____

The embryo develops areas of dense tissue running the length of the center of the body. These are the *neural ridges* and *neural groove*, which will form the spinal cord.

6. Observe the tissues running the length of the embryo that will form the spinal cord.

7. Find the structures at the anterior end of the brain that will develop into eyes.

c. *Describe the developing eyes.*

_____

_____

The body of the embryo develops somites, blocks of dense tissue that extend in pairs along the center line. The age of the embryo can be recognized by the number of pairs of somites present. The somites develop into the backbone and skeletal muscles.

8. Identify the somites in the region of the heart and posterior to it. Count how many somites are present in the embryo.

d. *Record the number of somites present.*

_____

9. Using Figures 3 and 4, estimate the age (in hours) of the embryo.

e. *Record the estimated age (in hours).*

_____

f. *Make a sketch of an embryo on a separate sheet of paper. Label any structures you can identify. Record the age of the embryo.*

_____

Analysis and Interpretations

1. List the major organ systems that you were able to see in the embryos in Parts II and III.

_____

_____

_____

2. In what order did these organ systems appear? Compare your findings with other groups in the class.

_____

_____

_____

_____

3. What can you conclude about the order of development of structures in chick embryos?

_____

_____

_____

_____

The Human Menstrual Cycle

Lab 31

Background

When a human female is born, her ovaries already contain the primary oocytes that will mature and produce eggs during her lifetime. Maturation of primary oocytes generally begins between the ages of 12 and 14, when the female reaches sexual maturity. Most commonly, eggs usually mature every 28 days or so, usually one at a time, in alternating ovaries. The rhythmic maturation of eggs and the events that accompany the process are termed the *menstrual cycle*.

Each egg matures inside an egg sac, or *follicle,* near the surface of one of the ovaries. When the egg is fully mature, the follicle bursts. The egg is released in a process called *ovulation.* Cilia sweep the egg into the Fallopian tube, which leads to the uterus. An unfertilized egg will pass from the female's body within a short time. The lining of the uterus, which had been prepared for the arrival of an embryo, deteriorates and also passes out of the body. This periodic loss of tissues and fluids from the uterus is a normal function known as *menstruation.* A menstrual cycle is considered to begin at the onset of menstruation.

Hormones carried in the bloodstream bring about the changes in the menstrual cycle by means of "feedback mechanisms." The pituitary gland below the brain secretes hormones that signal the growths and secretions in the ovary. Later, when the ovarian secretions reach low levels, these low levels stimulate the pituitary gland to secrete more hormones, which stimulate the development of another egg.

Objectives

In this activity you will:
1. Examine the events that occur in a 28-day menstrual cycle.
2. Graph the changing levels of four hormones in the bloodstream.
3. Study how hormone feedback mechanisms control a cyclic function.

Procedures and Observations

PART I.   THE FOLLICULAR PHASE

1. Look at Figure 1. Notice that it is made up of four parts—A, B, C, and D. Parts B and D show events occurring during the menstrual cycle. Parts A and C are graphs, which you will complete, that show the levels of hormones secreted during the menstrual cycle. Notice that each graph has two different y-axes. Each y-axis will be used to plot the level of a different hormone.

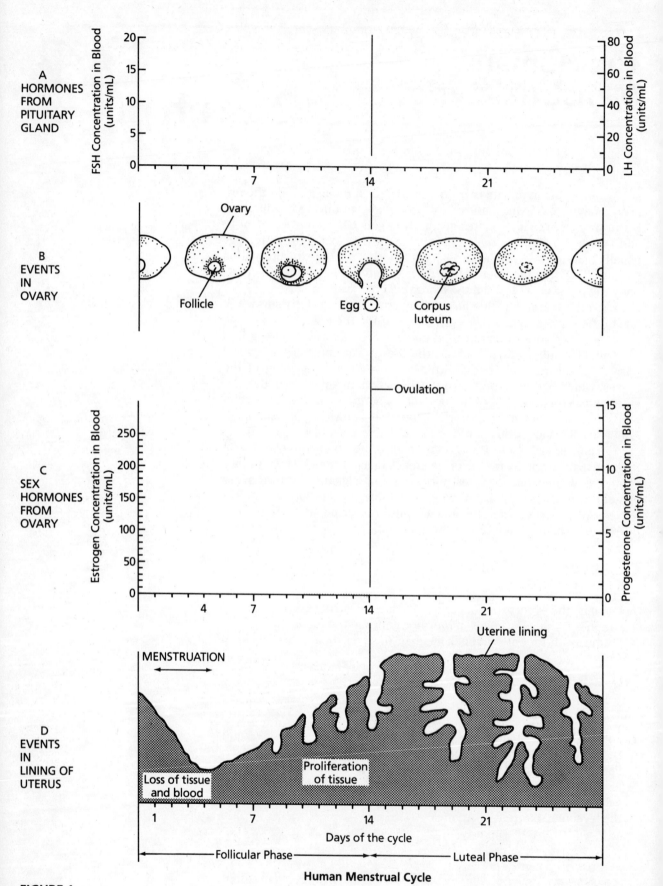

FIGURE 1

The Human Menstrual Cycle (continued)

Inside the follicle of the ovary is a single maturing egg, or ovum. On day 1 of a cycle, the follicle of a new egg is about to be stimulated to grow by an increase in the amount of follicle-stimulating hormone (FSH) in the blood. FSH is secreted by the pituitary gland.

2. Using the data in Table 1 on page 176, plot points in Part A of Figure 1 to indicate the concentrations of follicle-stimulating hormone in the blood. Remember to use the left-hand vertical axis. Check the points, then use a pencil to draw a curve. (Do not "connect the dots." Draw a smooth curve.)

   a. *On what day does follicle-stimulating hormone reach maximum concentration?*

   _____

   b. *What happens to the follicle during the 14 days that you plotted in Step 2, above? What causes these changes?*

   _____

   _____

   _____

   _____

   _____

The growing follicle secretes *estrogen,* a sex hormone, in increasing amounts. By the 13th day, the concentration of estrogen has increased to the point that it causes FSH secretion to decrease.

3. In Part C, use the data in Table 1 to plot points indicating concentrations of estrogen in the blood. Use the left-hand vertical axis for this plot. Draw a curve for the estrogen, as you did for follicle-stimulating hormone in Step 2.

The increased estrogen in the blood stimulates the cells of the uterus to form new tissue containing capillaries. In this way, the uterus is prepared for the arrival of an embryo.

4. Look at Part D of Figure 1. Notice that during menstruation the lining of the uterus decreases; between days 5 and 15, the lining reforms.

   c. *What happens in the ovary (Part B) and in the bloodstream (Part C) that brings about this change in the uterus?*

   _____

   _____

   _____

   _____

The increased concentration of estrogen that occurs during the follicular phase also stimulates the secretion of another pituitary hormone, *luteinizing hormone* (LH). By day 14 or 15, ovulation has occurred, and luteinizing hormone has reached its highest concentration.

5. On Part A of Figure 1, plot the points indicating the concentrations of LH for days 1–14. See Table 1 for data. Remember to use the right-hand vertical axis. Check the points, then draw the curve showing the changes in concentration of luteinizing hormone, or LH.

   d. *On what day of the cycle does luteinizing hormone reach maximum concentration?*

   _____

By the 14th day, the egg has developed sufficiently for fertilization to be possible. Ovulation occurs at some time between the 10th and 15th days. Ovulation ends the follicular phase.

PART II. THE LUTEAL PHASE

During the luteal phase, the ruptured follicle that remains in the ovary is stimulated by luteinizing hormone. The follicle grows and becomes a hollow, yellow mass of tissue called the *corpus luteum* ("yellow body"). The corpus luteum acts as an endocrine gland, secreting the hormone *progesterone*. Progesterone stimulates the uterus to maintain its thickened lining, and to develop pockets that contain glands.

1. Find the 15th day in Part B of Figure 1. Note the changes in the follicle tissue between days 15 and 28.

By the time ovulation has occurred, the secretion of estrogen by the follicle has stopped. The decrease in estrogen concentration causes the production of luteinizing hormone to decrease. The corpus luteum then deteriorates and stops producing progesterone.

2. In Part C of Figure 1, plot points indicating the concentrations of estrogen on Days 15–28. See Table 2 for data. Draw the remainder of the curve for estrogen. Label the curve.

Table 1. Concentrations of Hormones in Blood: Follicular Phase

Units per Milliliter				
Day	FSH	Estrogen	LH	Progesterone
1	9	30	9	0.6
2	11	40	12	0.8
3	13	50	16	1.0
4	14	70	18	1.0
5	15	80	19	1.0
6	14	100	16	1.0
7	14	130	12	1.2
8	15	140	19	1.2
9	13	180	15	1.3
10	11	200	16	1.5
11	9	220	20	1.5
12	18	230	30	1.6
13	13	220	75	1.8
14	9	200	58	2.0

Table 2. Concentrations of Hormones in Blood: Luteal Phase

Units per Milliliter				
Day	FSH	Estrogen	LH	Progesterone
15	9	180	30	2.3
16	8	150	14	3.7
17	8	120	10	5.8
18	8	100	9	8.3
19	8	50	7	10.4
20	7	30	5	12.0
21	7	25	3	12.0
22	6	25	3	11.8
23	5	25	2	10.3
24	5	25	3	7.2
25	6	20	3	4.0
26	7	20	4	3.0
27	7	25	5	1.5
28	8	25	7	0.8

3. In Part A of Figure 1, plot data from Table 2 to show concentrations of luteinizing hormone on days 15–28. Draw and label the curve for luteinizing hormone.

4. In Part C of Figure 1, plot points indicating the concentrations of progesterone for the entire 28-day cycle. Obtain data from both Table 1 and Table 2. Use the right-hand vertical axis for this plot. Draw and label the curve.

If an embryo becomes embedded in the uterine wall, the new glandular pockets will be stimulated to secrete hormones similar to progesterone and estrogen, and the uterine lining will be maintained all through the pregnancy.

If no embryo arrives in the uterus, the concentration of progesterone in the blood decreases rapidly. By day 28, both estrogen and progesterone in the blood are at their lowest combined levels. This condition signals the onset of menstruation—the end of the current cycle and the beginning of the next.

Since the secretion of *follicle-stimulating hormone* (FSH) is also triggered by simultaneously low concentrations of estrogen and progesterone, a new follicle will be stimulated to develop only when the ovarian hormones are both at very low levels of concentration in the blood.

5. In Part A of Figure 1, plot points for the concentrations of follicle-stimulating hormone on days 15–28. Data are given in Table 2. Draw and label the curve.

   a. *Why does the level of follicle-stimulating hormone decrease and remain at a relatively low level during the luteal phase of the cycle?*

_____

_____

_____

_____

Analysis and Interpretations

1. What process signals the end of one cycle and the beginning of another?

_____

_____

2. Why are the interactions of hormones and tissues in the menstrual cycle considered to be feedback mechanisms?

_____

_____

_____

_____

3. How does estrogen play a role in a feedback mechanism?

_____

_____

_____

_____

_____

_____

4. How does progesterone play a role in a feedback mechanism?

_____

_____

_____

_____

_____

Classification of Fruits

Lab 32

Background

A fruit is a ripened ovary that surrounds one or more seeds. While a seed develops, its surrounding ovary begins to thicken and enlarge, developing into a fruit. There are three major types of fruit produced by the flowering plants: *simple fruits*, *aggregate fruits*, and *multiple fruits*. All fruits have one main function—to disperse the seeds produced by the parent plant.

Objectives

In this activity you will:
1. Study the major types of fruits.
2. Determine the flower parts that make up a fruit.
3. Note how fruits are adapted for seed dispersal.

Materials

fresh, unopened pea pod
fresh string bean
sunflower seed
1/2 ear of fresh corn
winged maple samara
acorn (or chestnut or beechnut)
apple
cherry (or olive, peach, or plum, with "seed")
tomato
cucumber (or acorn squash)

fresh orange (or lemon or grapefruit)
fresh strawberry
1/4 fresh pineapple, cut lengthwise
preserved fig
knife
nutcracker
hammer
hand lens
paper towels

Procedures and Observations

PART I.   SIMPLE FRUITS

A simple fruit is a fruit that develops from a single pistil in a flower. There are two kinds of simple fruits—dry and fleshy. Some dry fruits split open when mature; others do not. Legumes are dry simple fruits that split open when they are mature. Peas and string beans are examples of legumes.

In legumes, each fruit develops from a single ovary. The stem of the fruit develops from the peduncle, or upper stalk, of the flower. The swollen receptacle can be seen below the sepals that surround the base of the pod.

1. Examine a fresh pea pod. Note the stem, receptacle, and the sepals.

   a. *How many sepals remain on the specimen?*

_____

Seamlike joints run the length of the pod. These are called *sutures*. The sides of the pods are called *valves*. When the fruit matures, the valves become dry. The pod then splits along both sutures and disperses the seeds.

2. Compare the pea pod with a string bean. Note the sutures and valves.

   b. *Sketch the pea pod. Label the* stem, receptacle, sepal, sutures, *and* valve.

Some dry simple fruits do not split open when mature. Fruits of this type include the achene, the grain, the samara, and the nut.

The *achene* contains a single seed and has a dry, hard outer coat. This outer coat is the ovary wall. The seed is attached to the wall at only one point. The buttercup, sunflower, and buckwheat flower produce achenes.

3. Examine a sunflower seed. Carefully break open the ovary wall and observe how the seed is attached to it.

   c. *Does the seed separate easily from the wall or is it firmly attached?*

   _____

   d. *Is the entire seed coat attached to the wall or is it attached at only one point?*

   _____

   _____

The ovary wall of a *grain* is completely joined to the seed coat. Corn, wheat, rice, and oats have this type of fruit.

4. Examine a grain, or kernel, of corn. Each kernel attached to the corn cob is a fruit. Try to peel off the outer layer of the grain.

   e. *Describe what happens.*

   _____

   _____

   _____

Classification of Fruits (continued)

The *samara* has a prominent wing, which is an outgrowth of the ovary wall. The maple tree fruit is a well-known samara.

5. Examine a maple samara. Carefully open it to find the seed.

f. *Is the seed coat firmly attached to the ovary wall or can it be separated easily?*

_____

g. *At how many points is the seed attached?*

_____

h. *Sketch the samara. Make it about 5 cm long. Label the* wings *and* ovary wall.

The *nut* contains one seed and has a tough, crusty coat. Nuts develop from cuplike structures composed of modified leaves. The acorn, walnut, and chestnut are typical nuts.

6. Examine an acorn. Note its hard coat. This was the ovary wall. Also note the cup that is still attached to it. Crack the nut with a nutcracker.

i. *How many seeds are in the nut?*

_____

j. *Describe the seed coat.*

_____

_____

Some simple fruits are fleshy, rather than dry. The ovary wall and other flower parts develop into a thick, watery, fleshy layer as the fruit matures. The fleshy simple fruits are the pome, the drupe, and the berry.

In a *pome*, the receptacle develops into the fleshy part of the fruit as it grows and surrounds the ovary. The ovary develops into the inner core, which is the true fruit. Examples of pomes are apples and pears.

7. Study an apple. Cut one apple in half lengthwise through the center of the core. Cut a second apple crosswise through the center of the fruit. See Figure 1.

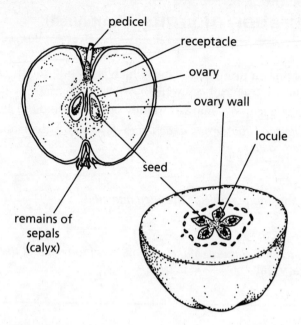

Figure 1

8. Compare the cut apple surfaces. Note the pattern of the locules in the two apples.

   k. *How many locules are present in the apple?*

   _____

   l. *How many seeds are in one locule?*

   _____

A *drupe* is known as a "stone fruit." All parts of the fruit form from the ovary only. The skin and fleshy layer are the two outer layers of the ovary wall. The hard part of the "stone" is the inner layer of the ovary wall. Cherries, peaches, plums, and olives are drupes.

9. Cut a cherry lengthwise through the center, separating the flesh from the stone.

10. With a hammer, tap the stone gently until it breaks open.

    m. *Describe what you observe.*

    _____

    _____

A true *berry* is a fleshy, enlarged ovary. The seeds are embedded in the flesh. A thin skin covers the fruit. Grapes, tomatoes, and blueberries are examples of berries.

11. Cut a tomato crosswise through the center. Note the many seeds embedded in the pulpy flesh. Try to peel off the skin.

    n. *Can you peel off the skin?*

    _____

    _____

Classification of Fruits (continued)

A *pepo* is a type of berry that has a firm rind. The rind does not separate from the flesh. Cucumbers, squash, melons, and pumpkins are pepos.

12. Cut a cucumber in half crosswise. Note the numerous seeds.

    o. *Sketch the cut surface of the cucumber. Label a seed, the* fleshy tissue, *and the* rind.

A *hesperidium* is a type of berry that has a leathery rind. The rind is formed from the ovary wall and contains oil glands. Citrus fruits, such as oranges, lemons, and grapefruits, are in this group.

13. Cut an orange crosswise through the center. Examine the inner structure.

    p. *Where in the ovary are the seeds attached?*

_____

    q. *Does the rind separate easily from the flesh ?*

_____

PART II.   AGGREGATE FRUITS

An *aggregate* fruit develops from a single flower that has many separate pistils. The pistils develop into a number of small fruits (fruitlets) that mature together on a common receptacle. The raspberry and blackberry are aggregate fruits.

The strawberry is also an aggregate fruit. The fruits of the strawberry are achenes, spread over the surface of the fleshy receptacle. The green, leaflike hull of the strawberry was the calyx of the flower.

1. Examine a strawberry.

    a. *How many sepals make up the calyx?*

_____

    b. *Where are the strawberry seeds?*

_____

_____

c. *Approximately how many fruitlets make up the strawberry?*

2. Cut the strawberry lengthwise through the center. Observe the structure of the receptacle. Note the conducting tissue.

   d. *How does the conducting tissue seem to be related to the achenes on the surface?*

PART III.   MULTIPLE FRUITS

A *multiple fruit* forms from the ovaries of many flowers closely clustered on a central stalk. The pineapple and the mulberry are multiple fruits.

1. Examine the cut section of a pineapple. Note the central core. It was a central stalk that bore a number of separate flowers.

2. Observe the outside of the fruit. Each rounded section came from one flower.

   a. *How many flowers were clustered to form your section of pineapple?*

   b. *If you have 1/4 of a pineapple, how many flowers grew together to form the whole fruit?*

The fig is an unusual multiple fruit called a *synconium*. The peduncle (central stalk) of the flower cluster becomes fleshy and completely encloses the fruits.

3. Examine a fig. Cut it in half lengthwise and look inside at the fruits. They are usually thought to be seeds.

4. Remove several fruits. With the flat side of a knife, gently crush the coat of the fruit.

5. With a hand lens, examine the crushed ovaries and the seeds within. Note that the seed is free of the ovary wall except at the one point where it is attached.

Analysis and Interpretations

1. The hull you peeled off the corn grain had two layers. What were they?

2. Approximately how many pistils were in the strawberry flower that produced your strawberry?

Classification of Fruits (continued)

3. Consider how the seed was attached inside the fig fruit. What type of fruit is found inside a fig?

_____

4. Explain how simple, aggregate, and multiple fruits are formed. Give two examples of each.

_____

_____

_____

_____

_____

5. What characteristics of each of the following fruits are adaptations for seed dispersal?

a. legume _____

_____

_____

b. achene _____

_____

_____

c. samara _____

_____

_____

d. nut _____

_____

e. fleshy fruit _____

_____

_____

6. Some fruits are brightly colored and some taste sweet. How would these qualities aid in dispersal of seeds?

_____

_____

_____

7. Many animals store achenes, grains, and nuts for winter food. What makes these fruits suitable for storage?

_____

_____

_____

8. The raspberry is an aggregate fruit. It is made up of many simple fruits attached to a receptacle. Each simple fruit is called a *drupelet*. Where are the raspberry seeds? (Be precise.)

_____

_____

Computer Activity

In Laboratory Experiment 32 you examined and classified plant fruits according to their forms. *Family Identification* is a database of 80 plant families and their identifying characteristics. It can be used to identify unknown plants or review the characteristics of plant families. Fruit type is one of the identifying characteristics.

Seeds of Flowering Plants

Lab 33

Background

In the flowering plants, the angiosperms, seeds develop from the ovules of flowers, after pollination and fertilization have occurred. Each seed consists of three fundamental parts: a plant embryo, a supply of nutrients for the embryo, and a protective coat. The seed coat prevents the seed from drying and protects it from other unfavorable environmental conditions.

The angiosperms include two major groups, which are identified partly by the structure of their seeds. The seeds of the *monocotyledons* (monocots) have one cotyledon, or seed leaf; the seeds of the *dicotyledons* (dicots) have two cotyledons.

Objectives

In this activity you will:
1. Study the structure of monocot and dicot seeds.
2. Examine the arrangement of the plant embryos inside monocot and dicot seeds.
3. Identify the embryonic plant tissues that develop into leaves, stems, and roots.

Materials

corn grain soaked in
    water overnight
lima bean soaked in
    water overnight
hand lens

dissecting needle
scalpel
Lugol's iodine solution in
    dropper bottle
paper towels

Procedures and Observations

PART I.   A MONOCOT SEED _____

The corn seed is a *monocot* seed—it has one cotyledon. The corn grain is a ripened ovary of a corn flower. Each grain is a fruit of the corn plant, containing a single seed. The seed coat is completely joined to the ovary wall, which is the outer covering of the grain. Within the seed coat is the plant *embryo* and its food supply, the *endosperm*. The point where the grain was attached to the cob is called the *pedicel*.

1. Examine the soaked corn grain. Note that it has two broad, flat sides. Observe the tough outer coat. Find the pointed pedicel.

2. Lay the corn grain on a paper towel, pedicel toward you, and look for the plant embryo on one broad side of the grain. You can see the embryo, a light-colored, shield-shaped structure, through the outer coat. Examine the embryo with the hand lens.

The endosperm surrounds most of the embryo and makes up the major portion of the corn grain. Endosperm from corn is the source of cornstarch, commonly used for thickening sauces and puddings.

3. Find the endosperm. Note its relationship to the embryo. Note also how it fills the corn grain.

A *silk scar* can be seen on the grain, where a "corn silk" was attached. A corn silk is a long, flexible style of a corn flower. Its stigma is outside of the leafy "corn husks" that cover the cob. Each "silk" extends to an ovule inside each grain on the cob.

4. At the end of the embryo opposite the pedicel, feel for a tiny, raised point. This is the silk scar.

  a. *In the box, sketch the embryo side of the corn grain. Make it about 4 cm high, pedicel at the bottom. Label* ovary wall, pedicel, silk scar, embryo, *and* endosperm.

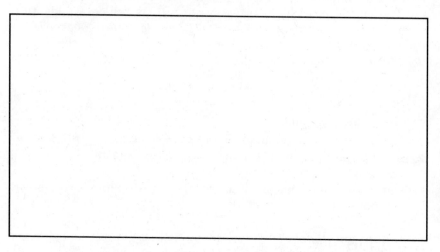

5. With a scalpel, make a firm cut lengthwise through the center of the grain. The cut should divide the embryo exactly in two, as in Figure 1.

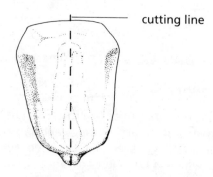

cutting line

Figure 1

A monocot embryo consists of three parts —the *cotyledon,* the *epicotyl* ("above cotyledon"), and the *hypocotyl* ("below cotyledon"). The cotyledon, or seed leaf, absorbs food from the endosperm and transfers it to the embryo during the early growth of the seedling. The epicotyl and hypocotyl are both attached to the cotyledon.

The epicotyl grows upward from the cotyledon and becomes the pointed shoot, the first part of the corn plant to sprout above ground.

Inside the protective covering of the shoot are the tissues that will become the first leaves of the plant, and the stem. The tissue of the epicotyl that develops into the first leaves is called the *plumule*.

The *hypocotyl* grows downward from the cotyledon. The very tip of the hypocotyl is the *radicle*. It is the first part of the embryo to break through the seed coat and ovary wall, when the seed germinates. In the corn plant, the hypocotyl and radicle give rise to the primary root.

6. Examine the cut surfaces of the corn grain with a hand lens. You can see the tissues of the embryo plant embedded in the endosperm.

7. "Paint" the cut surface of one-half of the grain with as small an amount of Lugol's iodine solution as possible. Observe it and then set it aside.

   b. *Which parts of the corn grain contain starch? Which do not?*

   _____

   _____

8. Examine the surface of the other half of the corn grain with the hand lens. Hold it with the pedicel down. On the embryo, find two tips of tissue, one pointing upward and one pointing downward.

   c. *Which is the epicotyl and which is the hypocotyl?*

   _____

   _____

9. With a dissecting needle, try to separate the tip of the epicotyl from the tissue behind it. The epicotyl will bend outward. Do not break it off. Note that it is firmly attached to the cotyledon.

   d. *What parts of the corn plant develop from the epicotyl?*

   _____

   _____

10. Gently separate the tip of the hypocotyl from the cotyledon with the dissecting needle. Be careful not to break off the tip. Note that the hypocotyl is firmly attached to the cotyledon.

    e. *What parts of the corn plant develop from the hypocotyl?*

   _____

   _____

11. Examine the cotyledon. Notice how its broad surface is firmly attached to the endosperm.

    f. *Sketch the cut surface of the corn grain. Label the* ovary wall, endosperm, cotyledon, epicotyl, plumule, hypocotyl, *and* radicle.

PART II.   A DICOT SEED

The bean seed is a *dicot* seed—it has two cotyledons. Bean seeds are produced in a pod, the fruit of the bean plant. Each seed is covered by a hard, protective seed coat, or *testa,* and is attached to the pod at the *hilum.* At one end of the hilum is a small pore called the *micropyle,* where the pollen tube entered the ovule of the flower. The micropyle is the only place where water can enter the seed.

1. Examine the soaked lima been seed. Locate the hilum, a scar on one side of the seed.

2. Use a hand lens to examine the micropyle.

   a. *Does the micropyle seem to extend all the way through the seed coat?*

   _____

   b. *Sketch the bean seed with the hilum facing you. Label the* hilum, seed coat (testa), *and* micropyle.

3. Peel the seed coat from the seed very carefully. Near the hilum and micropyle a part of the inner seed may break easily. Try not to break it off. If the two halves of the seed seem to be coming apart, hold them together. Place the inner seed on a paper towel.

The seed coat can prevent the drying out of the seed for years. It can also withstand the digestive juices of birds, allowing the seed to pass through their digestive tracts without change. In fact, many seeds are dispersed by birds. Birds eat the seed, carry it a distance, and then drop it with their digestive wastes. The seed can then grow in a new environment.

190

Seeds of Flowering Plants   (continued)   33

4. Examine the seed coat. Hold it up to the light to see the tissue structure.

The inner seed of the bean is made up entirely of embryo. The embryo consists of the two large cotyledons and the primary tissues of the new plant, the epicotyl and hypocotyl. The cotyledons contain stored food, which is transferred to the epicotyl and hypocotyl at the point where all are attached together.

5. Look at the plant embryo on the paper towel.

   c. *What are the two large "halves" of the inner seed?*

_____

6. Slowly and gently separate the cotyledons until you feel the point of attachment break. Look for the breaking point to see where the tissues were connected. Then lay the two sides flat on a paper towel, like an open book, with the primary tissues of the embryo at the top. Examine the opened embryo.

   d. *Are the two cotyledons alike?*

_____

_____

The hypocotyl, once attached to both cotyledons, is a long, curved structure that might have broken off easily when the seed coat was removed. In the early growth of bean plants, the hypocotyl forms the lower stem and the root. The radicle is the pointed tip of the hypocotyl. Inside the seed, the radicle is very close to the micropyle. It is the first tissue to break through the seed coat when germination occurs.

7. Find the pointed radicle extending outward from one of the cotyledons.

8. Above the hypocotyl is the broken point of attachment for the two cotyledons.

The plumule in the bean seed consists of the tiny leaves. They are part of the epicotyl, covering its tip. When the epicotyl grows, it will form the upper stem of the plant, and the plumule will become the first leaves.

9. Use the hand lens to locate the epicotyl and the plumule lying against the cotyledons.

   e. *How many leaves are there in the plumule?*

_____

   f. *Do they have leaf structure? Can you see veins?*

_____

   g. *Sketch the two halves of the bean seed. Label the* epicotyl, plumule, cotyledons, hypocotyl, radicle, *and* point of attachment.

Dicot seeds do not contain endosperm. The dicot embryo develops much more than does a monocot embryo, during the formation of the seed. Recall the differences you observed in the epicotyls, hypocotyls, and cotyledons of the corn and bean seeds. Much of the endosperm of the early dicot seed is consumed during this development. The remainder is converted mainly to starch, a nutrient stored in the cells of the cotyledons, and available for the growth of the embryo after germination of the seed.

10. With a scalpel, cut off a small portion of one of the cotyledons. Then slice that piece into smaller pieces. Put a drop of Lugol's iodine solution on the pieces.

h. *Is starch present in the cotyledon?*

_____

Analysis and Interpretations

1. Name the parts of the monocot seed and the dicot seed and state their differences.

_____

_____

_____

_____

_____

_____

_____

2. What is the function of the epicotyl? The hypocotyl?

_____

_____

_____

_____

Seeds of Flowering Plants   (continued)

3. What is the function of the micropyle when a seed is planted? Of what advantage to the plant is the position of the radicle, in relation to the micropyle?

_____

_____

_____

4. How is the seed coat related to the survival of a plant species?

_____

_____

_____

Probability and Inheritance

Background

In 1866 *Gregor Mendel*, an Austrian monk, published the results of his study of inheritance in garden peas. Although Mendel did not understand the mechanisms of inheritance, his work became the basis for the modern study of genetics. From his studies on the inheritance of certain traits in pea plants, Mendel formulated three laws of inheritance: the law of dominance, the law of segregation, and the law of independent assortment.

Mendel thought that every trait was controlled by a pair of factors, which we now call *genes*. The *law of dominance* states that one gene, the dominant gene, prevents the appearance of the trait controlled by the other gene, the recessive gene. The *law of segregation* states that during gamete (egg and sperm) formation, the pair of genes for a trait separate, so that each gamete has only one of the genes for the trait. The *law of independent assortment* states that as gametes are being formed, the genes for various traits separate independently of one another.

In this activity you will learn some principles of probability. You will use these principles and Mendel's laws to predict the inheritance of traits.

Objectives

In this activity you will:
1. Predict the probability of the occurrence of a single event.
2. Predict the probability of two independent events occurring at the same time.
3. Apply Mendel's laws to predict the occurrence of certain traits in the offspring of parents exhibiting particular traits.

Materials

two pennies
masking tape

Procedures and Observations

PART I.   OCCURRENCE OF A SINGLE EVENT _____

1. Toss a penny 20 times. Have your partner count how many times it lands heads up and how many times it lands tails up.

   a. *Write the totals under the Observed column for 20 tosses in Table 1.*

The law of probability states that when a procedure can result in two equally likely outcomes (in this case, heads or tails), the probability of either outcome occurring is 1/2, or 50%.

2. Using the law of probability, decide how many times out of 20 tosses you would expect heads to appear and how many times you would expect tails to appear.

   b. *Write your answers in the Expected column for 20 tosses in Table 1.*

   c. *Calculate the deviation by subtracting the expected number from the observed number. Record these in the Deviation column for 20 tosses in Table 1. Make all numbers positive.*

3. Have your partner repeat Step 1, but tossing the penny 30 times. Count how many times heads and tails appear.

   d. *Record the observed numbers in the Observed column for 30 tosses in Table 1.*

   e. *Calculate the expected numbers of heads and tails and record them in the proper column in Table 1. Then calculate the deviations, and enter these in the proper column.*

4. Now repeat Step 1, tossing the penny 50 times. Your partner should keep track of the number of heads and tails.

   f. *Record the observed numbers, expected numbers, and deviations in the columns for 50 tosses in Table 1.*

   g. *Add the observed numbers of heads and tails from the three trials and record the totals in the Total columns in Table 1. Then calculate the deviations and record these numbers.*

Table 1. Probability of the Occurrence of a Single Event

		Heads	Tails
20 Tosses	Observed		
	Expected		
	Deviation		
30 Tosses	Observed		
	Expected		
	Deviation		
50 Tosses	Observed		
	Expected		
	Deviation		
Total	Observed		
	Expected		
	Deviation		

PART II.   INDEPENDENT EVENTS OCCURRING SIMULTANEOUSLY ____

1. Toss two pennies simultaneously 40 times. Have your partner keep track of how many times headsheads, tailsheads, headstails, and tailstails occur. Count tailsheads and headstails together.

   a. *Record the numbers for each combination in the Observed column in Table 2.*

Probability and Inheritance (continued)

    b. *Calculate the percent of the total that each combination (heads-heads, heads-tails, or tails-tails) occurred and record it in the proper column. To find the percent, divide each observed number by 40 and multiply by 100.*

According to the law of probability, when there are four equally likely outcomes from a procedure, the probability that one of the outcomes will occur is 1/4 or 25%. We can see how this is calculated. For example, we know that in tossing two pennies, the probability of heads occurring on one penny is 1/2. The probability of heads occurring on the other penny is also 1/2. The probability of heads occurring on both pennies in one toss is $1/2 \times 1/2 = 1/4$.

2. Using the law of probability, predict the expected outcomes of tossing two pennies.

    c. *Record the expected numbers in the proper column in Table 2.*

    d. *Calculate the percent of the total that each combination is expected to occur, as you did above (problem 1-b). Enter these numbers in the proper column.*

    e. *Calculate the deviation by subtracting the expected from the observed and enter your results in Table 2.*

Table 2. Probability of Independent Events Occurring Simultaneously

Combinations	Observed	%	Expected	%	Deviation
Heads Heads					
Heads Tails Tails Heads					
Tails Tails					
Total	40	100%	40	100%	

PART III. PROBABILITY AND MENDELIAN GENETICS _____

We can use the law of probability to predict the probability of given genetic traits appearing in the offspring of particular parents. Punnett squares can also be used to make these predictions.

When gametes are formed, the pair of genes that determine a particular trait separate, and one gene goes to each gamete. When fertilization occurs, a male and a female gamete fuse. The resulting zygote, which develops into the new individual, now contains two genes for the trait. Which two of the parents' genes appear in the zygote is a result of chance.

In this case we will consider the inheritance in pea plants of round and wrinkled peas. *R* will represent the dominant gene for round peas and *r* will represent the recessive gene for wrinkled peas.

1. Put a small piece of masking tape on each side of two pennies. On one penny write *R* on each side. On the other penny write *r* on each side.

2. Toss the pennies several times.

   a. *What combinations of genes always appears?*

   _____

   b. *Would the offspring with these genes be round or wrinkled?*

   _____

3. Replace the old tape with new tape. On each penny, write *R* on one side and *r* on the other side. Toss the coins simultaneously until all possible combinations of genes have appeared.

   c. *What combinations of genes appear?*

   _____

   d. *For each of the combinations, would the offspring be round or wrinkled?*

   _____

Analysis and Interpretations

1. In Part I, what was the expected ratio of heads to tails for tosses of a single coin? Did your results always agree with the expected ratio? If not, what would be a reason for the deviation?

   _____

   _____

   _____

2. Compare the deviations from the expected for 20, 30, and 50 tosses. What seems to be the relationship between the sample size and deviation?

   _____

3. In Part II, what was the probability that tails would appear on both coins? How did you arrive at this answer?

   _____

4. What was the probability that heads-tails (or tails-heads) would appear? Show your calculations. (Hint: The probabilities for these two combinations must be added together because they were recorded together.)

   _____

   _____

5. If you tossed two coins simultaneously 400 times, would you expect the deviation to be greater or less than it was in tossing them 40 times?

   _____

6. In Part III, when an RR plant was crossed with an rr plant, would the offspring have round peas or wrinkled peas?

_____

7. Which of Mendel's laws did you apply to answer question 6?

_____

8. Complete the Punnett square for the cross of RR and rr plants.

9. Complete the Punnett square for the cross of Rr and Rr plants.

10. Draw a Punnett square to illustrate an Rr X rr cross. Show the genes of the parents, the possible gametes, and the types of offspring.

For Further Investigation

Mendel tested several different traits of peas. One of these traits was for the color of the pod. Green is the dominant trait; yellow is the recessive trait. Use *G* to represent the gene for green pods and *g* for yellow pods. Complete Punnett squares to show the expected offspring of a mating of a plant having yellow pods and one having green pods. (Hint: the green plant may be GG or Gg.)

Human Inheritance

Lab 35

Background

With an understanding of heredity and probability, biologists have learned about the genetics of many human traits. In many of these traits, several pairs of genes are involved and the pattern of inheritance is complex. For this activity we will assume that the traits we are studying are regulated by the alleles of only one gene, with one allele from the father and one from the mother.

Objectives

In this activity you will:
1. Determine your phenotype for several traits.
2. Determine (as far as possible) your genotype for the same traits.
3. Interpret the genotypes of individuals in a pedigree.

Procedures and Observations

PART I.   PHENOTYPES AND GENOTYPES OF COMMON TRAITS _____

You will determine your phenotype and try to determine your genotype for the traits listed in Table 1. Remember, if you show a dominant trait, you may be homozygous or heterozygous for that trait. Suppose, however, that one of your parents shows the recessive trait. In that case, the parent would have passed on a gene for the recessive trait and you would be heterozygous for that trait. If neither of your parents shows the recessive trait, you may not know whether you are heterozygous or homozygous for the trait. In this case, put a blank (_) for the unknown allele. If you show the recessive trait, record it as the phenotype as well as the genotype, with two recessive alleles.

Free earlobes, *L,* are dominant. People whose earlobes are attached directly to the side of the head have the recessive genotype, *ll*.

1. Have your partner check your earlobes.

   a. *Record your phenotype and genotype in Table 1 on the next page. (If you cannot determine whether your genotype is homozygous dominant or heterozygous, record* L_ *in the table.)*

Inheritance of eye color is controlled by multiple genes, but people having the homozygous recessive genotype, *bb*, have blue eyes. People who have a dominant allele, *B*, may have different shades of brown, hazel, or green eyes.

2. Check your eye color.

   b. *Record your phenotype and genotype in Table 1 on the following page.*

Table 1.   Phenotypes and Genotypes of Some Human Traits

Trait and Symbols for Genes	Phenotype	Genotype
Shape of ear lobe *L, l*		
Eye color *B, b*		
Shape of hairline *W, w*		
Ability to roll tongue *R, r*		
Ability to fold tongue *T, t*		
Shape of little finger *F, f*		
Ability to taste PTC *A, a*		
Hair on middle joint of fingers *H, h*		
Hair color *N, n*		
Hair curliness *C, c*		
Eyelash length *S, s*		

Human Inheritance (continued)

A widow's peak is a hairline that forms a downward point in the middle of the forehead. This is caused by a dominant allele, *W*. A smooth hairline is caused by the recessive genotype *ww*.

3. Have your partner check your hairline.

    c. *Record your phenotype and genotype in Table 1.*

A dominant allele, *R*, gives some people the ability to roll their tongues into a "U" shape when it is extended. People with the recessive alleles, *rr*, cannot roll their tongues.

4. Check to see if you can roll your tongue.

    d. *Record your phenotype and genotype in Table 1.*

A dominant allele, *T*, gives some people the ability to fold their tongues over. People with the recessive genotype, *tt*, cannot.

5. Check to see if you can fold your tongue.

    e. *Record your phenotype and genotype in Table 1.*

A dominant allele, *F*, results in the end joint of the little finger of each hand bending inward. Straight little fingers are a result of the recessive genotype *ff*.

6. Place your hands on a flat surface, palms down, and relax. Check to see if the first joints of your little fingers are bent or straight.

    f. *Record your phenotype and genotype in Table 1.*

Individuals who can taste the bitter chemical phenylthiocarbamide, PTC, have at least one dominant allele, *A*. Those with the recessive genotype, *aa*, cannot taste it.

7. Taste PTC paper to find out if it tastes bitter to you.

    g. *Record your phenotype and genotype in Table 1.*

Individuals who have hair on the middle joints of their fingers have at least one dominant allele, *H*. Those with two recessive alleles, *hh*, do not have hair on that joint.

8. Check to see if you have hair on the middle joints of your fingers.

    h. *Record your phenotype and genotype in Table 1.*

Individuals with red hair have the recessive genotype *nn*. Those with any other color hair have at least one dominant allele, *N*.

9. Check your hair color.

    i. *Record your phenotype and genotype in Table 1.*

Individuals having curly hair have at least one dominant allele, *C*. People having straight hair have the recessive genotype *cc*.

10. Check your hair type.

    j. *Record your phenotype and genotype in Table 1.*

Long eyelashes are the result of the dominant allele *S*. Short eyelashes are the result of the recessive genotype *ss*.

11. Have your partner check your eyelashes.

    k. *Record your phenotype and genotype in Table 1.*

PART II. HUMAN PEDIGREE

A diagram showing the transmission of a trait through several generations of a family is called a pedigree. In Figure 1, generation I is made up of grandparents, generation II is their children, and generation III is their grandchildren.

1. Study the pedigree diagram and the key in Figure 1 to learn the symbols.

Symbol	Meaning
○	Female without trait
□	Male without trait
●	Female with trait
■	Male with trait
•	Female, died in infancy
▪	Male, died in infancy
◌◌	Identical twins

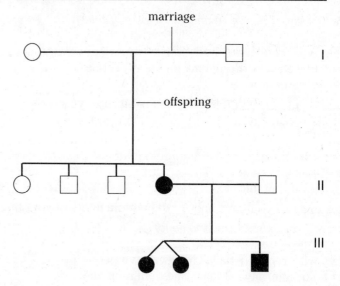

Figure 1

Individuals who lack an enzyme needed to form the skin pigment melanin are called albinos. Normal skin pigmentation is dominant.

2. Use *D* to represent the allele for normal skin and *dd* to represent the genotype for albinism. Where you cannot be sure whether an individual with the dominant trait is heterozygous or homozygous, show the genotype as *D_*.

    a. *List the genotype of each individual in Figure 2 on the next page.*

Human Inheritance (continued)

Individual		Genotype
I	1	
	2	
	3	
	4	
II	1	
	2	
	3	
	4	
	5	
	6	
	7	
III	1	
	2	

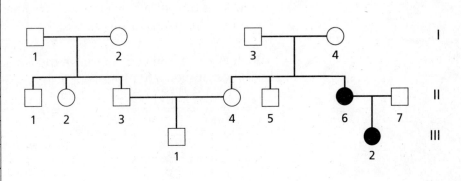

Figure 2

3. Use *A* to represent the allele for the ability to taste PTC, a dominant allele. Use *aa* for the PTC nontaster, who exhibits the recessive trait. Use *A_* where the genotype is uncertain.

   b. *List the genotypes of each individual in Figure 3.*

Individual		Genotype
I	1	
	2	
	3	
	4	
II	1	
	2	
	3	
	4	
	5	
	6	
	7	
	8	
III	1	
	2	
	3	
	4	

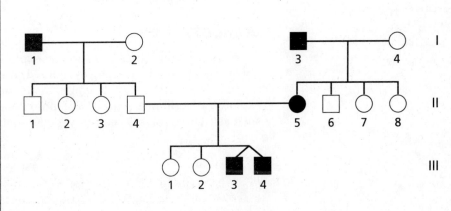

Figure 3

Analysis and Interpretations

1. Do you think that anyone in the class has all the same traits that you have? Why?

_____

_____

2. In the pedigree in Figure 2, if individuals 6 and 7 have another child, what is the chance that it will be an albino?

_____

3. In Figure 2, can you determine the genotypes of individuals 1 and 2 in generation I? Explain.

_____

_____

_____

_____

4. In the pedigree diagram in Figure 3, if individuals 4 and 5 in generation II have another child, what is the probability that it will be a taster?

_____

5. In Figure 3, if individual 8 in generation II married a man with genotype AA, what is the probability that she will have a nontaster child? Illustrate your reasoning with a Punnett square.

_____

Computer Activity

In Laboratory Experiment 35 you explored the inheritance of a variety of human traits including eyecolor, the ability to taste PTC, and the shape of the earlobe. The computer simulation _Human Genetic Disorders_ explores inheritance patterns of potentially lethal genetic disorders such as Huntington's Disease, Cystic Fibrosis, and Sickle Cell Anemia.

Extracting DNA

Lab 36

Background

Deoxyribonucleic acid, or DNA, is the largest type of molecule found in the cells of living organisms. An individual molecule of DNA can be several thousand times larger than a protein molecule.

To study DNA, scientists must extract it from cells without destroying its structure. In bacterial cells, which have no nuclei, the DNA is concentrated in a chromosome in a particular region of the cell. In chromosomes, DNA is chemically bound to proteins. Therefore the DNA must be separated from all cell materials, and then from the proteins to which it is bound.

Objectives

In this activity you will:
1. Extract DNA from bacterial cells.
2. Observe the DNA strands with the unaided eye, and also with the use of the compound microscope.

Materials

Escherichia coli culture in nutrient broth
250-mL flask
glass-marking pencil
10-mL and a 100-mL graduated cylinder
lysozyme
flat toothpick
incubator
sodium lauryl sulfate solution
oven mitt or tongs

paper towels
large test tube
test tube rack
100-mL beaker
ethyl alcohol
glass stirring rod
microscope slide
dissecting needle
cover slip
compound microscope

Procedures and Observations

PART I. SEPARATING DNA FROM BACTERIAL CELLS _____

In order to observe DNA, you must first release it from within bacterial cell walls, and then separate it from the proteins to which it may be attached. Lysozyme is an enzyme found in human tears and other body fluids. At human body temperature, 37° C, lysozyme breaks down bacterial cell walls, causing the release of cell contents. Work in pairs for this procedure.

1. Obtain a 250-mL flask. Use a glass-marking pencil to write your team name on the flask.

2. **CAUTION:** *Although* E. coli *do not cause disease, treat all bacteria as if they were harmful. Be sure to wear your lab coat and*

safety goggles during this activity. Use a graduated cylinder to measure 100 mL of bacterial broth into the flask.

3. Use a toothpick to add some lysozyme to the broth in the flask. Use only the amount of lysozyme that you can pick up with the flat end of the toothpick.

4. Gently and carefully swirl the flask to mix the lysozyme with the broth. Continue to swirl the mixture for about 1 minute, or until the lysozyme dissolves.

5. Place the flask in an incubator at 37° C. Incubate the flask for 30 minutes. During the 30 minutes, study the procedure for the remainder of this lab.

6. At the end of 30 minutes, remove the flask from the incubator. The flask will feel warm to the touch.

Your teacher will set the temperature of the incubator up to 56° C as soon as the flasks are removed. This higher temperature is needed for the next incubation step. The next substance you will add to the flask is sodium lauryl sulfate. This substance is a detergent, which will help to break down the cell walls and dissolve membranes present within the cells.

 7. Use a graduated cylinder to measure 4 mL of sodium lauryl sulfate solution into the flask . Gently swirl the flask for 1 minute.

8. Check the temperature of the incubator. It should be 56° C. When the temperature is correct, place the flask in the incubator. Incubate the flask for 10 minutes.

 9. At the end of 10 minutes, use an oven mitt or tongs to remove the flask from the incubator. **CAUTION:** *The flask will be hot to the touch.*

10. Cool the flask by holding the lower part of the flask under cold running water. Turn the flask gently to allow it to cool evenly. Be careful not to allow any water to run into the flask. Cool the flask in this way for 2 to 3 minutes. Dry the outside of the flask.

At the end of the second incubation, DNA will be dissolved in the broth. Now the DNA must be changed to a solid so that it can be seen and removed from the liquid. Since DNA is not soluble in ice-cold ethyl alcohol, this substance is added to bring the DNA out of solution. The alcohol is less dense than the broth solution, so it will float on the broth if added gently. The lowest layer of alcohol will rest directly on the surface of the broth. This creates an interface, an area where two different substances come into such close contact that they can interact. It is at interfaces that chemical reactions take place. As the dissolved DNA comes in contact with the cold alcohol, DNA comes out of solution. It will form a thin layer at the interface.

11. Obtain a large, chilled test tube. Pour cooled broth into the test tube until it is half full.

 12. Obtain a 100-mL beaker, and measure 20 mL of cold alcohol into it. Slant both the test tube and the beaker, as shown in Figure 1. Slowly pour the alcohol down the side of the test tube. The alcohol should run down the test tube so slowly that it does not mix into the broth. Continue to add alcohol until the test tube is two-thirds full. Set the test tube upright in a test tube rack.

Extracting DNA   (continued)

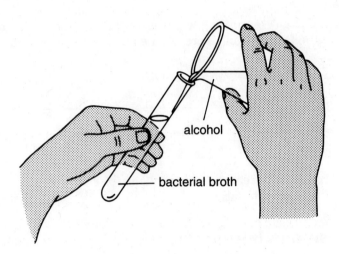

alcohol

bacterial broth

Figure 1

13. Use Figure 2 to show the layers in your test tube.

   a. *Draw lines on Figure 2 to indicate the upper and lower levels of the alcohol, and the upper level of the broth.*

   b. *Label the parts of your drawing* alcohol, broth, *and* interface.

   c. *Indicate the region where you observed the DNA.*

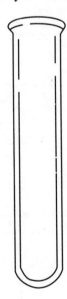

Figure 2

PART II.   COLLECTING AND OBSERVING DNA _____

It is possible to wind strands of DNA onto a dry glass rod. This process is like winding thread onto a spool, and is called spooling.

1. Insert the end of a dry glass stirring rod into the cloudy DNA layer in the test tube and slowly twirl the rod in one direction only. Strands

of DNA will stick to the rod. Spool the strands onto the rod until you have collected enough DNA to transfer to a microscope slide.

2. With a dissecting needle, gently spread the DNA into a single layer, if possible. Try not to break the strands. Place a cover slip over the DNA.

3. Observe the DNA under low power of the microscope. Find a field where the DNA is thinly spread. Then observe this area under high power.

   a. *Describe the appearance of the DNA.*

   _____

   _____

   _____

4. Follow your teacher's instructions for cleaning up and disposing of all materials.

Analysis and Interpretations

1. What was the effect of adding lysozyme to the bacterial broth?

   _____

   _____

   _____

2. Why was the broth incubated at 37° C after the lysozyme was added?

   _____

   _____

   _____

   _____

3. What was the effect of adding sodium lauryl sulfate to the broth?

   _____

   _____

   _____

4. Why was DNA visible at the interface between the alcohol and the broth, but not visible in the broth?

   _____

   _____

   _____

   _____

5. Describe the color of the DNA after you had spooled it onto the glass rod.

   _____

Extracting DNA (continued)

6. What was the source of the DNA that you used in this lab? Were the cells living when you obtained them?

_____

_____

7. Suppose you had carried out these procedures using cells of *Euglena,* or of some species of bacteria other than *E. coli.* Would you expect the color of the DNA to be the same? Explain your answer.

_____

_____

_____

For Further Investigation

1. If a centrifuge is available, place 15 mL of *E. coli* broth in a centrifuge tube, and centrifuge it for about 5 minutes. Gently pour off the clear liquid at the top, and discard it. Bacterial cells are at the bottom of the tube. Add a volume of sodium lauryl sulfate solution equal to the volume of bacterial cells, and incubate at 56° C for 10 minutes. Cool the tube, and add 2 to 4 drops of acridine orange fluorescent stain. **CAUTION:** *Acridine orange may stain your hands and clothing. Be sure to wear your lab coat and safety goggles when doing this activity.* Stir gently. Add cold ethyl alcohol as in Part I, Step 12. Remove strands of DNA as in Part II, and place some strands on a microscope slide. In a darkened room, illuminate the slide by a lamp equipped with a blue light. Describe what you see.

2. To learn more about the people who worked to discover the structure of the DNA molecule, read *The Double Helix,* by James Watson, a member of the team that devised the Watson-Crick model of DNA.

3. Construct a model of DNA nucleotides. Show how the paired bases of DNA fit together.

Protein Synthesis

Lab **37**

Background

DNA carries the information for the synthesis of all the proteins of an organism. Protein molecules are large and complex, composed of hundreds of amino acid units. In each kind of protein, the amino acid units are linked together in a definite sequence. The sequence of amino acids in a protein molecule is determined by the sequence of the nucleotides in the DNA of the organism. All the different proteins that occur in organisms are composed of only twenty kinds of amino acids.

In the first step leading to protein synthesis, the nucleotide sequence of the DNA is *transcribed* (the process is called *transcription*) into a long single-stranded molecule of RNA, termed *messenger* RNA (*m*RNA). The mRNA moves out of the nucleus into the cytoplasm through pores in the nuclear membrane.

In the cytoplasm, ribosomes temporarily attach to the mRNA. Triplet sequences of nucleotides, called codons, in the mRNA form a sort of pattern, or code, that specifies the order in which the amino acids of a protein are to be linked. While a ribosome is attached at each codon along the mRNA, molecules of another kind of RNA—*transfer* RNA (*t*RNA)—bring amino acids into place, each according to the code or sequence in the mRNA. As the ribosomes move along the mRNA from codon to codon, the appropriate amino acids are brought into place and linked together according to the sequence of codons. Thus, the code in the mRNA is *translated* into a special sequence of amino acids. The order of the amino acids in the protein, therefore, is specified by the mRNA, which in turn is transcribed from the DNA.

Objectives

In this activity you will:
1. Follow the steps of protein synthesis.
2. Translate the genetic code for specific amino acids.
3. Use paper models to simulate protein synthesis.

Materials

1/2-inch transparent tape   scissors

Procedures and Observations

During transcription, the DNA double helix unwinds and "unzips." The two strands separate as the hydrogen bonds binding the nitrogen bases break. Then, nucleotides present in the cell line up along one strand of the DNA, the order of the nucleotides determined by the order of the nucleotides in the DNA. As the mRNA forms, uracil (U) nucleotides match with adenine (A) nucleotides; cytosine (C) nucleotides match with guanine (G) nucleotides. **Note:** *RNA contains uracil (U) nucleotides where thymine (T) nucleotides would occur in DNA.*

The nucleotides in the newly formed mRNA are *complementary* to the nucleotides of the DNA segment on which it formed. For example, where the DNA contained guanine, the mRNA contains cytosine. Where the DNA contained adenine, the mRNA contains uracil. After the single-stranded molecule of mRNA is formed, it moves out of the nucleus into the cytoplasm.

1. One strand of DNA has the base sequence: C G A T T G G C A G T C A T. Determine the sequence of bases in the complementary strand of mRNA that would form next to this DNA strand.

   a. *Write the sequence of bases in the complementary mRNA strand below.*

   _____

The information carried on the mRNA is in a code—the *genetic code*. A group of three nucleotides on a molecule of mRNA is called a *codon;* each codon specifies one of the 20 amino acids, except for three codons that are stop, or termination, signals. There are 64 codons in the genetic code.

2. The 64 codons are shown in Table 1. Notice that the first two nucleotides of each codon (abbreviated by their first letter) are shown in the column on the left. To find out the amino acid specified by a given codon, find the first two letters in the column on the left, then follow that row to the column showing the last nucleotide (letter) of the codon. Note that most amino acids are coded for by more than one codon.

Table 1. The Genetic Code: Codons and Their Amino Acids

First Two Nucleotides of Codons	Last Nucleotide of Codons				The Amino Acids	
	U	C	A	G		
UU	phe	phe	leu	leu	*Abbreviations*	*Names*
UC	ser	ser	ser	ser	gly	glycine
UA	tyr	tyr	term	term	ala	alanine
UG	cys	cys	term	trp	val	valine
CU	leu	leu	leu	leu	ile	isoleucine
CC	pro	pro	pro	pro	leu	leucine
CA	his	his	gln	gln	ser	serine
CG	arg	arg	arg	arg	thr	threonine
AU	ile	ile	ile	met	pro	proline
AC	thr	thr	thr	thr	asp	aspartate
AA	asn	asn	lys	lys	glu	glutamate
AG	ser	ser	arg	arg	lys	lysine
GU	val	val	val	val	arg	arginine
GC	ala	ala	ala	ala	asn	asparagine
GA	asp	asp	glu	glu	gln	glutamine
GG	gly	gly	gly	gly	cys	cysteine
					met	methionine
					trp	tryptophan
					phe	phenylalanine
					tyr	tyrosine
					his	histidine
					term	termination

Protein Synthesis (continued)

3. Use Table 1 to read the codons below. Find the name of the amino acid and write it in the space provided. If the letters code for more than one amino acid, separate the names by dashes.

b. U U A: _____

c. G A G: _____

d. U A U C U A: _____

e. A U C U U G: _____

f. A A G A G U U C G: _____

g. A A A U U U G G G: _____

h. C C A G C U A G A G G G U G G C U G U C A:

_____

_____

    Molecules of transfer RNA (tRNA) are formed in the nucleus and migrate into the cytoplasm. There are twenty different types of tRNA, one for each kind of amino acid. The tRNA molecule has two ends. One end can carry only one kind of amino acid molecule. The opposite end has a three-base segment called an *anticodon,* which is complementary to a codon on mRNA.

    In protein synthesis, with a ribosome attached to an mRNA, a tRNA molecule carrying its special amino acid molecule briefly attaches to mRNA at its complementary codon. Next, a tRNA molecule complementary to the <u>adjacent</u> codon briefly attaches to the mRNA. The ribosome moves along the mRNA to that point of attachment. During each brief attachment among tRNA, mRNA, and ribosome, peptide bonds form between the amino acids. As these bonds form, the tRNA molecules are released from their amino acids, and also from the mRNA. Each is free to attach to another molecule of its special amino acid and carry it to another point along the mRNA. The ribosomes move along the mRNA as amino acids are added, one at a time, to a growing chain. This continues until a termination codon is encountered.

4. Determine the anticodon for each codon below. Write it in the space provided.

i. G G U: _____

j. C G C: _____

k. A U G: _____

l. U C G: _____

m. A A A: _____

n. C U G: _____

5. Cut out the tRNA models with amino acids attached, found in Figure 1 on the last page of this activity. Then cut out the mRNA strands and tape them together, so that strand 1 forms the left end of a long strand, strand 3 forms the right end, and strand 2 is between them.

6. Starting at the left of the mRNA strand, find a tRNA molecule with an anticodon complementary to the first codon. With a small piece of tape, attach the tRNA to the mRNA strand, anticodon to codon.

7. For the next codon, find a tRNA with the complementary anticodon. Tape the tRNA in place to the mRNA. Also, use a small piece of tape between the two amino acids to represent a peptide bond.

8. Once the peptide bond has been formed, the tRNA molecule attached first is released. Carefully cut the tape attaching the first tRNA to the mRNA, and cut the line that separates the tRNA and the amino acid. You may set the tRNA model aside and discard it later.

There are three termination codons in the genetic code. When a termination codon is read, the strand of amino acids is released, folding and twisting to form the final, complex structure of the protein.

9. Repeat Steps 7 and 8 along the mRNA strand. When you have used up all the tRNA-amino acid models provided, you will notice that there is one codon left on the mRNA—a termination codon. Cut the tape between the mRNA and the tRNA, and the line between the last tRNA and amino acid, thus releasing the chain of amino acids.

   o. *Starting at the left, write the sequence of the amino acids formed by translation of the mRNA strand.*

Analysis and Interpretations

1. Write the order of nucleotides in mRNA that would be transcribed from the following strand of DNA:

   G T A T A C C A G T C A T T T G T C

   Then list in order the amino acids coded by this sequence.

   mRNA _____

   amino acids _____

2. Sometimes a mistake occurs in the translation of an mRNA strand. Suppose that the reading of the mRNA strand in question 1 began, by mistake, at the second nucleotide instead of the first. The first codon would be AUA. Write the sequence of amino acids that would be formed.

---

3. Suppose the bases of the DNA strand in question 1 were not transcribed correctly and the mRNA read:

   C A C A U G G U U A G U A A G C A G

   How many mistakes were made in transcription? Write the abbreviations for the amino acids that would be formed by translation of the mRNA.

Protein Synthesis (continued)

Models for tRNA attached to amino acids:

cys — ACA

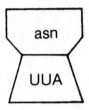
cys — ACG

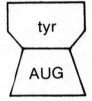
ala — CGA

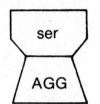
ser — AGG

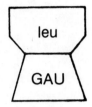
cys — ACG

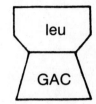
leu — GAC

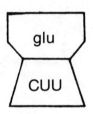
cys — ACG

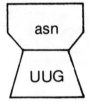
asn — UUA

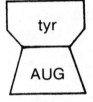
tyr — AUG

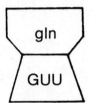
gln — GUU

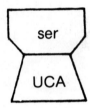
leu — GAU

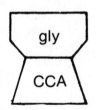
glu — CUU

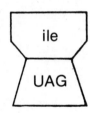
asn — UUG

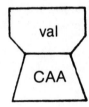
tyr — AUG

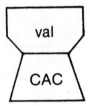
val — CAC

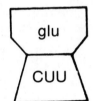
ser — UCA

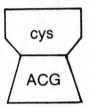
gly — CCA

ile — UAG

val — CAA

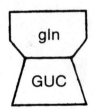
glu — CUU

gln — GUC

Models for mRNA (tape these, left to right, into one long strand):

GGU	AUC	GUU	GAA	CAG	UGU	UGC	GCU

UCC	GUG	UGC	AGU	CUG	UAC	CAA

CUA	GAA	AAC	UAC	UGC	AAU	UAA

Evidence of Evolution

Lab 38

Background

Much evidence has been found to indicate that living things have evolved or changed gradually during their natural history. The study of fossils as well as work in embryology, biochemistry, and comparative anatomy provides evidence for evolution.

Objective

In this lab you will learn about homologous, analogous, and vestigial structures and their significance in evolution theory.

Materials

colored pencils

Procedures and Observations

PART I.   HOMOLOGOUS STRUCTURES _____

1. Carefully examine the drawings of the bones shown in Figure 1 on the next page. Look for similarities among the various animals.

    a. *Color each part of the human arm a different color. (All bones of the wrist should be a single color, the bone groups of the hand should be a different single color.) Then color the corresponding bone in each of the other animals the same color as the human bone.*

    b. *Describe the function of each set of bones below:*

Animal	Function
human	
whale	
cat	
bat	
bird	
crocodile	

    c. *Are the bones arranged in a similar way in each animal?*

    _____

These structures are formed in similar ways during embryonic development and share like arrangements; however, they have somewhat different forms and functions. They are called *homologous structures*.

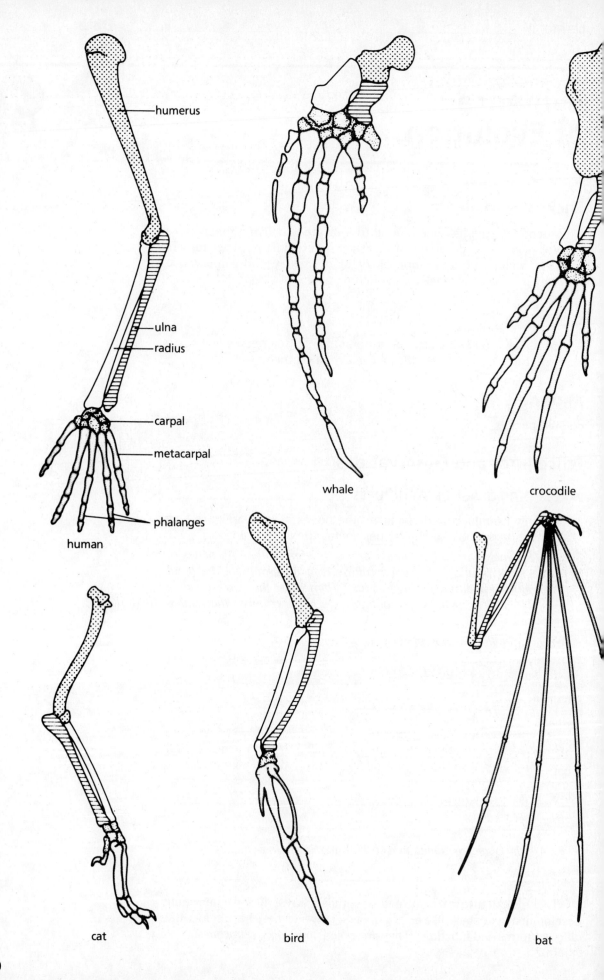

humerus

ulna

radius

carpal

metacarpal

phalanges

human

whale

crocodile

cat

bird

bat

220

Name _____

PART II. ANALOGOUS STRUCTURES _____

1. Examine the butterfly wing and the bird wing shown in Figure 2.

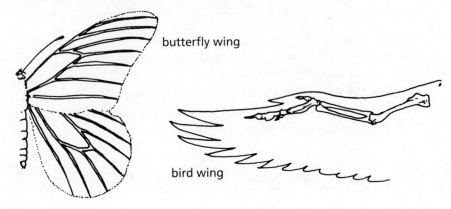

butterfly wing

bird wing

Figure 2

    a. *What function do these structures share?*

_____

    b. *How do the structures differ?*

_____

_____

    c. *Do birds and insects share any structural similarities that would suggest they are closely related taxonomically?*

_____

    Some apparently unrelated animals have organs with similar functions, yet are very different in structure and form. These structures are called *analogous structures.*

PART III. VESTIGIAL STRUCTURES _____

    Gradual changes have occurred through time that have in some cases reduced or removed the function of some body structures and organs. The penguin's wings and the leg bones of snakes are examples of this phenomenon.

1. The cave fish and minnow shown in Figure 3 are related, but the cave fish is blind.

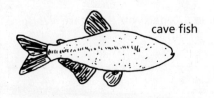

cave fish

minnow

Figure 3

a. *Explain why eyesight is not an important adaptation to life in a cave.*

_____

b. *Does the appearance of the cave fish and minnow suggest common ancestry? Why?*

_____

Organs or structures that have lost their function in the organism and become reduced in size (because of efficiency) are called vestigial structures. Human vestigial organs are well documented.

2. Read the list of human *vestigial structures* shown in Table 1.

   c. *Suggest a possible function for each structure and explain why it became vestigial. Record your answers in the table.*

Table 1.

Structure	Probable Function	Why Vestigial?
appendix		
coccyx (tail bones)		
muscles that move ears		
muscles that make hair stand up		
little toe		
wisdom teeth		

Analysis and Interpretations

1. Explain why the homologous structures in Part I are evidence of evolutionary relationships.

_____

_____

2. Explain the evolutionary relationship between the fin of a fish and the flipper of a whale.

_____

_____

3. List two structures (not from Table 1) that you think are vestigial and explain why.

_____

_____

_____

Evidence of Evolution   (continued)

For Further Investigation

1. Collect various flying insects and, using a microscope, compare their wing structure. Report on your results.

2. Investigate divergent, parallel, and convergent evolution, and explain how homologous and analogous structures are used to describe these concepts.

3. Construct a "Geologic Time Scale" using an appropriate reference showing geologic ages. Use a scale (such as 1 cm = 45,000,000 years) to draw in events that occurred millions of years ago.

4. How does the *modern theory of evolution* explain the loss of vestigial organs? How does this compare with Lamarck's *theory of use and disuse*?

Computer Activity

In Laboratory Activity 38 you studied homologous, analogous, and vestigial structures and their significance as evidence of evolutionary development. Charles Darwin defined evolution as the result of *natural selection*—that process that results in members of successive generations of a species becoming better adapted to survive within their environment.

The computer simulation *Survival of the Fittest* is a game in which you will direct the evolution of a predator population to capture as many prey as possible over a span of five generations. The prey population also evolves, challenging the predators to either adapt or perish. The program is both fun and instructive in the fundamentals of natural selection, adaptation, and mutation.

Investigating Spontaneous Generation — Lab 39

Background

In 1668 Francesco Redi performed an experiment to try to disprove the idea of *"spontaneous generation"*—that is, the idea that living things can come from nonliving things. At that time it was widely believed, for example, that mice arise from sweaty shirts, frogs from mud, and maggots from decaying meat. Redi's experiments showed that maggots do not arise from rotting meat, but many people continued to believe that microscopic organisms arose by spontaneous generation. In 1864 Louis Pasteur performed experiments that finally convinced scientists that organisms come only from parent organisms.

Objective

In this activity you will:
1. Perform an experiment similar to Redi's.
2. Perform an experiment similar to Pasteur's.
3. Use the results of your experiments to decide if spontaneous generation occurs.
4. Learn about sterilization.

Materials

2.5-cm cubes of raw meat	scalpel
3 wide-mouth jars	cheesecloth
plastic wrap	rubber bands
scissors	paper towels
labels	hand lens
beef broth	dropper bottle of water
glass-marking pencil	3 one-holed rubber stoppers
3 250-mL flasks	fitted with an S-shaped glass
50-mL graduated cylinder	tube, an L-shaped glass tube,
hot water bath	and a straight glass tube
thermometer	

Procedures and Observations

PART I.   REDI'S EXPERIMENT

Cutting a substance into several pieces increases *surface area*. When the cubes of meat are cut into smaller pieces, more meat molecules are exposed to the air and can be released into it.

1. Obtain three 2.5-cm cubes of raw meat and place them on a folded paper towel. Using the scalpel, cut each cube into two or more pieces.

2. Obtain three wide-mouth jars. Put three pieces of meat in each jar.

Organisms that cause decay need water for their life processes.

3. Put about 15 drops of water on the meat in each jar.

4. Place labels on the jars and number them 1, 2, and 3. Then add such information as the date, time, group number, and a description of the contents of the jar.

Cheesecloth has tiny openings that allow molecules to pass through it.

5. Leave jar 1 open to the air. If the meat becomes dry during the experiment, add a few drops of water to it.

6. Cover jar 2 with a piece of cheesecloth. Use a rubber band to hold the cloth in place. See Figure 1. Be careful not to spread apart the threads of the cheesecloth. Flies must be kept out.

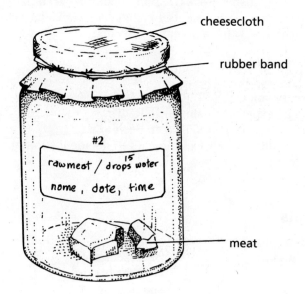

Figure 1

7. Cover jar 3 with plastic wrap and secure it with a rubber band.

8. Place the jars on a table or counter near an open window. Observe the jars. If any flies appear, note their behavior. If they seem to leave deposits anywhere, examine them with a hand lens.

   a. *Record your observations, starting with the first day of the experiment, in Tables 1, 2, and 3.*

9. Compare your results with those of other students in the class.

Investigating Spontaneous Generation (continued)

Table 1. Observations–Jar 1

Date	Time	Temp (°C)	Observations

Table 2. Observations–Jar 2

Date	Time	Temp (°C)	Observations

Table 3. Observations–Jar 3

Date	Time	Temp (°C)	Observations

PART II.   PASTEUR'S EXPERIMENT _____

1. Obtain three 250-mL flasks and three rubber stoppers each fit with a different type of glass tubing. Pour 50 mL of beef broth into each flask.

2. Put the stopper back in each flask. Label each flask as shown in Figure 2, and add your initials. Write with a pencil, not with a pen, as the ink would blur.

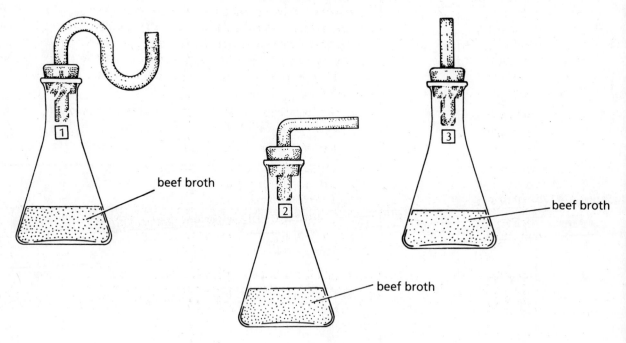

beef broth

beef broth

beef broth

Figure 2

Sterilization is the killing of all living organisms in or on something. It is usually done with heat. Something that has no living organisms in or on it is *sterile*.

 3. Carefully place the flasks in a hot water bath. Keep the water in the bath boiling for 2 hours.

4. After 2 hours, carefully remove the flasks to cool. **CAUTION:** *Use the proper tools and follow your teacher's instructions for removing the hot flasks.* Be careful not to disturb the stoppers. Be especially careful of the S-shaped tube.

As the vapor in the S-shaped tube cools, water will collect in the "U" part of the tube. This water should seal off the tube and prevent the entry of air into the flask.

5. Check the seal in the S-shaped tube.

6. Observe the flasks daily for any changes.

   a. *Record your observations in Tables 4, 5, and 6.*

7. Compare your results with other students in the class.

Investigating Spontaneous Generation (continued)

Table 4. Observations–Flask 1

Date	Time	Temp (°C)	Observations

Table 5. Observations–Flask 2

Date	Time	Temp (°C)	Observations

Table 6. Observations–Flask 3

Date	Time	Temp (°C)	Observations

Analysis and Interpretations

1. Explain the advantage of cutting the cubes of meat into smaller pieces.

_____

_____

2. What was the purpose of jar 1? jar 2? jar 3?

_____

_____

_____

3. Describe what happened to the meat in each jar.

_____

_____

_____

4. Describe the activities of any flies that you observed around the jars with the meat.

_____

_____

_____

5. If you saw maggots, answer the following questions:
   a. Did you actually see where they came from?

_____

   b. How long from the start of the experiment did it take them to appear?

_____

   c. Did they grow?

_____

   d. If you watched them over a long period of time, describe what happened to them.

_____

_____

6. Do you think that maggots arise from rotting meat? Why or why not?

_____

_____

7. Explain why the flasks in Part II were heated.

_____

Investigating Spontaneous Generation (continued)

8. Which of the flasks, if any, remained sterile? Why?

_____

_____

_____

9. How long did it take for cloudiness (turbidity) to appear in any of the flasks?

_____

10. Did the cloudiness increase, decrease, or stay the same as time passed?

_____

11. Explain what you think caused the cloudiness in each flask. How could you prove this?

_____

_____

_____

_____

Variation in Grasshopper Legs

Lab 40

Background

As you know, all members of a species do not look exactly alike. Variations within a species can have many forms. For example, variations can involve differences in the sizes and shapes of body parts, in the strength of muscles, or in the speed of flight. There can also be variations in biochemistry, in behavior, and in resistance to disease.

The continuation of any species depends upon individual organisms living long enough to reproduce. The offspring must also be able to survive and to reproduce. Which individuals survive to reproduce depends, in part, on the variations that those individuals possess. Some variations have greater survival value than others. You will observe a variation that can affect the survival of grasshoppers.

Objectives

In this activity you will:
1. Measure variations of one trait in a single species of grasshopper.
2. Collect class data on these variations and graph these data.

Materials

3 or 4 preserved adult   dissecting tray
    grasshoppers   metric ruler
graph paper

Procedures and Observations

PART I.   MEASURING GRASSHOPPER LEGS _____

A grasshopper has three pairs of legs; the back pair are the jumping legs. The jumping legs of a grasshopper are important to the insect's survival. By jumping, the grasshopper escapes from predators.

1. Obtain 3 or 4 grasshoppers, and place them in a dissecting tray.

2. Study Figure 1, and identify the jumping legs of your grasshoppers.

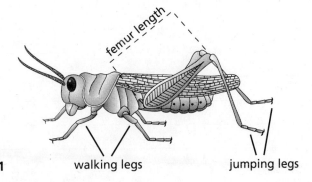

Figure 1   walking legs   jumping legs

3. The upper part of the jumping leg is called the *femur*. Locate the femur of one of your grasshoppers. **Note:** *As you work with the grasshoppers, do not damage them in any way.*

4. Use a metric ruler to measure one femur on each grasshopper. See Figure 1 to locate the exact points where you should start and end your measurement. Use these same points on each femur you measure. The measurements should be accurate to the nearest 0.1 cm.

a. *Record each measurement in Table 1.*

Table 1. Measurements of Femurs

Grasshopper	Length of Femur (cm)
1	
2	
3	
4	

5. Return the specimens to your teacher.

6. Wash your hands and follow your teacher's instructions for cleaning up your work area.

PART II.   ORGANIZING AND GRAPHING DATA _____

The different femur lengths will be listed on the board, in order, from the shortest to the longest. Opposite each measurement, a tally will be kept, to record the number of grasshoppers found to have femurs of that length. Be ready to report your data when called upon.

1. Follow your teacher's instructions for reporting your data.

2. When all data are recorded, complete Table 2. In the first column record the femur length. In the second column record the number of grasshoppers with femurs of that length. **Note:** *You may not need all of the spaces in Table 2.*

Table 2. Femur Lengths

Femur Length (cm)	Number of Individuals

AnalyzingVariations (continued)

3. On a sheet of graph paper, plan a graph to display the class data. Label the x-axis *Femur Length*. Label the y-axis *Number of Individuals*. Along the axes of the graph, write the numbers that correspond to your data.

   a. *Plot the class data as points on your graph.*

   b. *After you have plotted all the points, draw a smooth curve that best represents the data. This curve can pass through points or between them.*

4. Calculate the average length of the femurs. To calculate such an average, multiply each length by the number of times it occurred. Add these products together. Then divide by the total number of femurs measured.

   c. *What was the average femur length?*

   _____

   _____

Analysis and Interpretations

1. How did the most common femur length compare with the average length that you calculated?

   _____

2. What is the shape of the curve on your graph? What does the curve tell about variation of leg length within a species of grasshopper?

   _____

   _____

   _____

   _____

   _____

3. Why was it important to measure the femurs of adult grasshoppers only?

   _____

   _____

   _____

4. How might a longer femur help a grasshopper survive?

   _____

   _____

   _____

   _____

5. Compare the number of grasshoppers having a shorter than average-length femur with those having a longer than average-length femur. Why do you think a species of grasshopper might not evolve longer and longer femurs?

_____

_____

_____

_____

_____

_____

_____

_____

For Further Investigation

1. Study variations in the sizes of all the bean seeds in 0.5 kg of dried lima beans. Set up 10 large test tubes in a row. Measure the shortest bean you can find and place it in the test tube at the left end of the row. Label the test tube with that measurement, accurate to the nearest millimeter. Measure the largest bean you can find and place it in the test tube at the right end of the row. Label the test tube with that measurement. Label the eight remaining test tubes with measurements between the two extremes. You may have to place a range of measurements in each tube, to accommodate all measurements. Measure the beans, being sure to measure each one between the same points. Place each bean in the correct tube. Examine the distribution of different bean seed lengths in the tubes. Notice that a graph of the heights of the beans in the test tubes forms a curve. Compare this curve to the curve you produced in your graph of grasshopper femur lengths.

2. Study variations in the lengths of the littlest finger on the left (or right) hands of all the members of your biology class. Before measuring your fingers, agree on where the measurements will begin and end. Graph your findings as you did with grasshopper femur lengths and compare the curves.

3. If a balance accurate to 0.01 g is available, compare the masses of corn seeds. Use test tubes to collect seeds of different masses, as in the bean study above. Compare these results to your other variation studies.

A First Look at Bacteria

Lab 41

Background

Bacteria are the smallest and most abundant organisms on the earth. They are so small that 600 billion (6×10^{11}) average sized bacterial cells can fit in 1 cubic centimeter. Round bacteria are called cocci, rod shaped bacteria are called bacilli, and spiral shaped bacteria are called spirilla. Bacteria can grow in pairs, chains, and clusters. Under ideal conditions, bacteria can divide every 15 to 20 minutes.

Most bacteria are harmless to humans; some are even helpful. Disease-causing bacteria are called pathogens. When handling any bacteria, it is important to use sterile technique to prevent the possible spread of disease. Since bacteria are usually colorless, simple stains are often used to make them more visible.

Objectives

In this activity you will:
1. Learn the sterile technique for working with bacteria.
2. Stain bacteria using simple staining techniques and observe the bacteria under the microscope.
3. Observe some bacteria found in the human mouth.

Materials

stoppered test tube of
    bean culture
test tube rack
flat toothpick
Bunsen burner
facial tissue
bottle of tincture
    of Merthiolate
control bottle of tincture
    of Merthiolate

disinfectant solution
inoculating loop
clothespin
staining trays
slides
methylene blue stain
    in dropper bottle
wash bottle of water
microscope
paper towels

Procedures and Observations

PART I.   STERILE TECHNIQUE _____

The sterile technique is a way of preventing contamination and the spread of dangerous organisms while studying bacteria.

 1. Wipe your work area with a disinfectant solution before starting your work. Let it dry. Then light the Bunsen burner, obtaining a blue flame. **CAUTION:** *Use care in working with the Bunsen burner.*

A bean culture provides plenty of bacteria to study.

2. Hold the stoppered test tube of bean culture with one hand. Gently tap it with a finger of the other hand to resuspend any material that has settled out. The bean culture should not splash onto the stopper.

3. Pick up the inoculating loop with your free hand. Hold the loop in the blue part of the Bunsen burner flame until it glows bright red. This sterilizes it.

4. Still holding the loop, remove the stopper of the test tube with the last two fingers of the same hand. Carefully pass the top of the test tube through the flame several times. See Figure 1.

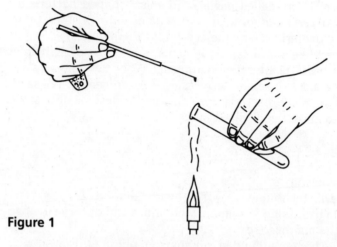

Figure 1

5. Then quickly dip the sterilized inoculating loop into the culture in the test tube. Try not to touch the sides of the test tube. Make sure a drop of culture stays on the loop. Do not set the inoculating loop down.

6. Pass the top of the test tube through the flame two more times. Then restopper the test tube and set it in the test tube rack.

7. Transfer the drop of culture to the center of a clean slide. Spread the drop into an even-layered smear. Then hold the inoculating loop in the flame until it glows red again. After sterilizing it, you may set the loop down.

8. When the smear appears dry, attach a clothespin to the edge of the slide. Holding the clothespin, pass the slide through the flame several times to fix the smear. Do not hold the slide over the flame—you do not want to burn the smear. Then set the slide down and turn off the Bunsen burner.

PART II. SIMPLE STAINING TECHNIQUE

Bacteria are colorless and so tiny that they are difficult to see under a microscope. A simple stain allows them to be observed more easily.

1. Place your slide in a staining tray. Completely cover the smear with several drops of methylene blue stain. Wait 1 minute. **CAUTION:** *Use care to avoid allowing methylene blue to stain hands or clothing.*

2. After a minute, use a wash bottle of water to gently wash the excess stain off the smear. Then blot the smear dry with a folded facial tissue. Do not rub.

3. Observe the stained smear under the microscope at low power, then high power.

   a. *What shapes of bacteria do you observe?*

   _____

   b. *Make a drawing of the bacteria as seen under high power. Record the magnification.*

   +---+
   | |
   | |
   | |
   | |
   | |
   | |
   | |
   | |
   | |
   +---+

   c. *Describe how the bacterial cells are arranged—singly, in pairs, or in chains.*

   _____

   _____

PART III.   BACTERIA OF THE HUMAN MOUTH

Many bacteria live in the human body. The intestines, for example, normally contain a wide variety of bacteria. Some synthesize vitamins; others help in digestion. The human mouth also contains many bacteria.

1. Hold a clean, flat toothpick by its pointed end. With the broad end, gently scrape some material from your teeth at the gum line. Swirl the material in a drop of water on a clean slide. Do this several times, adding additional material to the slide. Be careful not to scrape or injure your gums.

2. Spread the material into a thin layer. When you have finished using the toothpick, break it in half and discard it. Then allow the smear to dry. You may not be able to see it when it is dry.

3. Use the applicator in the bottle to paint a very thin layer of tincture of Merthiolate onto the smear. Use only enough to add color to the slide—do not make droplets. Also be careful not to scrape the smear off the slide. Replace the cap on the bottle. **CAUTION:** *The tincture of Merthiolate is a laboratory material. It must not be used for first aid purposes. Be careful not to stain your hands or clothing with the tincture of Merthiolate.*

4. Let the stained smear dry.

Any large cells that you see are probably epithelial cells from your gums. They may be single or in groups. Their nuclei are stained pink or brown by the Merthiolate.

5. Observe the slide under low power. Look for some large, flat epithelial cells. They may be torn or whole, folded or flat. Then switch to high power and observe them.

Bacteria should be visible around and on the epithelial cells. The pink Merthiolate clings to bacteria, so they appear as pinpoints of light surrounded by pink.

6. Observe the bacteria under high power. Note the shapes of the bacteria. Some chains may be seen on the surface of the epithelial cells. Move the fine adjustment knob back and forth to see the light change in the bacterial cells.

   a. *Make a drawing of bacterial and epithelial cells as seen under high power. Contrast their sizes as accurately as possible.*

7. Compare the diameter of an epithelial cell to the diameter of your high power field. Estimate (in micrometers) the diameter of the epithelial cell. Then, comparing the size of the epithelial cell to the bacterial cell, estimate the diameter of a bacterial cell.

   b. *Record the estimate (in micrometers) of the diameter of an epithelial cell. Then record the estimate (in micrometers) of the diameter of a bacterial cell.*

8. Observe the slides made by some other people in your class.

   c. *Are the bacteria similar to yours or different?*

9. Place a thin layer of Merthiolate from a control bottle on a clean slide. Let it dry.

A First Look at Bacteria (continued)

10. Observe the slide under low power, then high power.

    d. *Describe what you see.*

    _____

 11. Dispose of your materials as instructed by your teacher. Then wipe your work area clean with disinfectant and wash your hands thoroughly.

Analysis and Investigation

1. What are two ways to kill bacteria?

_____

2. Why is sterile technique important when studying bacteria?

_____

_____

3. Explain how each step of sterile technique helps to prevent contamination of objects and the spread of bacteria.

_____

_____

_____

_____

4. When people used ice boxes instead of refrigerators, they allowed dinner leftovers to cool to room temperature before placing them in the ice box. This helped to conserve ice. Why is this not a good idea, knowing how frequently bacteria reproduce?

_____

5. What was the purpose of the slide prepared with only tincture of Merthiolate?

_____

_____

6. If there were bacteria on the slide prepared with only tincture of Merthiolate, how can you explain their presence?

_____

7. Why should the tincture of Merthiolate not be used for first aid purposes once it has been used in this experiment?

_____

_____

_____

8. After observing several slides, what is your opinion about the number of bacteria in the human mouth?

_____

9. What are some possible sources of bacteria on human teeth?

_____

10. What function might bacteria be performing on the surface of a loose epithelial cell?

_____

For Further Investigation

Design an experiment to test the effectiveness of disinfectants and antibiotics in killing bacteria. Write down the procedure and check it with your teacher before trying your experiment.

Looking at Blue-Green Bacteria

Lab 42

Background

Blue-green bacteria make up the phylum Cyanobacteria, which is a large group of organisms in the kingdom Monera. Blue-green bacteria are found all over the world, wherever there is water and light—in salt and fresh water, in polar ice caps, and in hot springs. All blue-green bacteria are photosynthetic. Some are capable of using atmospheric nitrogen; these organisms are nitrogen-fixers, like some other types of bacteria. In this activity you will learn about some characteristics of cyanobacteria by observing representatives of two families: the family Oscillatoriaceae (ah-sil-uh-tor-ih-*ace*-ih-ee)—either the genus *Oscillatoria* or *Lyngbya*—and the family Nostocaceae (nah-stahk-*ace*-ih-ee)—either the genus *Anabaena* or *Nostoc*.

Objectives

In this activity you will:
1. Observe a blue-green bacterium of the family Oscillatoriaceae.
2. Observe a blue-green bacterium of the family Nostocaceae.

Materials

cultures of *Oscillatoria* and/or *Lyngbya* (family Oscillatoriaceae) OR prepared slides of each
cultures of *Anabaena* and/or *Nostoc* (family Nostocaceae) OR prepared
  slides of each

Petri dish	hand lens
Syracuse dish	dissecting microscope
slides	dissecting needles
cover slips	pipettes
compound microscope	sheet of white notebook paper

Procedures and Observations

PART I.   OBSERVATION OF THE FAMILY OSCILLATORIACEAE _____

1. Obtain a specimen of the family Oscillatoriaceae and some culture water in a Petri dish.

2. Place the Petri dish on a sheet of white notebook paper for con-trast. Observe the specimen with a hand lens. Note the filaments. Try to see the ends of the filaments. Use a dissecting needle to work the ends out of the tangled mass until you can see them.

3. Place the Petri dish under a dissecting microscope. Focus on the free ends under low power.

   a. *Are the ends moving?*

b. *Can you detect any movement of the entire mass of filaments?*

_____

4. Remove the Petri dish from the stage. Then place a clean slide in the center of the dissecting microscope stage. With a pipette, pick up a few filaments of the bacteria and place them on the slide with about 2 drops of culture water.

5. Observe the bacteria under low power. While looking through the eyepieces, use two dissecting needles to separate and spread the bacteria filaments over an area about the size of a cover slip. Try to free some of the ends of the filaments. Then add a cover slip.

6. With the compound microscope, examine the slide under low power. Look first at individual cells.

   c. *What color are the cells?*

   _____

   d. *Is the colored matter in separate bodies within the cells or is it distributed throughout the cell?*

   _____

   _____

A chain of cells in a filament is called a trichome.

7. Observe the trichomes.

   e. *Are the cells of the trichome in a single row, or are they several rows wide?*

   _____

   f. *Are all the cells in the trichome alike?*

   _____

   g. Are all the cells the same width or does the trichome taper?

   _____

   _____

   h. *Are the filaments branched?*

   _____

8. Switch to high power and examine the edge of a trichome.

   i. *Can you see a clear sheath surrounding the trichome?*

   _____

The end cell, the *apical cell*, is used to identify the genus of a cyanobacterium in the family Oscillatoriaceae.

9. Focus on the tip of a filament under high power.

   j. *In the box on the following page, draw the apical cell of the filament as accurately as possible. Also include a few cells of the filament.*

Looking at Blue-Green Bacteria (continued)

[blank box]

The apical cell seen in members of the genus *Oscillatoria* is shown in Figure 1. Members of the genus *Lyngbya* have a clear sheath that surrounds the trichome and extends beyond the apical cell.

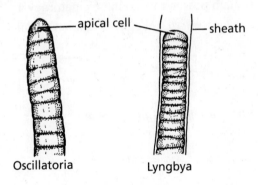

Oscillatoria   Lyngbya

Figure 1

10. Compare your drawing of bacterial cells to Figure 1.

   k. *Identify the genus of your specimen. Add the name under your drawing.*

11. Observe a specimen of a different genus under a nearby microscope.

12. Return the bacterial specimen to your teacher.

PART II.   OBSERVATION OF THE FAMILY NOSTOCACEAE _____

1. Obtain a specimen of the family Nostocaceae with some culture water in a Syracuse dish.

2. Using a pipette, place some of the bacteria in 2 drops of culture water on a clean slide. Add a cover slip.

3. Using a compound microscope, examine the slide under low power.

   a. *What color are the cells?*

b. *Is the colored matter in separate bodies within the cell or is it distributed throughout the cell?*

_____

c. *Are the cells in a trichome in a single row or are they several rows wide?*

_____

d. *Are all the cells in the trichome alike?*

_____

e. *Are the trichomes tapered or are the cells the same width?*

_____

Along the trichome are empty-looking cells called heterocysts. Recently it has been discovered that nitrogen fixation—the transformation of atmospheric nitrogen into forms usable by the blue-green bacteria— occurs in the heterocysts.

4. Locate some heterocysts. They are enlarged cells that look empty.

5. Switch to high power and examine a heterocyst.

f. *Is the cell wall clear or colored? Is it thin or thick?*

_____

6. Look at each end of the heterocyst where it is connected to the cells next to it.

g. *Describe the cell wall of the heterocyst where it is connected to another cell.*

_____

_____

h. *Draw a heterocyst with several cells on each side of it. Show the differences in the shapes, sizes, and structures of the cells.*

An akinete is a type of cell that forms in a trichome during unfavorable environmental conditions. It forms from an ordinary cell and contains stored food. Akinetes can survive heat, cold, and drying and can produce new trichomes after long periods of time.

7. Under low power, look for akinetes. They are enlarged cells that are dense and granular with thick walls. They do not look empty.

Both *Anabaena* and *Nostoc* have the family characteristics that you have observed so far. You can distinguish between them, however. Bacteria of the genus *Anabaena* have separate, solitary trichomes. The cells are beadlike or barrel-shaped.

A member of the genus *Nostoc* has filaments entangled in a firm, gelatinous mass that is globular or egg-shaped. *Nostoc* colonies, which may be up to 10 cm in diameter, are sometimes called "mare's eggs."

8. Examine your specimen and compare it to the descriptions above.

   i. *Identify the genus of your specimen.*

   _____

   j. *Make a drawing of the bacteria as seen under high power. Label a trichome, heterocyst, and* akinete. *Show the shape and relative sizes of the unspecialized cells of the trichome. Indicate the gelatinous mass of Nostoc, if your specimen is of that genus. Then place the correct genus name under the drawing.*

9. Observe a specimen of a different genus under a nearby microscope.
10. Return your bacterial specimen to your teacher.

Analysis and Interpretations

1. In plant cells, the pigments are contained in chloroplasts or other plastids. How did the pigments seem to be distributed in the monerans you observed?

   _____

   _____

   _____

2. What characteristics do *Oscillatoria* and *Lyngbya* have in common?

_____

_____

_____

3. What characteristics place *Oscillatoria* and *Lyngbya* in different genera?

_____

_____

4. What characteristics do *Anabaena* and *Nostoc* have in common?

_____

_____

5. What characteristics place *Anabaena* and *Nostoc* in different genera?

_____

_____

6. What did you notice about the cell wall at each end of a heterocyst? Was this a characteristic of all the heterocysts that you observed?

_____

7. What is the function of an akinete?

_____

_____

_____

Looking at Protists

Lab 43

Background

Members of the kingdom Protista are all either unicellular or very simple multicellular organisms. The **euglenoids** (phylum Euglenophyta); the chrysophytes (phylum Chrysophyta), or **golden algae**, which include the **diatoms**; and the **dinoflagellates** (phylum Dinoflagellata) are all unicellular algae. Most of these algae are motile. Many contain chlorophyll and are photosynthetic; others are heterotrophic some or all the time.

The euglenoids are bright green because they contain chlorophyll in numerous chloroplasts. They live in fresh water, in marshes and ponds, and in slow, shallow streams where the water is clear.

The chrysophytes contain chlorophyll, but they contain more of the yellow-brown pigment, *fucoxanthin*. Their food is produced by photosynthesis and is stored in the form of oil droplets or a starchlike carbohydrate. The cell walls of the chrysophytes are composed of carbohydrate, and many contain silica compounds, forming a glasslike shell. The diatoms, the most numerous members of the phylum, are found throughout the world, in fresh and salt water, in mud flats, on floating wood, or any surface that is constantly wet and exposed to light.

The dinoflagellates are mostly marine organisms, found in the warmer regions of the ocean. Many are yellow-brown or yellow-green in color, but some are bright red or yellow. Some types are photosynthetic, while others are heterotrophic. The cells contain chlorophyll as well as other pigments. Food is stored as starch, or as bright red or yellow oil droplets. Sometimes red dinoflagellates produce "blooms" (population explosions) that are responsible for the poisonous red tides along ocean shores.

Objectives

In this activity you will:
1. Observe two members of the phylum Euglenophyta.
2. Observe diatoms, the most numerous organisms in the plankton of the ocean.
3. Observe one member of the phylum Dinoflagellata.

Materials

live cultures of:
  Euglena acus
  Phacus, sp.
  Pinnularia nobilis or
    Isthmia nervosa
  Cyclotella bodanica
  Gyrodinium or
    Peridinum, sp.

5% glycerin solution in
  dropper bottle
0.01% methylene blue
  stain in dropper bottle
1% aniline blue stain in
  dropper bottle
2-centimeter squares of
  black construction paper

microscope
pipettes
paper towels

cover slips
slides
sheet of white notebook paper

Procedures and Observations

PART I.   EUGLENOIDS

1. Place 1 drop of 5% glycerin solution on a clean slide. Using a pipette, add 1 or 2 drops of the *Euglena* culture. Then add a cover slip.

2. Examine the slide under low power. Look for slender, green cells with a small clear area at their anterior end. Try to find a *Euglena* that has been slowed down or stopped by the glycerin. Then switch to high power.

The clear space at the anterior end of the *Euglena* is the *reservoir*. The flagellum is attached at the base of the reservoir. See Figure 1.

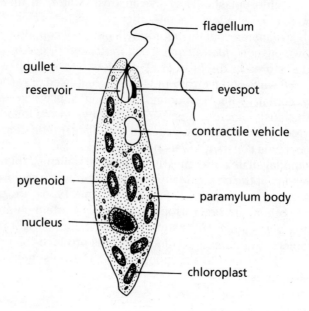

Figure 1

3. Examine the reservoir of the *Euglena* under high power.

Euglena is remarkably responsive to light. A red *eyespot*, or *stigma*, is present on one side of the reservoir near the base of the flagellum. The red pigment blocks light on one side of a nearby light receptor, so that the *Euglena* can receive light from only one direction.

4. Under high power locate the eyespot.

A contractile vacuole empties excess water from the cell into the reservoir on the side opposite the eyespot.

5. Locate the contractile vacuole. Watch to see if it empties and fills up.

   a. *Can you see the contractile vacuole working? If so, describe it.*

Looking at Protists (continued)

Chlorophyll in *Euglena* is found in the green chloroplasts. Food is stored as paramylum, a carbohydrate similar to starch but found only in euglenoids. Paramylum is stored in round *pyrenoid bodies* at the centers of the chloroplasts.

6. Identify the chloroplasts. Then try to locate some pyrenoid bodies at their centers.

Euglena cells have no cell wall. Just under the cell membrane is a pellicle, formed of strips of protein. The pellicle, which is flexible, maintains the shape of the cell and makes it possible for the *Euglena* to contract and elongate in a peculiar motion known as *euglenoid motion*.

7. Observe a *Euglena* that has been stopped by the glycerin and is trying to move.

   b. *Describe the motion of the Euglena.*

   _____

8. Try to locate the nucleus of the *Euglena*, near the center of the cell. It may be difficult to see because of the numerous chloroplasts.

9. Set the slide on a sheet of white notebook paper. Cover half of the cover slip with a square of black construction paper. Leave the slide undisturbed.

10. Place 1 drop of 5% glycerin on another clean slide. Using a clean pipette, add 1 or 2 drops of *Phacus* culture. Then add a cover slip.

11. Observe the slide under low power. Note the leaflike shape of *Phacus*.

   c. *Describe how Phacus swims.*

   _____

12. Find an organism that has been slowed down. Locate the reservoir.

   d. *Can you see an eyespot?*

   _____

   e. *Can you see a flagellum moving in a whiplike fashion?*

   _____

13. Switch to high power. Examine the eyespot.

   f. *Describe the location of the eyespot in relation to the base of the flagellum.*

   _____

14. Look for rings or disks (like doughnuts) of paramylum.

   g. *Are chloroplasts visible?*

   _____

   h. *In the box on the following page sketch the Phacus as seen under high power. Make it about 5 cm across.*

15. Set the *Phacus* slide next to the *Euglena* slide on the sheet of white paper. Cover half the cover slip with a piece of black construction paper, as in Step 9. Leave both slides undisturbed while you prepare to perform Part II.

16. After 10 minutes, examine the *Euglena* and *Phacus* you set aside.

    i. *Where on the slides are the organisms located?*

    _____

17. Remove the pieces of black paper.

    j. *Were there any organisms under the black paper?*

    _____

PART II. DIATOMS _____

Diatoms make up one class of the phylum Chrysophyta, the class Basillariophyceae. The class is divided into two orders: *Pennales* and *Centrales*. See Table 1 for a comparison of the characteristics of the two orders. You will study one genus of each.

1. Set up your microscope in the best light possible and with the diaphragm at the widest opening.

2. Prepare a wet mount of *Pinnularia* (order Pennales) on a clean slide. The space under the cover slip should be just filled with water.

Table 1. Characteristics of Diatoms

Order	Characteristics
Pennales	Bilateral symmetry Found on surfaces of plants, mud flats, etc.
Centrales	Radial symmetry Free-floating, with flotation devices, such as oil droplets, gas bubbles, etc.

Looking at Protists (continued)

Millions of diatoms rise to the surface of mud flats at every low tide. As the water returns, they migrate down a few centimeters, remaining below the surface until the next low tide. The movements of diatoms have been measured at 20 μm per second.

3. Observe *Pinnularia* under low power. Watch the cells for a few moments.

  a. *Are the diatoms moving?*

  _____

  b. *If so, describe the motion.*

  _____

4. Center your specimens, then switch to high power and observe them. Use maximum light.

  c. *Describe the color of the diatoms. Are they yellow-brown, olive-green, or yellow-green?*

  _____

5. Estimate the length of the diatoms. Count how many would fit end-to-end across the diameter of your high-power field.

  d. *Record the number of diatoms that would fit across the diameter of the high power field. Then calculate (in micrometers) the length of a diatom.*

  _____

  _____

  _____

Figure 2 shows the structure of a diatom. The glasslike cell wall, the *frustule,* is secreted by the living cell within it. It is composed of the carbohydrate *pectin* and a silica compound similar to opal. The upper part of the frustule fits over the lower part in the same way that the cover of a Petri dish fits over the bottom of the dish. Each half of a frustule is called a *valve.*

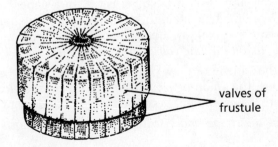

valves of frustule

Figure 2

If you look down at a diatom from the top, you see the *valve view*. See Figure 3. If you look at a diatom from the side and see the valves over-lapped, you are seeing the *girdle view*. These two views account for the different appearances of diatoms under the microscope.

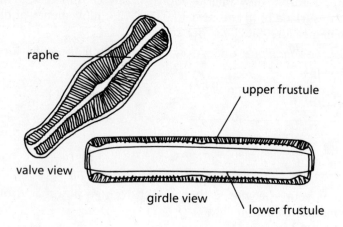

raphe

upper frustule

valve view

girdle view

lower frustule

Figure 3

6. Examine your specimens, using the fine adjustment. Note the appearance of diatoms in the valve view and in the girdle view.

A long, central groove, the *raphe,* can be seen on a diatom only in the valve view. The raphe has slitlike openings. Cytoplasmic streaming in the cell close to the raphe is thought to be the cause of the jerky move-ments by which the members of the order Pennales propel themselves.

7. Observe your specimens as you turn the fine adjustment knob small amounts in each direction. Try to locate the raphe on some diatoms.

The fine lines perpendicular to the raphe are tiny perforations. Each perforation is a complex, sievelike structure called an *areola.* Areolae permit the diffusion of materials between the cell and its environment. The sculptured patterns of areolae are used to classify diatoms. The closely spaced areolae in two genera of diatoms, *Amphipleura* and *Pleurosigma,* are used to test the resolving power of microscope lenses.

8. Note the fine lines perpendicular to the raphe in a valve view of a diatom. These are the areolae.

9. Remove your slide from the stage. Set it on a paper towel. Put 1 drop of 1% aniline blue stain on one side of the cover slip. Using a paper towel on the other side, draw the stain through. **CAUTION:** *Use care to avoid staining your hands or clothing.*

10. Examine the slide under low power, then high power. Look for col-ored bodies, the *chloroplasts* within the diatoms. Chloroplasts in diatoms are yellow-brown. Note their shape and distribution.

   e. *Describe the shape and distribution of the chloroplasts within the diatoms.*

Looking at Protists (continued)

f. *Draw a valve view of a Pinnularia as seen under high power. Label a chloroplast, areola, the frustule, and raphe.*

11. Make a new wet mount of *Pinnularia,* using 2 drops of culture and 1 drop of 0.01% methylene blue stain.

12. Observe the slide under low, then high power. Note that the nucleus and nucleoli of the diatoms become stained and visible.

g. *Are the chloroplasts stained?*

_____

h. *Are oil droplets visible?*

_____

i. *Add any additional structures that you see in the cells stained with methylene blue to your drawing of the diatom. Label them.*

13. Make a wet mount of *Cyclotella* (order Centrales). Examine the slide under low power.

j. *Are the diatoms moving?*

_____

14. Note the radial symmetry of the diatoms. They are disc-shaped with very precise lines of areolae. Note also that the discs tend to cling together in filaments.

15. Find a single *Cyclotella* and center it. Switch to high power. Look for chloroplasts, oil droplets, and areolae.

k. *Describe the color, form, and distribution of chloroplasts in Cyclotella.*

_____

_____

_____

_____

1. *Draw a valve view of Cyclotella as seen under high power. Label a* chloroplast, areola, *and the* frustule.

PART III.　DINOFLAGELLATES

Dinoflagellates make up the class Dinophyceae in the phylum Dinoflagellata. They are tiny cells that move through the water with a complex spinning motion.

1. With a clean pipette, place 1 or 2 drops of *Gyrodinium* culture on a clean slide. Add a cover slip. If the area under the cover slip is not filled, add some culture water.

2. Examine the slide under low power. Look for small, spinning cells.

3. If the dinoflagellates swim too rapidly to see, make a new mount using 1 drop of glycerin, 1 drop of culture, and a cover slip.

A groove called the *girdle* goes across the center of the cell. The ribbon-shaped *transverse flagellum* beats within the girdle, causing the cell to rotate. See Figure 4.

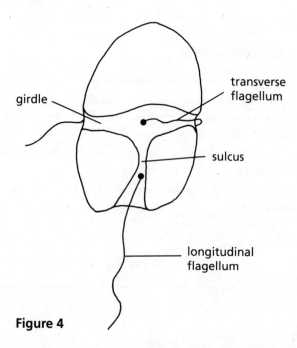

Figure 4

Looking at Protists (continued)

4. Find a slow-moving *Gyrodinium* and focus on it. Then switch to high power. Locate the girdle.

    a. *Can you see the transverse flagellum beating?*

_____

The *sulcus* is a groove that runs at right angles to the girdle. It contains the longer *longitudinal flagellum*, which pushes the cell from behind.

5. Locate the sulcus. Try reducing the light to get a better view of the flagellum.

    b. *Can you see the longitudinal flagellum beating?*

_____

    c. *What color is your specimen? How is the pigment distributed?*

_____

_____

_____

    d. *Describe any colored bodies that you see inside the dinoflagellate.*

_____

6. Prepare another mount of the dinoflagellate. Use 1 drop of 0.01% methylene blue stain and 2 drops of the culture. Add a cover slip.

7. Observe the slide under low power. Then switch to high power. As the stain gradually reacts with the cell, the nucleus should become visible. Note the chromosomes, which look like beaded threads, and the nucleolus.

    e. *Sketch the Gyrodinium in the box below. Make it about 5 cm high. Label all structures that you see.*

Analysis and Interpretations

1. Name some structures that are common to *Euglena* and *Phacus*. Describe some differences between them.

_____

_____

_____

_____

2. Euglenoids have chloroplasts. Why is it advantageous for these photosynthetic organisms to have light receptors and a means to detect the direction of the light?

_____

_____

3. Explain the effect you observed when you examined the slides that had been half covered with black construction paper.

_____

_____

4. What function does the contractile vacuole serve?

_____

_____

_____

5. Why would it be advantageous for a photosynthetic cell such as a diatom to migrate to the surface of a mud flat at low tide?

_____

6. Of what advantage might it be for a diatom to migrate down into the mud as the tidewater returns?

_____

_____

7. If you can see the raphe of a diatom in the order Pennales, are you observing a valve or girdle view?

_____

8. Why are certain species of diatoms useful in testing the resolving power of microscope lenses?

_____

_____

_____

_____

Looking at Protists (continued)

9. Describe the movements of *Gyrodinium*. Make a sketch of the positions the cell assumes as it swims.

_____

_____

_____

_____

10. How would you describe the nucleus of *Gyrodinium*? Is it large or small? Does it have a membrane around it?

_____

_____

Observing Fungi

Lab 44

Background

The Kingdom Fungi includes a wide variety of species. Fungi lack chlorophyll, and thus are heterotrophs: they must take in food from other sources. Most fungi are saprobic, obtaining their nutrients from dead organisms.

Individual fungi are made up of threadlike filaments called *hyphae*. The growth and branching of many hyphae produce a netlike mat, or *mycelium*, which spreads over the surface of a food supply. The hyphae of the mycelium secrete enzymes that digest the food. The hyphae then absorb the products of digestion.

Some fungi live in a symbiotic association with autotrophic green algal cells or blue-green bacterial cells. These associations are called *lichens*. You will be able to see the hyphae of the fungus when you observe a lichen under the microscope.

Objectives

In this activity you will:
1. Identify the parts of a mushroom.
2. Observe basidia and spores of a mushroom.
3. Observe the structure of lichens.

Materials

mushroom	scalpel
hand lens	dissecting needles
paper	cover slip
microscope slide	compound microscope
water	lichens
bulb pipette	

Procedures and Observations 🔳

PART I.   STUDYING MUSHROOM STRUCTURE _____

The mushrooms commonly sold in markets are the fruiting bodies, or reproductive structures, of fungi in the genus *Agaricus*, of the phylum Basidiomycota. The mycelium, from which these mushrooms arise, lies just under the surface of the ground. As the cap of the mushroom matures, gills on the underside produce spores.

1. Obtain a mushroom. Examine it and locate the stalk, or *stipe*, and the top, or *cap*. The lower surface of the cap is filled with structures called *gills*. Locate the gills of your specimen.

2. In an immature mushroom, the gills are covered by a thin sheet of tissue called the *veil*. When a mushroom is mature, the veil breaks,

and the gills become visible. The remnants of the veil are called the *annulus*, and may be found clinging to the stipe. Locate the veil or annulus on your specimen.

a. *Has the veil broken on your specimen?*

_____

b. *In the space provided, make a drawing of the mushroom. Label the* stipe *and* cap. *If your specimen is mature, draw and label the* annulus *and* gills. *If your specimen is not mature, draw and label the* veil.

3. Remove the cap from the stipe. Use a hand lens to examine the gills.

c. *Describe the gills.*

_____

_____

4. Tap the mushroom cap on a piece of paper, and look for any material that falls from the gills.

d. *Describe what happened.*

_____

_____

5. Place a microscope slide on a piece of paper. Using a bulb pipette, place one drop of water on the slide. Using a scalpel, cut the free edges from a few gills, and transfer them to the drop of water on the slide. **CAUTION:** *Use care when handling the scalpel.*

6. Separate the gills into a single layer on the slide. Use dissecting needles to tease the gills apart. Touch the gills on the cut edges only. Add another drop of water to the slide, then add a cover slip.

7. Examine the gills at low power. Look at the two edges of one section of a gill. Determine which edge is the free edge, and which was formed when the gill was cut from the mushroom cap. Focus on a free edge. Look for rounded cells, side-by-side along the edge of the gill. These are *basidia*, the structures that bear the spores.

8. Change to high power, and note the arrangement of spores on the basidia.

   e. *How many spores are there on each basidium?*

   _____

   f. *In the space provided, draw a row of basidia, as seen under high power.* Label *basidia and* spores.

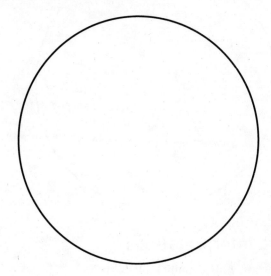

PART II.   STUDYING LICHENS _____

   A lichen is an association of a fungus with an autotrophic green alga or blue-green bacterium. Lichens are classified as if they were single organisms, according to the fungus species of their association. Three types of lichen body are recognized: *crustose*, in which the body is a thin, flat crust; *fruticose*, in which the body is erect and branching, like a small shrub; and *foliose*, in which the body is a series of flat, leaflike layers.

1. Select a specimen of lichen.

2. Examine the structure and color of the specimen. Use a hand lens to study the lichen in greater detail.

   a. *Describe the color and appearance of your specimen.*

   _____

   _____

   b. *Which of the three types of lichen is your specimen?*

   _____

3. Place a microscope slide on a piece of paper. Using a bulb pipette, place one drop of water on the slide. Use a scalpel to cut off a small section of the lichen, and to transfer it to the water on the slide. Use two dissecting needles to gently tease the lichen apart until it is in a thin layer. Add another drop of water and a cover slip.

4. Observe the lichen under low power. Find a field that has a single layer of filaments and cells, and change to high power. You should be able to see threadlike filaments that surround green or blue-green cells. The filaments are the hyphae of the fungus. The green or blue-green cells are the autotrophs (green algae or blue-green bacteria).

   c. *In the space provided, draw the forms that you see. Label* hyphae of fungus *and* autotrophs.

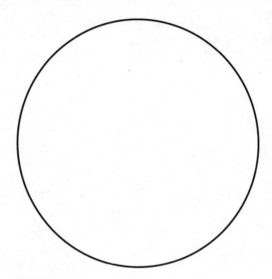

Analysis and Interpretations

1. Why do mushroom gills usually look dusty?

_____

2. Mushroom spores are very small and light. How is this an adaptation for reproduction?

_____

_____

_____

_____

3. Mushrooms produce many thousands of spores. Why, then, is the world not covered with mushrooms?

_____

_____

_____

_____

Observing Fungi (continued) 44

4. Why are lichens a lighter shade of green than are mosses and other plants?

_____

_____

_____

_____

5. Lichens readily absorb substances dissolved in rainwater, including sulfur dioxide, an air pollutant. Lichens are particularly sensitive to such chemicals. How might lichens serve as pollution indicators?

_____

_____

For Further Investigation

1. Make a mushroom spore print. Place a sheet of white paper in the bottom of a dissecting tray, or similar container. Set a mushroom cap, gill side down, on the paper. Cover the container with a sheet of waxed paper. After a few days, lift the cap and see if any spores have fallen onto the paper. Compare the pattern of spores to the pattern of the gills of the mushroom.

2. Try growing mushrooms, using one of the kits that are available from biological supply houses. Follow the instructions furnished with the kit. **CAUTION:** *Do not collect or grow spores of mushrooms growing in the wild, as many of these mushrooms are poisonous.*

Looking at Hydra

Lab 45

Background

The hydra is a small animal, only 6–10 mm long and about 1 mm in diameter. Hydras belong to the phylum Coelenterata, which also includes jellyfish, sea anemones, the Portuguese man-of-war, and the coral animals that build coral reefs. All members of this phylum have specialized stinging cells, called *cnidoblasts,* with which they paralyze their prey.

Coelenterata means "hollow intestine," which describes the bodies of these animals. Most coelenterates live in the ocean, but hydras live in freshwater ponds and slow-running streams. Though they live attached to twigs, leaves, or rocks, hydras are also able to move about, gliding on their bases, or turning "handsprings" on their tentacles. Sometimes the hydra secretes a bubble from its base and floats about, buoyed up by the bubble. The hydra feeds on small swimming animals. It first paralyzes the prey with the stinging cells, then draws it to its mouth with its tentacles.

Objectives

In this activity you will:
1. Study the structure of hydra.
2. Note some characteristics of members of the phylum Coelenterata.

Materials

hydra culture   pipette
slide   cover slip
single-edged razor blade   microscope

Procedures and Observations

1. Your teacher will place a hydra, with 2 or 3 drops of culture water, on your clean slide. Do not add a cover slip.

2. Observe the hydra under low power. The animal may remain contracted for a while, so watch as it relaxes and stretches out.

The body form of hydra is called a *polyp.* At the anterior end of the cylindrical *body stalk* is a cone-shaped *hypostome,* in which the *mouth* is located. Around the base of the hypostome is a circle of *tentacles.* The hydra attaches to surfaces by the *basal disk* at the posterior end of the body stalk.

The body of hydra shows *radial symmetry*, a characteristic of all coelenterates. Radial symmetry is most often found in sessile animals—it enables them to respond to environmental stimuli from all directions.

3. Observe the structure of the hydra.

    a. *Sketch the outline of the hydra in the space provided below—you will fill in more structures as you go through the activity. Label the* basal disk, body stalk, hypostome, mouth, *and* tentacles.

The body of hydra is a hollow sac, with the mouth the only opening. The cavity inside the hydra is the *gastrovascular cavity*, where *extracellular digestion* takes place.

The body wall is composed of two cell layers. The outer layer, the *ectoderm,* has five different kinds of cells. Each kind of cell has a special function, such as contraction, regeneration, mucus secretion, sensing of stimuli, and defense.

The inner cell layer is the *endoderm.* It lines the gastrovascular cavity. Specialized cells in this layer can either contract, secrete enzymes for extracellular digestion, or engulf food particles for *intracellular digestion.* Some cells have *flagella* that protrude into the gastrovascular cavity. The beating of the flagella mixes the contents of the cavity. The endoderm also has some cells that sense stimuli and act like nerve cells.

Looking at Hydra (continued)

Between the ectoderm and endoderm is a thin layer of jellylike material, the *mesoglea*. In jellyfish, this mesoglea is very thick.

4. Focus on any part of the hydra. The tissue that you see in a live hydra (its outer layer) is part of the ectoderm. You will not be able to distinguish the different types of cells.

   b. *Add some details to your drawing of the hydra. Sketch and label the ectoderm, endoderm, and gastrovascular cavity.*

Each tentacle of hydra contains *cnidoblasts,* or stinging cells. A cnidoblast contains a *nematocyst,* which is a capsule with a threadlike tube that can be discharged. Some nematocysts shoot a thread that entangles prey; some inject a paralyzing poison into prey; and some give off a sticky substance used to anchor the hydra when it turns handsprings. After a nematocyst is discharged, the cnidoblast disintegrates. However, it is replaced with a new one, complete with nematocyst, in a few hours.

5. Focus on one tentacle of the hydra. The small bumps on the tentacle are cnidoblasts.

   c. *Sketch some cnidoblasts on a tentacle in your drawing of the hydra. Label one of them.*

The hydra can reproduce both asexually and sexually. It reproduces asexually by *budding.* This usually occurs in the spring and summer. The bud grows out near the middle of the body stalk.

6. Observe the hydra to see if it is budding.

   d. *Does your hydra have a bud? If so, sketch it on your hydra drawing and label it.*

In the fall, the hydra reproduces sexually. Most species of hydra have separate male and female animals. However, some species are *hermaphroditic*—each animal has both male and female reproductive organs. *Testes* are cone-shaped structures on the upper half of the body stalk. Sperm from the testes are released into the water. An *ovary* is formed on the lower half of the body stalk and produces one egg. When the egg is fertilized, a shell forms around the hydra embryo. This shell-enclosed egg drops to the bottom of the pond or stream and remains there during the winter. In the spring the egg hatches and develops into a new hydra.

7. If your hydra is not budding, check to see if it has developed testes or an ovary (or both).

   e. *Is the hydra reproducing sexually? If so, sketch the reproductive structure(s) on your hydra and label it (them).*

8. With a single-edged razor blade, cut off the ends of several tentacles of the hydra. **CAUTION:** *Handle the razor blade with care.* Push the ends of the tentacles to one edge of the slide in a drop of water.

9. Place a cover slip over the tentacle pieces. Then, using a pipette, return the hydra to the hydra culture. It will soon replace the tentacle parts that you removed.

10. Using a pipette, fill the space under the cover slip with culture water.

11. Observe the slide under low power. Locate the cnidoblasts. Then focus on one that you can see well.

12. Switch to high power. Carefully examine the structure of the nematocyst inside the cnidoblast.

    f. *Sketch a cnidoblast below the hydra drawing. Make it 2 or 3 cm across. Label the* cnidoblast *and* nematocyst.

Analysis and Interpretations

1. Describe the symmetry found in the hydra.

_____

2. Name the two cell layers that make up the hydra body wall. What kinds of cells are in each?

_____

_____

_____

_____

3. What takes place in the gastrovascular cavity?

_____

4. How does sexual reproduction take place in hydra?

_____

_____

_____

_____

_____

5. Why is the winter egg produced by the hydra an adaptive advantage for species living in cold climates?

_____

_____

Anatomy of the Earthworm

Lab 46

Background

The earthworm is the best-known member of the phylum Annelida, the segmented worms. Annelids are bilaterally symmetrical, and their bodies are divided into segments both externally and internally. They have a tube-within-a-tube body structure. The outer tube is the body wall, while the inner tube is the digestive tract. The cavity between the outer and inner tubes is the *coelom*.

Objectives

In this activity you will:
1. Study the external and internal anatomy of the earthworm.
2. Observe some characteristics of annelids.

Alternate Approach: In Part I, examine the external anatomy of an earthworm, using a live specimen or a model. In Part II, use a dissection guide or a model of an earthworm to study the organism's internal anatomy. Ask your teacher about additional alternatives.

Materials

preserved earthworm   scalpel
   (*Lumbricus,* sp.)   straight pins
dissecting tray   hand lens or dissecting microscope
dissecting scissors   dissecting needles
forceps   probe
latex gloves

Procedures and Observations

PART I.   EXTERNAL ANATOMY OF THE EARTHWORM _____

1. Put on your gloves and wear them throughout this lab activity. Examine the external structure of the earthworm. The thickened region, the *clitellum*, is closer to the anterior end of the animal. The clitellum secretes a cocoon around the fertilized eggs. The *prostomium* is the anterior tip of the earthworm. The upper, or dorsal, surface of the worm feels smooth, while the lower, or ventral, surface feels rough because of the *setae*, or bristles, on each segment. Determine which is the dorsal and which is the ventral surface of the worm.

   a. *Count and record the number of segments between the prostomium and the clitellum.*

b. *Using your hand lens to see, how many setae are on each segment?*

_____

2. Examine the anterior and posterior ends of the worm.

    c. *What are the two openings you see?*

_____

In addition to the openings in the first and last segments of the body, the earthworm has several other types of openings. On the sides of most segments there are excretory pores. On the ventral surface of segment 14 are pores through which eggs are discharged. On the ventral surface of segment 15 are pores through which sperm are discharged.

3. Using a hand lens or dissecting microscope, examine each surface of the worm.

    d. *Can you see any of the openings described above? If so, which ones?*

_____

_____

PART II.   INTERNAL ANATOMY OF THE EARTHWORM _____

1. Place your earthworm in the dissecting tray with the dorsal surface up and the anterior end facing away from you. Place dissecting needles through the first and last segments to hold the worm in position. In making an incision you must be careful to cut only the body wall. If you cut too deeply, you will damage the internal organs. The incision should be slightly to one side of the midline. Using a sharp scalpel or dissecting scissors, make an incision from behind the clitellum to the anus. **CAUTION:** *Handle the scalpel and scissors with caution throughout this lab activity.* Then turn the tray around and extend the incision to the mouth. Holding the body wall with your forceps, use a scalpel or dissecting needle to cut the membranes that separate the segments of the earthworm. Starting at the anterior end, separate the body wall along the cut, and pin it down, as shown in Figure 1.

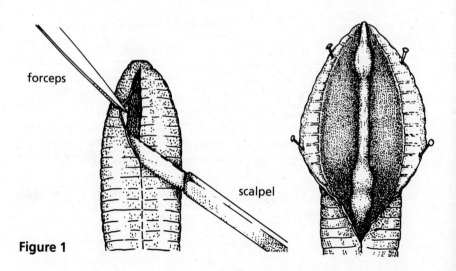

forceps

scalpel

Figure 1

Anatomy of the Earthworm (continued)

a. *How does the internal segmentation of the earthworm compare with the external segmentation?*

_____

_____

_____

_____

The mouth of the earthworm opens into the muscular pharynx, which sucks food into the digestive tract. The pharynx is found within the first 5 or so segments. See Figure 2. Posterior to the pharynx is the esophagus, which extends for about 10 segments. The esophagus is a narrow tube that widens where it enters the crop, a thin-walled organ in which food is temporarily stored. Posterior to the crop is the thick-walled gizzard, where food is broken down mechanically. From the gizzard, food passes into the intestine, which extends posteriorly to the anus.

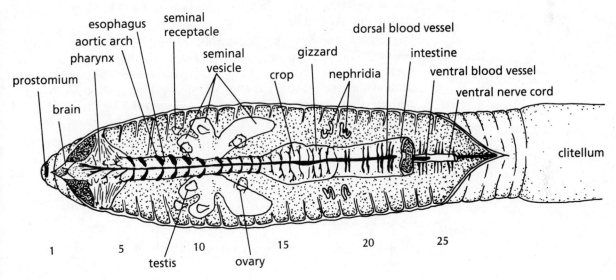

Figure 2

2. Beginning at the anterior end of the worm (segment 1), identify the organs of the digestive system. Use a probe to feel the relative thick-nesses of the walls of the crop and gizzard. Use your scalpel to make a cross-sectional cut through the intestine about half way along its length. Make sure you cut only through the intestine; do not cut any other body part. Examine the cut end of the intestine with a hand lens or dissecting microscope.

b. *In the box on the following page, draw a cross section of the earth-worm. Label the body wall, setae, coelom, intestinal wall, and the intestinal opening.*

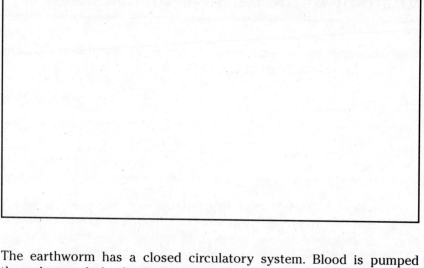

The earthworm has a closed circulatory system. Blood is pumped through vessels by five pairs of aortic arches, or hearts. The aortic arches encircle the esophagus between segments 7 and 11. From the aortic arches, blood flows into the ventral vessel, which runs beneath the organs of the digestive tract. The ventral vessel branches and divides into smaller vessels, eventually forming capillaries that serve the cells of the animal. The capillaries join, forming larger vessels. Blood is returned to the aortic arches through the dorsal vessel, which runs along the top of the digestive tract.

3. Identify the dorsal vessel, which runs along the top of the intestine. Follow it forward toward the esophagus. Gently move aside any organs that obscure your view so that you can see the aortic arches around the esophagus. Lift the cut end of the intestine so that you can see the ventral vessel, which runs along the ventral surface of the digestive tract.

c. *Describe the dorsal vessel, the aortic arches, and the ventral vessel.*

_____

_____

_____

d. *Add the dorsal and ventral blood vessels to your cross-sectional drawing.*

Earthworms are hermaphroditic—they contain both male and female reproductive structures. However, self-fertilization does not occur. When earthworms mate, they exchange sperm, which later will fertilize the eggs produced by the ovaries. Sperm are produced and stored in the *seminal vesicles*. Sperm received from another animal in mating are stored in the two pairs of *seminal receptacles*.

4. The most visible parts of the reproductive system are the pair of three-lobed seminal vesicles on either side of the esophagus. The seminal receptacles are in segments 9 and 10. The two pairs of testes are on the walls that separate segments 10 and 11, and the ovaries are in segment 13. Try to identify the various parts of the reproductive system. Use a hand lens or dissecting microscope where necessary.

Anatomy of the Earthworm (continued)

e. *List the parts of the reproductive system that you could see.*

_____

_____

_____

The excretory organs of earthworms are the *nephridia*, which are tiny, coiled, white tubules. Pairs of nephridia are found in all segments except the first three and the last.

5. Using a hand lens or dissecting microscope, try to identify a nephridium.

f. *Add a pair of nephridia to your cross-sectional drawing.*

The earthworm has a central nervous system made up of a brain and a pair of solid, ventral nerve cords. The brain is actually a pair of fused ganglia, and the nerve cords enlarge into ganglia in each segment. A peripheral nervous system consisting of nerves branching from the central nervous system serves all parts of the body.

6. The brain is a small mass of white tissue found on the dorsal surface of the anterior end of the pharynx. Extending from the brain and running around either side of the pharynx are nerve cords. Gently move the pharynx and trace the nerve cords. Beneath the pharynx is another pair of ganglia. Extending from these ganglia are the pair of ventral nerve cords. Gently move any organs that are in the way, and identify as many parts of the nervous system as you can.

g. *What parts of the nervous system could you see?*

_____

_____

h. *Add the ventral nerve cord to your drawing.*

Analysis and Interpretations

1. What advantage does hermaphroditism have for slow-moving organisms such as the earthworm?

_____

_____

_____

2. In what ways does the internal structure of the earthworm show development of a specialized "head" end?

_____

_____

_____

3. In terms of what you actually observed in your dissection, describe the tube-within-a-tube body structure of the earthworm.

_____

_____

_____

4. How do you think the setae on each segment function in locomotion?

_____

_____

_____

For Further Investigation

Draw cross-sectional views of earthworm anatomy at different segments of the worm, so different features of the anatomy are shown. Label the structures that you see at the different segments.

Anatomy of the Clam

Lab 47

Background

The clam is a member of the phylum Mollusca and shows many of the basic characteristics of its phylum. The clam has a muscular foot, a mantle, and a hard shell. It is a challenging invertebrate to study because its complex organ systems are crowded into a small container and are twisted in unique ways. Refer to the diagram of the clam in Figure 1 before and while you do this activity. Try to identify as many of its structures as you can.

Objectives

In this activity you will:
1. Observe the external and internal anatomy of a clam.
2. Identify characteristics of a mollusk.

Materials

clam	empty clam shell
broken clam shell	dissecting tray
dissecting scissors	screwdriver
glass stirring rods	scalpel
forceps	hand lens
slide	pipette
microscope	latex gloves

Alternate Approach: Use a model or a dissection guide of the clam to complete this lab activity. You may also wish to use a live clam for Part I and to observe the intake of water by the clam in Part II, Step 12. Ask your teacher about additional alternatives.

Procedures and Observations

PART I. EXTERNAL ANATOMY _____

The shells of a clam are called valves. The valves are held together at their dorsal surface.

1. Examine the closed clam.

   a. *How many valves enclose the body?*

_____

On the sides of the valves are growth lines, which are formed as the clam valves increase in size. The longest lines are the newest. The oldest part of each valve is the hump on the dorsal side, the *umbo*. The umbo points to the anterior end of the clam.

2. Identify the umbos. Observe the growth lines on the valves. Then hold the clam with its dorsal side toward you, anterior end up. Try to determine the right and left sides.

b. *Can you determine the right and left valves of the clam?*

_____

c. *What kind of symmetry is shown in the clam?*

_____

The hinge ligament connects the two valves between the umbos. It is composed of a tough, elastic material and tends to pull the valves open. the clam holds its valves tightly closed by means of two strong muscles, the anterior and posterior *adductor muscles*. When a clam dies, the muscles stop working against the hinge ligament and the valves open.

The shell is made up of three layers. The outer layer is composed of the same tough material as the hinge ligament. It protects the shell from the carbonic acid that forms when carbon dioxide reacts with water. The middle layer of the shell is composed of calcium carbonate crystals, which are aligned perpendicular to the surface of the shell. The inner layer of the shell, which is pearly and shiny, is composed of thin sheets of calcium carbonate that lie parallel to the surface of the shell.

3. Examine a broken clam shell. Note the hard outer layer, which may now be dried. Use a hand lens to see the crystalline structure of the middle layer.

PART II. INTERNAL ANATOMY

1. Place the clam on its right side, anterior end to your left, dorsal side away from you. Pry apart the ventral margins of the valves using a screwdriver blade as a wedge. **CAUTION:** *Be careful not to jab yourself with the screwdriver.*

a. *In a live clam, are the muscles holding the valves together strong?*

_____

2. Refer to Figure 1 on the next page to see where the anterior and posterior adductor muscles are. Note their size. Then slide a scalpel between the valves and cut each muscle with a clean, sideways cut. **CAUTION:** *Be careful using the scalpel throughout this lab activity.* Cut only the muscles of the clam. You will be able to feel the resistance of the dense muscle tissue and you will know when it is cut. When both muscles are cut, the clam will remain open.

The *mantle* is a thick layer of tissue that encloses the clam body. It is in two parts, one part against each valve. The mantle secretes the three layered shell, increasing the size of the shell as the clam grows.

3. Look inside the clam. When you open the valves, the mantle may cling to the left (upper) valve. If this happens, slide the scalpel between the mantle and valve. Then pull the mantle downward with forceps so that it covers the clam body.

Anatomy of the Clam   (continued)

4. Examine the internal surface of the left valve. Note the cut surfaces of the anterior adductor muscle and the posterior adductor muscle. You can see the scars of the attachment of these muscles on the empty clam shell. Also note the hinge teeth near the dorsal sides of the valves. They interlock and prevent the valves from sliding sideways when closed. Find the prominent *pallial line,* which is near the ventral margin of the clam shell and shows where the mantle was attached.

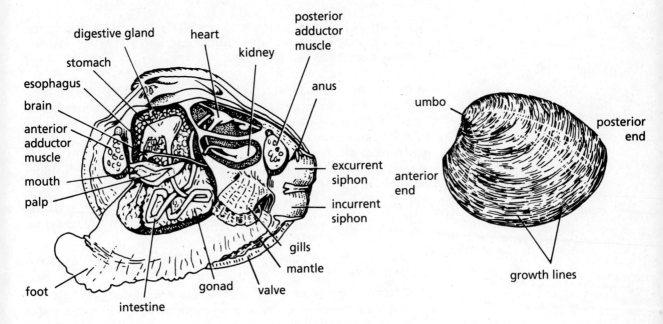

Figure 1

At the posterior end of the mantle are two pipelike siphons that carry water into and out of the clam. The clam is a filter feeder. The ventral siphon, the *incurrent siphon,* draws a stream of water into the body where it is filtered over the gills. The dorsal siphon is the *excurrent siphon* through which the stream of water leaves the clam body, carrying digestive and respiratory wastes. A 10-cm long clam filters 2 to 3 liters of water per hour.

5. Locate the dark colored incurrent and excurrent siphons where the left and right margins of the mantle join at the posterior end. Look at the ends of the siphons.

   b. *Describe how the ends of the incurrent and excurrent siphons differ.*

   _____

   _____

   _____

6. Detach the clam body from the shell. Grasp the mantle lobe at the dorsal side of the body and pull it away from the shell all along the dorsal midline.

7. Arrange the animal in the shell with its mantle surrounding it. Look at the anterior end.

    c. *Does the clam have a head?*

---

8. Note the mouth, a small tube near the anterior adductor muscle. Also find the palps, two folds of tissue, one on each side of the mouth. Use Figure 1 as a reference.

The *visceral mass,* or organ systems, of the clam are within the mantle cavity. This arrangement of organs is characteristic of mollusks. The muscular foot extends toward the anterior. The gills are very thin folds of tissue posterior and dorsal to the foot.

9. Lift the ventral edge of the mantle with the forceps, then snip the mantle away from the body with scissors. Observe the visceral mass. Locate the foot and gills.

The gills of the clam are the chief feeding and respiratory organs. They are living sieves, with rows of microscopic pores and comblike bands of ciliated tissue. The cilia create water currents, filter out food and sediments, and move waste materials out of the clam's body. Gill tissue also secretes mucus, which traps food and carries it to the mouth in the form of strings. Oxygen and carbon dioxide are exchanged by diffusion between the gill tissue and water passing through the gills.

10. Cut a 5-mm square of gill tissue with the scalpel or the scissors. Place it on a slide. Add a few drops of fluid from the clam with a pipette. Do not use a cover slip.

11. Examine the slide under low power. Look for the hairlike cilia moving in waves.

12. Observe the live clam set up under the dissecting microscope. Tiny particles of red, powdered carmine were added to the water in the demonstration. You should be able to see the water stream produced by the beating cilia.

13. Refer to Figure 1 to locate the digestive system of the clam. Then observe your specimen. Locate the dark *digestive gland* near the anterior end, dorsal to the mouth. The stomach is completely surrounded by the digestive gland.

The heart of the clam has three chambers. Two receiving chambers, *atria,* show bilateral symmetry, and one pumping chamber, the *ventricle,* is on the dorsal midline. The clam has an open circulatory system. The colorless blood is pumped into sinuses, or spaces, in the tissues. A large sinus is located in the foot. When it fills with blood, it helps to swell the foot for digging.

14. Locate the heart, which is posterior to the digestive gland and stomach on the dorsal side. Try to identify the two atria and the ventricle.

15. Find the intestine as it passes through the heart. Trace it to the anus, which is near the excurrent siphon at the posterior end.

The reproductive organs, or *gonads,* surround the coils of the intestine. You will find testes in a male clam and ovaries in a female clam. In some kinds of clams, the female carries her young, bivalved larvae, called

Anatomy of the Clam (continued)

glochidia, in her gills for a time. When the larvae are present, the gills of the female are swollen. The glochidia are shed into the water through the excurrent siphon. Within a few days, they clamp onto the gills or fins of a fish and live there as parasites for some weeks. After this period the tiny clams drop to the bottom of the water to take up their burrowing existence in muddy sediments. Perhaps you have caught fish with black "pinheads" in their gills and never knew that they were young clams.

16. Remove one side of the foot by snipping the tough tissue with scissors. Try to locate the grainy tissue of the reproductive organs surrounding the coils of the intestine.

Analysis and Interpretations

1. How can you tell whether or not a clam is alive just by looking at its exterior?

_____

2. Make a labeled diagram showing the structure of a clam shell. Be sure the layers have the appropriate thickness.

3. What structure produces the shell of the clam?

_____

4. What does the incurrent siphon end appear adapted to do?

_____

5. Explain the process of filter feeding.

_____

_____

_____

6. What functions are performed by the gills of a clam?

_____

_____

_____

7. The intestine of a clam passes through two organs in which you do not usually expect to see an intestine. What are they?

_____

_____

Comparative Anatomy of Two Arthropods

Lab 48

Background

The phylum Arthropoda includes at least 80 percent of all known animal species. More than a million species of arthropods occupy more kinds of habitats, and consume more varieties of foods, than any other group of organisms. The sorting and identification of this bewildering array of animals has occupied generations of biologists. In this laboratory activity, you will compare the external anatomy of members of two classes of arthropods, class Crustacea and class Insecta. You will perform studies similar to those employed by taxonomists as they attempt to classify and identify animals.

Objectives

In this activity you will:
1. Observe characteristics of crayfish and grasshoppers that identify them as members of the phylum Arthropoda.
2. Observe differences between crayfish and grasshoppers that place them in separate classes: the class Crustacea and the class Insecta.

Materials

preserved crayfish
   (large species)
dissecting tray
forceps
dissecting scissors
latex gloves

preserved grasshopper
   (large species)
dissecting needle (probe)
hand lens
Petri dish

Alternate Approach: Use a model or pictures and/or drawings of the crayfish and grasshopper to complete this lab activity. You may also wish to use a live crustacean to complete this lab, omitting Part I, Steps 3-5 and Part II, Steps 19-22. Ask your teacher about additional alternatives.

Procedures and Observations

PART I.   CHARACTERISTICS OF CRAYFISH AND GRASSHOPPERS _____

1. Place the crayfish and the grasshopper side by side in the dissecting tray, dorsal sides up and anterior ends away from you. Note that each animal has a head at its anterior end where sense organs are located. Observe that the bodies are streamlined. Imagine a line running down the middle of the dorsal side of each body, dividing it into right and left sides. Providing the crayfish has both claws, the sides of each body are mirror images. Also note the posterior parts of the two bodies.

a. *What kind of symmetry is characteristic of the crayfish and the grasshopper?*

_____

b. *Are any parts of the bodies divided into sections, or segments, similar to the segments found in an earthworm?*

_____

2. Turn both animals ventral sides up. Examine the ventral sides to see how the bodies are organized.

c. *Seen from the ventral sides, do the bodies appear to be segmented?*

_____

Arthropods are named for their jointed legs. "Arthro-" comes from the Greek word for *joint,* and "-pod" comes from the Greek word "pous," meaning *foot.* The paired, jointed legs are called *appendages,* as are the other paired structures that are attached to the body segments.

3. Turn the crayfish over and lift it up by the middle of its body. Notice how the pairs of legs hang downward. Turn the grasshopper over and lift it by its body and note how its legs are attached. Observe the joints in the legs of both animals.

d. *Are the legs attached to the dorsal or to the ventral sides of the animals?*

_____

e. *How are the leg attachments related to the segments?*

_____

Arthropods have an outside skeleton, the *exoskeleton,* that covers the body like armor. The exoskeleton is composed of *chitin,* a tough, flexible substance. Only the arthropods have this kind of exoskeleton. It is considered to be one of the reasons for their remarkable success.

4. Examine the outer covering of each animal. With the handle of your dissecting needle, or with the forceps, test the hardness and flexibility of the exoskeleton. Press gently on the dorsal and ventral sides of each animal in several places, proceeding from anterior to posterior.

f. *Which parts are harder than others?*

_____

g. *Which parts are more flexible than the others?*

_____

_____

5. Examine the legs of each animal. Feel the claws of the crayfish by holding them between your thumb and forefinger. Look at the form and arrangement of the claws.

h. *Is the exoskeleton on the legs firm enough to make a good pushing or walking leg?*

_____

i. *Do the claws of the crayfish seem like good pinchers? Explain.*

_____

6. Look at the grasshopper claws with the hand lens. Feel them with your forefinger. Then examine the wings of the grasshopper. They are also made of chitin. Feel the wings and test their strength.

  j. *How do you think chitin makes the claws suitable for clinging to grass and leaves?*

_____

  k. *What properties of chitin might make it a good wing material?*

_____

7. Find other pairs of jointed appendages on the bodies of these two animals. On the heads, find antennae. Proceeding posteriorly on both dorsal and ventral sides, note how the pairs of appendages differ from each other. Each pair is highly specialized for a specific use in the animal's environment.

PART II. COMPARISON OF A CRUSTACEAN AND AN INSECT _____

  The crayfish, classified in the Class Crustacea, is an example of an arthropod adapted for living in water. Crabs, lobsters, and shrimp are also crustaceans. The grasshopper, a member of the Class Insecta, is in many ways typical of the land-dwelling insects.

As you study these arthropods, enter your observations in Table 1 on the next page.

  1. Compare the exoskeletons of the crayfish and grasshopper. With the handle of your probe or with a pencil, tap on the exoskeleton of each animal. The difference in the sounds tells you that one exoskeleton is harder, or more crusty, than the other. Both exoskeletons contain chitin, but one also contains calcium salts, which make the exoskeleton hard. Animal parts hardened by salts such as calcium carbonate (lime) and calcium phosphate are said to be *calcified.*

  a. *Which animal has the crusty, calcified exoskeleton?*

_____

In general, the arthropod body is divided into three distinguishable regions—the head, thorax, and abdomen. (Thorax is the Greek word for "chest.") In the crayfish, the head and thorax are fused together, forming what is called a *cephalothorax.* The covering of the cephalothorax, called the *carapace,* covers the first 13 segments of the crayfish. The abdomen of the crayfish is clearly segmented.

  2. Determine the number of segments that make up the crayfish abdomen. The last segment is the *telson,* the single, flat structure at the center of the fanshaped posterior end.

  b. *How many segments make up the crayfish abdomen?*

_____

Table 1.   Comparison of Crayfish and Grasshopper

Characteristic		Crayfish (Class Crustacea)	Grasshopper (Class Insecta)
Composition of exoskeleton			
Body regions			
Sense organs	antennae		
	eyes		
	hearing organ		
Locomotor organs	Legs		
	wings		
Abdomen	Number of segments		
	appendages present		
	posterior segments		
Respiratory structures			

c. *How many segments make up the entire crayfish body?*

_____

The grasshopper body has three regions. The head is composed of six fused segments and is attached to the thorax. The thorax consists of three segments. The abdomen, posterior to the thorax, is made up of ten complete segments plus one incomplete segment.

3. Examine the segments of the thorax and abdomen on the ventral side of the grasshopper body. With the hand lens, examine the ventral side of the head. You will see paired appendages, each pair highly specialized.

d. *How many segments make up the grasshopper body?*

_____

The sense organs of the head are noticeable on both animals. The antennae are jointed, paired appendages. Each pair of antennae is attached to a segment.

4. Look closely at the bases of the antennae on each animal and count the pairs of antennae on each. The anterior, Y-shaped antennae of crustaceans are known as *antennules.*

e. *How many pairs of antennae does the crayfish have?*

Comparative Anatomy of Two Arthropods (continued) 48

f. *How many pairs of antennae does the grasshopper have?*

The large eyes on the head of the grasshopper are *compound eyes*, each made up of more than 2000 units, called *facets*. Each facet receives light from part of the surroundings and forms an image. The many separate images reach the brain by means of nerves. The "picture" received by the brain consists of as many small units as there are facets in the eye. This kind of vision is called *mosaic vision*, and is unique in arthropods. Animals with compound eyes are very sensitive to movements in their surroundings. As an object moves, its image moves from one facet of the compound eye to the next.

5. Look at the large eyes of the grasshopper. Note the curved surface of each eye, and the amount that the eye extends outward from the head. Also examine the eye with the hand lens. Be sure to have good light on the specimen.

    g. *Considering the structure and placement of the compound eyes, can the grasshopper see in all directions without moving?*

6. With the hand lens, examine the crayfish eyes. Look at the attachments of the eyes, also, observe where they are mounted on the head.

    h. *Are the crayfish eyes compound?*

    i. *How are the eyes attached to the head?*

    j. *Can the crayfish see in all directions without turning around?*

Some arthropods have simple eyes, called *ocelli (ocellus,* singular), in addition to the compound eyes. Such eyes are light sensors only and do not form images.

7. Pick up the grasshopper and look straight at its face. Using the hand lens, look for three simple eyes. One ocellus is in the center of the face between the antennae. The other two ocelli are above the bases of the antennae, close to the compound eyes.

    k. *How do the ocelli compare in size to the compound eyes?*

8. Look for ocelli near the crayfish antennae and eyes.

    l. *Does the crayfish have ocelli?*

The hearing organ of the grasshopper is the *tympanum,* a membrane stretched across a cavity. Sound waves cause the membrane to vibrate, stimulating nerve endings inside the cavity. The crayfish has no tympanum. However, the crayfish body has many bristles and fine, hairlike structures. Vibrations in the water vibrate such hairs. Some of them are thought to serve as hearing organs.

9. Find the first segment of the grasshopper abdomen. It is located under the wings, dorsal to the attachment of the large jumping leg. See Figure 1. The flat, oval structures on each side of the first abdominal segment are the tympana.

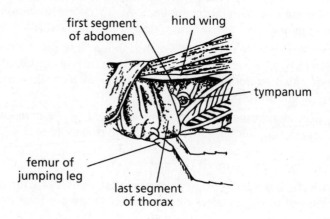

Figure 1

10. Look all over the crayfish body for bristles and hairs that might be vibrated by vibrations in water.

Crayfish, shrimp, lobsters, and crabs are classified as decapods (Order Decapoda). All have five pairs of walking legs, with the first pair often modified as pincers, or chelipeds. The legs are not all alike and are adapted for different functions. All of the pairs of legs are attached to the last five segments of the cephalothorax.

11. Look at the pairs of legs on the crayfish. The first pair, the *chelipeds,* are larger and heavier than the other legs. They are adapted for catching food and for offense and defense. The next four pair are the *walking* legs.

    m. *How many pairs of legs does the crayfish have?*

The thorax of the grasshopper has been called its "locomotor box." Two pair of *walking legs* are attached to the first two segments of the thorax. One pair of *jumping legs* is attached to the third (last) segment. *Wings* are attached to the dorsal side of the thorax.

12. Examine the legs and wings of the grasshopper. Notice the differences between the pairs of legs and the pairs of wings.

Comparative Anatomy of Two Arthropods (continued)

n. *How many pairs of wings are attached to the thorax?*

_____

o. *Where are they attached?*

_____

_____

p. *In all, how many pairs of locomotor appendages are attached to the three segments of the thorax of the insect?*

_____

Almost every segment of the abdomen of crustaceans bears a pair of appendages on the ventral side. Insects, however, have no abdominal appendages except on the last segment of the female.

13. Look at the ventral sides of the abdominal segments of the crayfish. The small, jointed appendages are called *swimmerets.*

In the male crayfish, the first pair of swimmerets are modified into pipelike *copulatory organs.* In the fall, the male deposits sperm through these organs into the body of the female. The female crayfish has paired openings between the last pair of walking legs where the sperm are received. The sperm remain in a pouch, the *seminal receptacle,* all winter. In the spring, 300 to 600 eggs are shed through the openings of the internal oviducts, located at the bases of the third pair of walking legs. As the eggs are released, the stored sperm are released simultaneously, resulting in fertilization. The mass of fertilized eggs becomes attached to the female's swimmerets. The eggs hatch in about 5 to 6 weeks, and the larvae remain attached to the mother for several more weeks.

14. Determine the sex of your crayfish specimen. Look for the modified first pair of swimmerets to see if the specimen is a male. If not, look for the paired openings between the last pair of walking legs of a female. If the specimen is female, try to find the openings to the internal oviducts at the bases of the third pair of legs.

15. Examine a specimen of the opposite sex to observe the reproductive structures.

The sex of a grasshopper can be determined from its external structure. In the female, the abdomen ends in a four-pointed structure called an *ovipositor.* The ovipositor is used to dig a hole in which the fertilized eggs are deposited. In the male, the abdomen ends in a single tip without the ovipositor.

16. Examine your grasshopper and determine its sex. Examine someone else's grasshopper of the opposite sex.

The abdomen of the crayfish is adapted for fast movement in water. Muscles extend the length of the abdomen, and the last two segments bear broad flippers, forming a fantail. When the abdominal muscles contract, the fantail pushes strongly against the water, sending the crayfish backwards at great speed.

17. Look at the last two segments of the crayfish abdomen. The last segment is the central telson, which you observed in Part II, Step 2. The segment to which the telson is attached bears a pair of broad, flat *uropods.* The uropods and the telson form the fantail.

The respiratory organs of the crayfish are the gills, where the exchange of carbon dioxide and oxygen takes place. Gills are adaptations for life in water.

18. Place the crayfish dorsal side up. Lift the right edge of the carapace slightly, just above the walking legs. Note its thickness.

19. With scissors, carefully cut off the right side of the carapace. See Figure 2. Cut only the carapace.

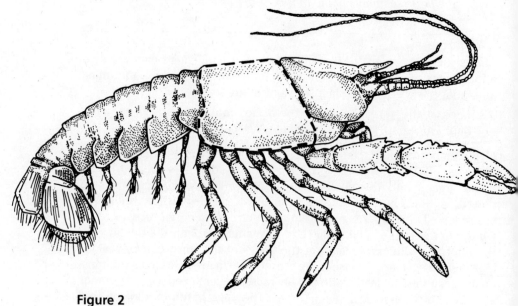

Figure 2

20. Observe the orderly arrangement of the gills. Note how they are attached to the legs.

q. *How many sets of gills can you see?*

_____

21. With thumb and forefinger, grasp the entire joint of the most posterior walking leg where it joins the body. Be sure you have a firm hold. Carefully twist and remove the leg with its attached gills. Be sure not to destroy the rest of the body.

22. Place the leg and gills in water in a Petri dish. Move the leg in the water so that the featherlike branches of the gill spread out. Note the large surface area provided by the fine branching.

The respiratory structures of the grasshopper are adapted for life on land. Insects are true breathers, forcing air into and out of their bodies by means of muscles. On each side of almost every abdominal segment is an opening called a *spiracle,* where air enters and leaves the insect. Each spiracle opens into a breathing tube, a *trachea.* The respiratory gases are not carried in the blood. They diffuse through the walls of the tracheae, which are supported by rings of chitin. There are also spiracles and tracheae in the thorax. Spiracles and tracheae are characteristic of insects.

Comparative Anatomy of Two Arthropods (continued)

23. Examine the lower sides of the abdomen and thorax.

  r. *How many spiracles can you see? How many are in the abdominal segments and how many are in the thorax?*

_____

_____

Analysis and Interpretations

1. For what anatomical characteristic are the arthropods named?

_____

2. Give three characteristics of arthropod bodies.

_____

_____

_____

3. What kind of symmetry is characteristic of arthropods?

_____

4. Give three characteristics of chitin that make it a good material for the exoskeletons and wings of arthropods.

_____

_____

_____

5. What three body regions are characteristic of insects?

_____

6. How do the body regions of the crayfish compare with those of the grasshopper?

_____

_____

_____

7. Give the meaning of this statement: "The crustacean exoskeleton is calcified."

_____

_____

8. Considering your own body, can you name any parts that are calcified?

_____

9. Discuss the vision of grasshoppers and crayfish. Confine your remarks to items you saw or read about during this laboratory activity.

_____

_____

_____

_____

_____

_____

10. How are the compound eyes of arthropods adaptive for catching prey and escaping predators?

_____

11. It has been said, "If humans could jump the way a grasshopper can, they could jump over barns." What characteristics of the grasshopper body help to accomplish such feats of jumping? (Think of the landing as well as the take-off.)

_____

_____

_____

12. What can a crayfish do well that a grasshopper cannot do at all?

_____

_____

Anatomy of the Starfish

Lab 49

Background

The starfish is a representative of the phylum Echinodermata, the spiny-skinned animals. Other members include brittle stars, sea urchins, sand dollars, sea cucumbers, and sea lilies. There are about 6000 species of echinoderms and all live in the ocean. The early life of a starfish is spent as a microscopic, bilaterally symmetrical, free-swimming larva. After a few weeks, the larva changes and becomes sessile, attaching to a surface on the ocean bottom. As further metamorphosis takes place, the right side of the larva becomes the upper surface of the starfish and the left side becomes the lower surface. The starfish continues to develop until it has short, stubby arms. At this stage it can move about, but it is still less than one millimeter in diameter.

Objectives

In this activity you will:
1. Study the external and internal anatomy of a starfish.
2. Observe characteristics of echinoderms.

Materials

preserved starfish   hand lens
   (*Asterias* species)   scissors
dissecting tray   dissecting needle
forceps   latex gloves

Alternate Approach: Use a model or a dissection guide of the starfish to complete this lab activity. If you have access to a salt-water aquarium, you may also wish to use a live starfish to complete this lab, omitting Part II. Ask your teacher about additional alternatives.

Procedures and Observations

PART I.   EXTERNAL ANATOMY _____

The starfish body consists of a *central disc* surrounded by a number of arms, or *rays.* There are most commonly five rays. But sun stars have 7 to 14 rays, and some sea stars found in Puget Sound have 15 to 24 rays and are almost a meter in diameter.

1. Examine the starfish. Refer to Figure 33-18 in your text for help in identifying structures. Distinguish between the ventral (oral) surface, where the mouth is located, and the dorsal (aboral) surface. Feel the spiny epidermis that covers and protects the body.

   a. *How many rays does the starfish have?*

_____

b. *What sort of symmetry does the starfish exhibit?*

___

2. Locate an ambulacral groove on each ray. The groove extends outward from the center on the oral surface. The edges of the groove have rows of movable spines that can close over the groove.

The starfish moves by means of *tube feet*. The tube feet are connected to a water-filled system of tubes and canals called the *water-vascular system*. A tube foot has a bulblike *ampulla* on one end and a sucker at the tip. When the ampulla contracts, water is forced into the tube, causing it to elongate. When the tube foot touches a surface, the sucker clings to it. When the tube foot contracts, water is forced back into the ampulla and the starfish moves forward. The tube feet also serve as a respiratory surface.

3. Look inside the ambulacral grooves. Locate the rows of tube feet.

c. *How many rows of tube feet does your specimen have?*

___

d. *Draw the oral surface of the starfish. Label the* mouth, ambulacral groove, *and* tube feet.

In the starfish, the only true sense organs are the *eyespots*. There is an eyespot on the oral surface of a small tentacle at the tip of each ray. An eyespot is made up of 80 to 200 *ocelli,* which contain granules of red pigment. The eyespots are sensitive to light, but no images are formed.

4. Find the small tentacle at the tip of each ray. Then locate the pink or red eyespot on the oral side of the tentacle.

Anatomy of the Starfish (continued)

49

5. Study the aboral surface of the central disc.

e. *What do you notice about the number of spines there?*

_____

6. Try to find the anus in the center of the aboral central disc. It opens out from the intestine.

Water enters the vascular system of the starfish through the *madreporite,* or *sieve plate.* Its surface is grooved, and more than 200 pores open downward from the bases of the grooves. The madreporite acts as a fine sieve or strainer for the water.

7. To one side of the central disc, between two of the arms, find the madreporite. Examine its surface.

f. *Draw the aboral surface of the starfish. Label a* ray, *the* central disc, madreporite, *and* anus.

The epidermis is spiny and irregular because parts of the endoskeleton protrude through the skin. The endoskeleton is an open framework of stonelike rods and plates called *ossicles.* The ossicles are composed of calcium carbonate and are embedded in connective tissue.

Around the base of the spines are *pedicellariae,* which are jawlike structures. They capture small animals and keep the epidermis free of foreign objects.

8. Feel the ossicles inside the starfish by pinching the rays.

9. Study the aboral surface with a hand lens. Locate a spine and the pedicellariae around it.

The *skin gills* are soft projections from the aboral surface, which are lined by tissue of the inner cavity. They provide a large surface area across which oxygen and carbon dioxide can be exchanged with the water. The skin gills are protected by the pedicellariae.

10. Using the hand lens, locate skin gills near some pedicellariae.

PART II.   INTERNAL ANATOMY

1. Without disturbing the madreporite, remove the skin from the aboral surface of the central disc. Use scissors and forceps. Be careful as you separate the skin from the digestive system underneath. Look for the intestine attached to the anus.

2. Remove the skin from the aboral surface of two rays. Note the animal's radial symmetry. Preserve all the internal connections to the central disc.

3. In the central disc region, note the short intestine with the *rectal caeca* on one side.

4. Locate the star-shaped *pyloric stomach* connected to the intestine from below.

A *pyloric duct* connects the pyloric stomach with the much-branched and pocketed *pyloric caeca*. There are two pyloric caeca in each arm. Their large surface areas are lined with secretory cells that secrete digestive enzymes.

5. Trace a pyloric duct from the pyloric stomach into one arm. Locate the pyloric caeca and remove them.

6. Locate the pair of gonads close to the central disc in the arm. They may be either testes or ovaries.

Starfish are famous for their method of feeding. Using the tube feet, a starfish attaches to a bivalve mollusk with its central disc opposite the *umbos*. It steadily pulls the valves of the mollusk until the valves open—an opening of 0.1 mm is enough. The starfish then everts its cardiac stomach (lower) and inserts it between the valves of the mollusk. Digestive enzymes are released and the mollusk is partly digested. The starfish absorbs the food and retracts the cardiac stomach into its normal position.

7. Underneath the pyloric caeca, find two gastric ligaments in each arm attached to the wall of the cardiac stomach. They serve to pull the cardiac stomach back into the body after feeding.

8. Cut away the gastric ligaments and look for the tubes of the water-vascular system.

9. Look underneath the madreporite. It leads into a *stone canal*. Trace the stone canal toward the oral surface. It leads to the *water-vascular ring* that surrounds the mouth.

10. Dissect out the water-vascular ring. Note a *radial canal* leading from the ring canal into each arm, connecting with the ampullas and the tube feet. Also note nine *Tiedemann's bodies* located along the water-vascular ring. The function of these structures has not been determined.

Anatomy of the Starfish (continued) 49

Analysis and Interpretations

1. Why can starfish move equally well in any direction?

_____

_____

2. What organs used for locomotion are seen only in echinoderms?

_____

3. What are two functions of the tube feet?

_____

_____

_____

4. Explain how a starfish feeds.

_____

_____

_____

_____

_____

_____

5. Describe the nature of the starfish skeleton.

_____

_____

_____

6. Give several functions of the pedicellariae.

_____

_____

7. How does respiration occur in the starfish?

_____

_____

8. What is the function of the pyloric caeca?

_____

_____

For Further Investigation

1. Find out the problems of maintaining a marine aquarium. Develop a plan that you will submit to your teacher for approval. Some questions to be considered are: What will you feed the animals in the marine aquarium? How will you maintain the required temperature? Who will care for the animals during vacations?

2. When you are at the ocean shore, try to find a live starfish and observe its behavior. Test its reactions to light by shielding it from the sunlight on one side. Test its reaction to being on the shore above water level by placing it about 3 meters (three long strides) above the water line. Find out what a starfish does when you turn it onto its aboral side. Does it turn itself over? How? Does it perform the same actions every time? After you have observed the starfish, be sure to return it to its normal environment.

Anatomy of the Perch

Lab 50

Background

The bony fishes, class Osteichthyes, are the largest group of living vertebrates. They are found in both fresh and salt water in all parts of the earth. The perch, a member of the order Perciformes, is often used as a representative bony fish.

Objectives

In this activity you will:
1. Observe the external and internal anatomy of the perch.
2. Identify basic characteristics of the bony fishes.

Materials

preserved perch	scalpel
dissecting tray	dissecting scissors
forceps	probe
hand lens	latex gloves

Alternate Approach: In Part I, use a dissection guide or observe a fish from an aquarium to study the specimen's external anatomy. In Part II, use a dissection guide or a model of a fish to study the organism's internal anatomy. Ask your teacher about additional alternatives.

Procedures and Observations

PART I.   EXTERNAL ANATOMY OF THE PERCH _____

1. Put on your gloves and wear them throughout this lab activity. Figure 1 on the next page shows the external structure of the perch. Compare your fish with the diagram and identify on your fish the parts labeled on the diagram.

   a. *Describe the general body shape of the perch.*

   _____

   b. *In what way does the body shape show adaptation for life in the water?*

   _____

   c. *Count the spines on each fin and write the number of spines on the line next to the name of the fin.*

   _____

EXTERNAL ANATOMY

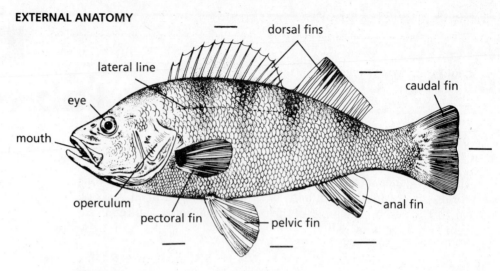

Figure 1

2. Examine the scales of your fish with a hand lens.

    d. *Describe the scales of the perch.*

_____

In fish, the position of the mouth is generally related to feeding habits. Where the mouth is on the ventral surface, the fish generally feeds on the bottom. Where the mouth is on the dorsal surface, the fish generally feeds at the surface of the water. In fish such as the perch, where the mouth is at the front of the head, the fish generally feeds by catching its prey from behind while swimming.

3. Examine the head and mouth of the perch. Using a scalpel or dissecting scissors, carefully slit the sides of the mouth if necessary to examine the throat. **CAUTION:** *Throughout this lab activity, use care when working with the scalpel.*

    e. *Describe the location of the eyes in the perch.*

_____

_____

    f. *Does the perch have any eyelids?*

_____

    g. *How many nostrils does the perch have?*

_____

    h. *Describe the teeth of the perch.*

_____

_____

The lateral line system consists of a network of tubules in the skin, which is beneath the outer covering of scales. Small branches of the tubules pass through the scales and open to the surface of the fish, forming the lateral lines visible on either side of the body. The lateral line system contains sense receptors sensitive to vibration.

Anatomy of the Perch   (continued)

50

4. Identify the lateral lines on your perch.

In the perch, water is drawn continuously into the mouth. The water passes through gill slits in the pharynx into the chamber that contains the gills. It flows over the gills and leaves the fish body through the opening created by the flap of the *operculum*, or gill cover. As the water flows over the gills, it gives up oxygen, which enters the gill capillaries, and picks up carbon dioxide that diffuses out of the gill capillaries.

5. Carefully cut off the operculum on one side of your perch. Do not damage the gills underneath.

6. Examine the gills, using a hand lens if necessary.

   i. *What characteristic can you observe in the gills that make them an efficient respiratory surface?*

_____

PART II.   INTERNAL ANATOMY OF THE PERCH _____

1. Figure 2 shows the incisions to be made for viewing the internal structure of the perch. Begin the incision on the ventral surface just forward of (anterior to) the anus. Be careful not to cut too deeply. You might destroy some of the internal organs. Use your scissors or scalpel and make an incision toward the head, as shown in the diagram. When you reach the gills, cut upward behind the gills. The incision along the side of the fish should be just below the lateral line. Very carefully lift away the cut section of the body wall. Use your scissors to cut any membranes that adhere to the body wall. Use your forceps to remove any fat covering the internal organs.

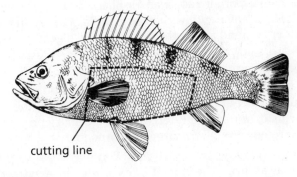

cutting line

Figure 2

2. Figure 3 shows the internal anatomy of the perch. Before you start to trace any of the organ systems, refer to Figure 3 and identify as many of the organs as you can in your fish.

   a. *Which organs could you see?*

_____

_____

_____

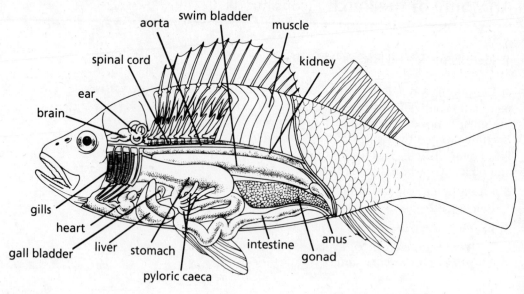

Labels on figure: aorta, swim bladder, muscle, spinal cord, kidney, ear, brain, gills, heart, gall bladder, liver, stomach, intestine, anus, gonad, pyloric caeca

Figure 3

From the mouth, food taken in by the perch passes into the short esophagus, which leads to the stomach. At the anterior end of the intestine, where it joins the stomach, are three pyloric *caeca*, which are digestive pouches. The liver, which is anterior to the stomach, is connected by ducts to the gallbladder. The pancreas is alongside the intestine but usually is hard to observe. The spleen is a dark red gland near the stomach.

3. Identify the organs of the digestive tract in your perch, including the liver and pancreas. Also identify the spleen. Cut open the stomach and examine the contents with a hand lens.

The swim bladder, or air sac, is an air-filled sac that enables the fish to maintain itself at any depth without expending energy. In the perch, the swim bladder is found above the organs of the digestive system.

4. Identify the swim bladder.

The kidneys are found against the body wall above (dorsal to) the swim bladder. Ducts carry urine from the kidneys to the urinary bladder. In the male, urine is excreted through a urinary pore. In the female, urine is excreted through the urogenital opening.

5. Identify the kidneys in your perch. You may have to pull the swim bladder away from the dorsal body cavity to expose the kidneys. Try to trace the ducts from the kidneys to the bladder and urinary opening.

b. *Describe the parts of the excretory system that you could identify.*

_____

_____

The heart of the perch has two chambers. Blood pumped by the heart passes into the ventral aorta, which carries it to the gills. From the gill capillaries, the blood passes into the dorsal aorta, which subdivides into an extensive arterial system. The arteries carry oxygenated blood from the gills to all the tissues of the body. Blood returns to the heart through the veins.

The two chambers of the perch heart are the atrium and the ventricle. The sinus venosus and bulbus arteriosus are enlargements of blood vessels leading to and away from the heart.

6. To see the heart, extend your ventral incision forward. With your forceps, gently remove the pericardial membrane covering the heart. Figure 4 shows the structure of the heart. Referring to the diagram, identify the two chambers of the heart and the vessels leading to and away from it.

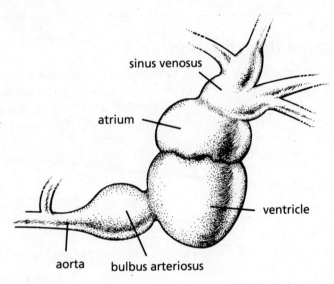

sinus venosus

atrium

ventricle

aorta   bulbus arteriosus

Figure 4

The sex organs, or gonads, of the fish are found in the trunk of the body posterior to the organs of the digestive system. In the male there is a pair of lobed testes. Ducts carry the sperm from the testes to the genital pore, which is located behind, or posterior to, the anus. In the female there is only one large ovary, which is a sac of eggs. The eggs pass from the ovary into the oviduct and leave the body through the urogenital pore located behind the anus.

7. Identify the ovary or testes of your perch. Study a fish of the opposite sex so that you have seen both the male and female reproductive systems.

   c. *Which sex is your perch?*

_____

_____

Analysis and Interpretations

1. What adaptation suggests that the perch is a predator?

_____

_____

2. What adaptations suggest that the perch is prey for other organisms?

_____

3. What did the stomach of the perch contain? What would you expect it to contain?

_____

_____

4. Organisms float more easily in salt water than in fresh water. Do you think the swim bladder would be larger or smaller in a saltwater species as compared to a freshwater species? Explain your answer.

_____

_____

For Further Investigation

Determine the age of the fish you dissected. Remove a scale from the perch with tweezers or forceps. Use a hand lens to observe the scales.The age of the fish can be estimated by counting the growth rings on its scales, which are comparable to growth rings on a tree.

Fish Respiration and Water Temperature

Lab 51

Background

Cold-blooded animals do not maintain a constant body temperature. Instead, the body temperature varies with the temperature of the environment. In these animals, the metabolic rate, which is also affected by temperature, can vary over a wide range.

The fish is a cold-blooded animal in which the exchange of respiratory gases occurs as water flows across the gills. The rate of respiration can be measured indirectly by observing how often the *operculum*, or gill cover, opens and closes. Changes in environmental temperature can affect the rate of respiration in fish.

Objectives

In this activity you will observe the effect of temperature on the respiration rate of a goldfish.

Materials

500-mL and 1-L beakers
aquarium water
thermometer
goldfish
fish net

crushed ice
stirring rod
water
hot plate

Procedures and Observations

1. Fill a 500-mL beaker about three-fourths full with aquarium water at room temperature. Using a thermometer, measure the water temperature.

   a. *Record the temperature of the water in the data table on page 307.*

2. With a fish net, remove a goldfish from the aquarium and place the goldfish in the beaker. **CAUTION:** *Be careful handling the fish throughout this lab activity to avoid injuring it.* Observe the behavior of the fish while it gets used to its new environment.

   b. *Record your observations in your data table.*

3. Count the number of times the fish opens its operculum in 15 seconds. Do this three times.

   c. *Record the respiration rate—operculum openings per 15 seconds—for each trial in the spaces below.*

   Trial 1: _____
   Trial 2: _____
   Trial 3: _____

   d. *Find the average respiration rate from the three trials and record it in your data table.*

4. Fill a 1-L beaker about one-third full with cold tap water and crushed ice. Use a glass stirring rod to gently stir the ice and water. Remove the stirring rod and place the beaker with the fish in the ice bath. Gently stir the water in the smaller beaker, being careful not to disturb the goldfish. Use the thermometer to check the water temperature in the beaker holding the goldfish. Observe the behavior of the fish while the water temperature drops. As soon as the temperature has dropped at least 10° C, remove the beaker from the ice bath.

   e. *In your data table, record the water temperature at which you removed the fish from the ice bath.*

5. Count the number of times the fish opens its operculum in 15 seconds. Do this three times.

   f. *Record the respiration rate per 15 seconds for each trial in the spaces below.*

      Trial 1: _____

      Trial 2: _____

      Trial 3: _____

   g. *Find the average respiration rate from the three trials and record it in your data table.*

   h. *How does this respiration rate differ from that at room temperature?*

   _____

   _____

   _____

6. Fill a 1-L beaker about one-third full with hot tap water. Heat the water on a hot plate. Stir the water with the glass stirring rod. Place the thermometer in the small beaker holding the fish, then place the small beaker in the hot-water bath. Use the glass stirring rod to carefully stir the water in the small beaker. Observe the behavior of the fish while the water temperature rises 10° C above the temperature of the water in the aquarium. **CAUTION:** *Do not allow the water temperature in the beaker holding the fish to rise above 35° C, or the fish may die.* Continue to record your observations in your data table. As soon as the temperature has risen sufficiently, remove the small beaker from the hot-water bath.

7. Count the number of times the fish opens its operculum in 15 seconds. Do this three times.

   i. *Record the respiration rate per 15 seconds for each trial in the spaces below.*

      Trial 1: _____

      Trial 2: _____

      Trial 3: _____

   j. *Find the average respiration rate from the three trials and record it in your data table.*

   k. *How does this respiration rate differ from that at room temperature?*

   _____

   _____

   _____

Fish Respiration and Water Temperature

51

8. Record your observations as you watch the respiration rate of the fish return to normal. Allow the temperature of the water to drop to room temperature gradually. Check the temperature of the water in the small beaker; when it returns to the temperature of the water in the aquarium, return the goldfish to the aquarium.

9. Graph your data in the space provided, showing how respiration rate changed with temperature. The x-axis of the graph shows the temperature in °C. Using the average respiration rate for 15 seconds, calculate the average respiration rate per minute. Add the appropriate numbers to the y-axis and plot your data.

Data Table

Temperature of Water (°C)	Average Resp./15 sec	Average Resp./min	Observations
At room temperature			
In ice bath			
In hot-water bath			

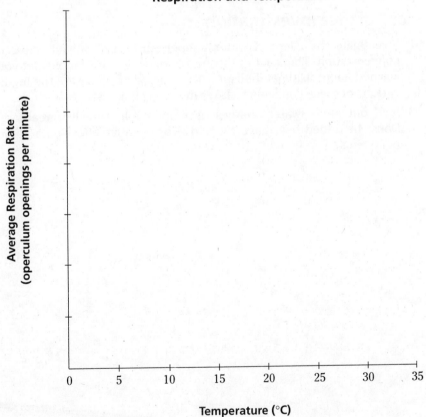

Respiration and Temperature

Analysis and Interpretations

1. How did the respiration rate change as the temperature changed?

_____

_____

2. At what temperature did the fish need the most food and oxygen? How can you tell?

_____

_____

_____

3. At what temperature was the fish's metabolic rate highest? Explain.

_____

_____

_____

4. What do you think happens to the activity of fish in cold climates during the winter months? Explain.

_____

_____

_____

For Further Investigation

1. Investigate the effect of water temperature on dissolved oxygen concentration. Think about this new information in light of what you learned about fish metabolism and temperature. What are the implications of these concepts to lakes in warm climates?

2. Find out about water sources used for cooling nuclear reactors. Does the added heat have a positive or negative effect on aquatic organisms?

External Anatomy of the Frog

Lab 52

Background

The frog is classified in the phylum Chordata because a gristly rod, the *notochord,* forms along the dorsal midline of the frog embryo. Frogs are classified in the subphylum Vertebrata because the adult frog has a segmented backbone, the *vertebral column*. Humans are also chordates and vertebrates. Although humans belong to the class Mammalia and frogs belong to the class Amphibia, their bodies show many similarities of structure and organization.

Objective

In this activity you will observe the external anatomy of the frog.

Materials

preserved frog (*Rana,* sp.)   hand lens
dissecting tray   forceps
scissors   dissecting needles
probe   latex gloves

Alternate Approach: Carefully examine the external anatomy of a live frog in Part I. Look for adaptations of the frog to its environment. Use a diagram or model of a frog for Part II. Check with your teacher about other alternatives.

Procedures and Observations

PART I.   EXTERNAL ANATOMY _____

1. Put on your gloves and wear them throughout this lab activity. Examine the body of the frog. It is mostly composed of a head and a trunk. Note that the neck is so short that it is almost nonexistent. But the frog can still move its head a limited amount.

   a. *What kind of symmetry is exhibited by the frog body?*

   _____

The frog skin has concealing coloration known as *countershading*. It tends to make the animal blend into its surroundings. Seen from above in dark water, the frog is hidden because its back is dark. Seen from below, the light-colored ventral skin blends with light coming from the sky. Seen from the side, the frog appears a perfectly even, camouflaged color—bright light from above illuminates the dark back of the frog while dimmer, reflected light from below illuminates the light underbelly.

The skin of the living frog is kept constantly moist and slippery with mucus secreted by mucus glands in the skin.

2. Observe the skin of the frog. Note the dark-colored dorsal side and the light-colored ventral side. With a hand lens, look closely at the skin surface.

   b. *Is the skin scaly or smooth?*

   _____

3. Observe the large mouth extending posteriorly on both sides of the head. Find the nostrils near the front tip of the head.

   c. *How many nostrils are there?*

   _____

The eyes of the frog protrude when they are open. The frog can close its eyes only by withdrawing them into their sockets. The upper eyelid is not movable, and the lower eyelid moves only slightly. The frog also has a third eyelid, a transparent *nictitating membrane* that closes upward over the eye. It protects the eye when the animal is on land, and allows the frog to see underwater. In the human eye, the "third eyelid" is a small fold of tissue in the corner of the eye next to the nose.

4. Examine the eyes of the frog. Try to identify the three eyelids.

The frog's outer ear is the *tympanum,* a flat, oval membrane. Sound waves cause the tympanum to vibrate. The vibrations are transferred to a small bone inside the ear, which in turn stimulates impulses in certain nerve endings.

5. Locate the tympanum, which is posterior to the eye on each side of the head.
6. Note the two dorsal folds of skin running from each eye to the anus, high between the hind legs.
7. Identify the two forelimbs and the two hind limbs.

   d. *Where are the four limbs attached?*

   _____

The forelimbs are used mainly to brace the body as the frog lands after a jump. They are also used for climbing, but not for swimming.

8. Observe a forelimb. Attached to the body is an upper arm. Find an elbow, a forearm, a wrist, a hand, and fingers.
9. Examine a hand.

   e. *How many fingers are on the hand?*

   _____

   f. *Is there any sign of a thumb?*

   _____

   g. *Are the fingers webbed?*

   _____

   h. *Are there claws on the fingers?*

   _____

External Anatomy of the Frog   (continued)

A living frog sits with its hind limbs folded and ready to jump.

10. Examine a hind limb. Attached to the body is the large thigh. The lower part of the limb is called the leg. Note the long ankle. The foot is attached to the ankle.

   i. *Describe the structure of the foot and toes of a hind limb.*

   _____

   _____

   j. *In the space below, draw a dorsal view of the frog, with the anterior end at the top. Label the* head, trunk, mouth, nostril, eye, tympanum, skin fold, anus, arm, hand, thigh, leg, *and* foot.

PART II.   MOUTHPARTS OF THE FROG

The mouth cavity of the frog is lined with a mucous membrane composed of ciliated cells. The large mouth surface is a part of the frog's respiratory system. Oxygen and carbon dioxide are exchanged across the lining of the mouth.

1. Place the frog ventral side up, anterior end toward you. With the scissors, cut the corners of the mouth on each side where the two jaws meet, so that you can open the mouth wide. Pull the lower jaw away from the upper jaw until you can see the back of the mouth. The back of the mouth becomes the pharynx (throat).

The frog can flip out its tongue to catch insects in flight. When extended, the tongue may be 6 to 8 cm long. A sticky mucus on the tongue helps to trap the insect. The insect is popped into the pharynx where it is swallowed whole. Frogs attempt to capture any moving objects small enough to be swallowed.

2. Examine the tongue.

   a. *Where is the tongue attached?*

   _____

   b. *Describe the shape of the free end of the tongue.*

   _____

3. Run your finger around the inside edge of the upper jaw. Use your hand lens to see the *maxillary teeth*. These hold a large insect in place until it can be swallowed. Then examine the lower jaw.

   c. *Are there any teeth on the lower jaw?*

   _____

The frog breathes through *nostrils*. To inhale, the frog lowers the floor of its mouth. The mouth fills with air through the nostrils. The nostrils then close by means of valves. To fill the lungs, the frog raises the floor of its mouth, pushing the air through the glottis. The air then passes through the larynx, or voice box, into the lungs.

4. The openings of the nostrils are near the anterior end of the roof of the mouth. Gently push the point of your probe into one nostril from the outside. Watch the tip enter the mouth. Then find the glottis, a slit in the raised area at the back of the mouth. Feel the opening with the point of the probe.

5. Between the openings of the nostrils in the roof of the mouth are paired *vomerine teeth*, bony ridges attached to the skull. Feel the vomerine teeth with the probe. Then examine them with the hand lens. These teeth are used for holding, not for chewing.

   d. *Describe the vomerine teeth.*

   _____

6. On each side of the upper part of the mouth, near the place where the two jaws meet, find the openings to the Eustachian tubes. The tubes connect the mouth with the middle ear.

7. At the back of the mouth, posterior to the glottis, is the opening to the esophagus, which leads to the digestive system. Push the handle of the probe into the pharynx to locate the opening. The wrinkled membranes indicate how much the pharynx can stretch to accommodate large pieces of food.

   e. *Make a drawing of the inside of the frog mouth. Label the* upper jaw, lower jaw, tongue, maxillary teeth, opening of nostril, glottis, vomerine teeth, opening to Eustachian tube, *and* opening to esophagus.

Analysis and Interpretations

1. Describe countershading in animal coloration. Of what advantage is it for an animal?

   _____

   _____

   _____

2. Describe the body covering of the frog.

   _____

   _____

3. How does a frog close its eyes? Describe the eyelids of a frog.

   _____

   _____

   _____

4. Describe the structure and functions of the forelimbs and hind limbs of the frog.

_____

_____

_____

_____

5. Explain how a frog captures and swallows an insect.

_____

_____

_____

Internal Anatomy of the Frog

Background

For many decades the study of the internal anatomy of the frog has been part of the laboratory program in biology courses. From a study of the frog, students can gain much information about the internal organization of vertebrate bodies in general. The structure and arrangement of organs and organ systems in the frog are very similar to those of the human body. When you have completed this laboratory study, you will know more about the organs and organ systems of your own body.

Objectives

In this activity you will:
1. Observe the internal anatomy of the frog.
2. Study the frog as a representative of the phylum Chordata, subphylum Vertebrata.

Materials

preserved frog (*Rana*, sp.)	dissecting tray with wax bed
dissecting scissors	dissecting needles
large dissecting pins	forceps
scalpel	hand lens
latex gloves	

Alternate Approach: Using a dissection guide or a model of the frog, examine the frog's internal anatomy. Using a chart of human internal anatomy, compare the frog to the human. How do the brains and hearts differ in the two organisms? Check with your teacher about additional alternatives.

Procedures and Observations

PART I.   DISSECTION OF THE FROG _____

1. Put on your gloves and wear them throughout this lab activity. Lay the frog in the dissecting tray, ventral side up, anterior end away from you. Look at Figure 1 on the next page to see where the incisions should be made. Each dissection line in Figure 1 has a dot where the cut should begin and an arrowhead indicating the direction of the cut. Pinch a bit of skin on the frog to feel its thickness. Note that the skin is free from the tissues underneath it.

2. Pinch up a bit of skin at the dot for line 1. Snip a V with the scissors. Cut through the skin only along line 1 shown in Figure 1, all the way to the chin. Then cut the skin along lines 2, 3, 4, and 5. This creates flaps of loose skin.

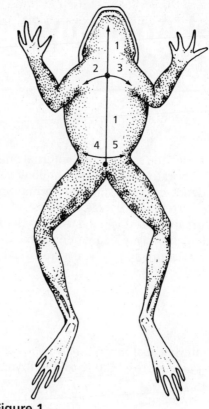

Figure 1

The skin of the frog is very important as a respiratory surface, especially in the winter when the frog hibernates in mud at the bottom of a pond or stream.

3. Lay back the skin flaps and examine the underside of the skin. Note the many fine blood vessels. Then cut off the skin flaps.

4. Examine the muscles of the ventral side of the frog. They are related to the head, thorax, and abdomen. Picture the movement of the frog body as each muscle contracts.

5. Look at Figure 1 again. With scissors, cut the muscle along line 1 just to the level of the forelimbs. Make a shallow cut so as not to damage the organs underneath. At the level of the forelimbs you have to cut through bone. The heart is directly beneath the bone, so work carefully. Slide the lower scissors blade just under the bone, forward toward the chin, until the scissors are opened quite wide. Then close the scissors together in one firm cut through the bone.

6. Continue to cut along line 1 all the way to the jaw bone. Cut through muscle only—do not destroy the floor of the mouth. Then make cuts along lines 2, 3, 4, and 5 through the muscles of the body wall.

7. Pin the specimen to the wax in the tray. Take hold of the two forelimbs and stretch them widely apart so that the chest cavity opens. See Figure 2. Place a large dissecting pin in each limb at an angle of about 45°. Push the pins firmly into the wax. Then pull the muscle flaps created by cuts 2 to 5 away from the body cavity. Place two large dissecting pins in each flap at 45° angles. Now the body cavity will be held open as you work.

Internal Anatomy of the Frog (continued)

Figure 2

8. If the frog is a female, two large masses of black eggs may be hiding the internal organs. The eggs are in thin ovary tissue so that you can see the separate eggs. After examining the egg masses, if you have a female, let other groups observe them. Then remove the egg masses by lifting them carefully and cutting the two ovaries free from the body.

The frog stores extra food at times of heavy feeding (in the summer) in the form of *fat bodies*. When food is scarce, or during hibernation, the fat bodies provide energy for life processes. They are necessary for the production of eggs and sperm in the spring breeding season.

9. Observe the yellow, finger-shaped fat bodies. If they are large, remove them. Then, at the anterior end of the abdominal cavity, find the two dark-red lungs. They may be deflated, long and thin, or inflated, like long, oval balloons. Note that the lungs connect anteriorly with the larynx and glottis.

The frog has a three-chambered heart. The two *atria* are the receiving chambers: one receives oxygenated blood from the lungs and one receives deoxygenated blood from the body. The *ventricle*, the pumping chamber, pumps the blood to the body.

10. Locate the heart. It is in a triangular *pericardial* sac in the center of the body between the forelimbs. Open the pericardial sac. Note the pointed ventricle. Anterior to the ventricle are the two atria.

The liver is the largest organ in the frog body. (It is also the largest gland in the human body.) Attached to the underside of the liver is the *gallbladder*, which stores *bile*. A *bile duct* connects the gallbladder to the intestine.

11. Locate the large liver. It is reddish-brown and has three lobes that overlie the abdominal organs and extend behind the heart. Carefully lift up the lobes of the liver and look at where they are connected to each other. Identify the gallbladder, which is a small, green-yellow sac attached to the liver. Then trim away most of the liver, leaving some tissue attached to the intestine.

12. Find the anterior end of the alimentary canal, the esophagus, posterior to the head. Trace the esophagus as it leads into the stomach, which is a curved, white sac. The stomach curves slightly to the frog's right side. The posterior end of the stomach leads into the small intestine, a small, coiled tube. Note that the liver is attached near where the stomach and small intestine join.

13. Find the pancreas. It is a feather-shaped organ located just dorsal to the stomach and is attached to the bile duct by a small tube, the *pancreatic duct*.

14. Trace the small intestine toward the posterior of the frog. Do not tear any tissue. Find where the small intestine joins the large intestine, a larger, shorter tube. The large intestine leads deep into the posterior abdominal cavity. Just anterior to the anus, between the hind limbs, the large intestine is joined by the urinary bladder, a two-lobed, thin-walled sac that may be lying on top or to one side of the large intestine.

15. Remove the alimentary canal from the abdomen. Hold the stomach as you snip the esophagus with the scissors. Gently free the tube from surrounding tissues in order to keep the organs intact. Then cut the posterior end of the canal as close to the anus as possible.

The small intestine is the principal organ of digestion and absorption of nutrients in the frog. As in most vertebrate digestive systems, it is held in place by a *mesentery* and supplied by blood vessels in the mesentery. The mesentery is a thin, fan-shaped membrane.

16. Examine the freed alimentary canal. Note the size of the stomach and the length of the small intestine. The small intestine is twisted into a helical form by the mesentery. Spread the coils of the small intestine a bit to see the shape of the mesentery and also to see the blood vessels in it.

17. Also attached to the mesentery is the small, spherical, dark-red *spleen*. Identify it. Normally it is centered in the abdominal cavity between the stomach and the large intestine.

The frog excretes one-third of its weight in urine each day because water is constantly entering the body through the skin. Urine is produced in the kidneys and passes through tubes to the *cloaca*, the posterior part of the large intestine. It can be released from the body through the cloaca, or it can be stored in the urinary bladder for a time. When frogs and toads are captured, they promptly empty their urinary bladder through the cloaca onto the captor. This often prompts the captor to release the animal—the desired response!

18. Locate the reddish-brown kidneys, deep in the posterior abdominal cavity on both sides of the backbone. Trace the path of urine from the kidneys through tubes to the cloaca.

19. On the ventral surface of each kidney, find a light-colored mass of tissue running almost the length of the kidney. These are the adrenal glands.

Internal Anatomy of the Frog (continued)

The male reproductive organs in the frog are the testes. In the frog and other amphibians, sperm travel to the cloaca through the same tubes as the urine.

20. If your frog is male, find the testes on the ventral side and anterior end of the kidneys. They are yellowish, oval bodies connected to the kidneys by tubes. Then observe a specimen of the opposite sex to see the reproductive organs.

In the female frog, the eggs produced by the ovaries are swept by cilia into the funnel-shaped openings of the oviducts near the tips of the lungs. The eggs pass through the oviducts in single file, all the way to the cloaca where they are released. As they pass through, they are coated with a jellylike material that swells as the eggs enter the water. Sperm from a male are released at the same time the eggs are released. Fertilization is external.

21. If your frog is a female, find the coiled, white oviducts. Then observe a specimen of the opposite sex to see the reproductive organs.

22. Examine the backbone, or vertebral column. Each bone is a *vertebra*. The vertebral column encases the spinal cord.

23. Note the stringlike pairs of spinal nerves emerging from between the vertebrae. There are 10 pairs of spinal nerves. Try to find the large *sciatic nerves* leading to the muscles of the thighs.

PART II. FURTHER INVESTIGATION IN THE FROG _____

1. With the scissors, cut the skin of the frog all the way around the top of one thigh where the leg joins the body. See Figure 3 on the following page.

2. Fold the skin downward, inside out, toward the knee, as in Figure 3. Then grasp the cuff of skin and pull firmly and steadily until the skin comes off over the knee. Be careful—if you pull too hard the skin might break. Also, if you hold the leg too firmly, the bone may break. A steady, firm pull is best.

3. The skin is difficult to detach at the ankle. Note its strength and its attachments. Continue to pull the skin until it comes off over the toes.

4. Examine the muscles of the thigh. Note that each muscle is separate. Pull on each muscle to find out what movement it produces when it contracts.

The calf muscle of the leg is called the *gastrocnemius*. It has the same name and same function as the calf muscle in the human leg. As in all muscles that move the skeleton, each end of the gastrocnemius muscle is attached to a bone by means of a *tendon*.

5. Examine the gastrocnemius. Find the upper tendon of the muscle and trace it to its attachment on a bone.

   a. *To which bone is the upper end of the gastrocnemius attached?*

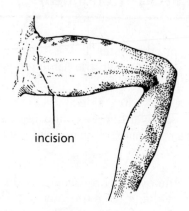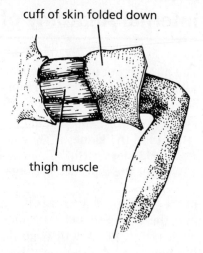

cuff of skin folded down

incision

thigh muscle

Figure 3

6. Cut the gastrocnemius free of its tendon near its upper attachment. Pull upward on the muscle to see how it moves the foot when it contracts.

7. Then pull down on the gastrocnemius, toward the foot and away from the skeleton. Firmly and steadily pull the lower tendon, the *Achilles tendon,* free from the ankle bone and remove the entire tendon from the foot.

b. *How is the tendon attached to the foot?*

---

8. Examine the foot and toe bones and the joints between them. All vertebrate skeletons are similar in form.

The lens of the eye in a living frog is crystalline and transparent. The lens does not change shape to focus as it does in the human eye. Frogs are nearsighted on land and farsighted under water.

9. With scissors, carefully dissect the eyeball. Remove the spherical lens. Note that it gathers light, even in its preserved condition.

10. With the tips of two dissecting needles, tease apart the lens to see its structure.

11. Place the frog dorsal side up and remove the skin from the skull with scissors or a scalpel.

12. With a scalpel, shave or whittle the bone of the skull between the eyes. **CAUTION:** *Use care in handling the scalpel. Direct the strokes of the scalpel away from your body.* Use very shallow strokes, peeling off the bone in layers or shavings. When the bone becomes thin, peel it off very carefully using forceps. Be sure not to dig the points of the forceps into the brain tissue. See Figure 4 on the following page.

The *cerebral hemispheres* of the brain control voluntary motion and conscious activities of the frog.

13. Identify the rounded cerebral hemispheres between the eyes.

The *olfactory lobes* are nerve centers for sensing odors. Nerves lead to these lobes from the nostrils.

Internal Anatomy of the Frog (continued)

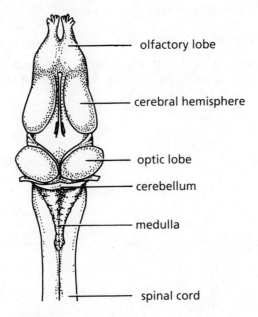

53

Figure 4

- olfactory lobe
- cerebral hemisphere
- optic lobe
- cerebellum
- medulla
- spinal cord

14. Continue to shave bone toward the anterior of the frog's head. Expose the olfactory lobes.

The *optic lobes* control the activities of the eyes.

15. Continue to shave bone, working posteriorly from the cerebral hemispheres. Locate the optic lobes, relatively large, hollow, rounded masses of midbrain tissue.

The cerebellum coordinates the muscular activities and controls the balance of the frog.

16. Posterior to the optic lobes, find the cerebellum, a very short section of the brain.

The *medulla* is the control center in the brain for breathing, swallowing, digestion, and reflexes.

17. Trace the cerebellum as it leads into the medulla.

18. Then locate the spinal cord as it begins at the posterior base of the medulla. Dissect a vertebra or two in order to see the spinal cord encased within the vertebral column.

Analysis and Interpretations

1. Explain how respiration occurs in three areas of the frog.

_____

_____

_____

_____

2. One atrium of the frog heart receives blood from the body, and the other receives blood from the lungs. Both atria deliver blood into the ventricle, which pumps the blood to the body. Is the blood pumped to the body oxygenated, deoxygenated, or both?

_____

3. List the parts of the frog alimentary canal, including the glands attached to it, beginning with the mouth and ending with the anus.

_____

_____

_____

_____

4. How does pancreatic juice get into the alimentary canal in the frog?

_____

_____

5. Describe the structure and function of the mesentery associated with the small intestine of the frog.

_____

_____

_____

_____

_____

_____

For Further Investigation

Save your frog specimen for additional study of the nervous system. After dissecting out the brain, continue dissecting the spinal cord. Follow as many spinal nerves as you can to see how the nerves are distributed into smaller nerves throughout the frog body.

Anatomy of the Fetal Pig (Part 1)

Lab 54

Background

Pigs are placental mammals and show the distinguishing characteristics of that group. In studying the anatomy of the fetal, or unborn, pig, you will see that its various organ systems are basically the same as those of humans.

To see the organs and organ systems discussed in this lab, you will have to do a very careful dissection. It is very easy to crush or remove important structures before you recognize what they are. You can avoid this problem by reading over the complete instructions for each part of the lab before beginning to work on the pig. You should also study accompanying diagrams and compare the structures you see with the diagrams. Except where you are instructed to use your scalpel or scissors, use forceps, probes, and dissecting needles to expose internal structures. Fatty and connective tissues should be removed carefully with a forceps.

Objectives

In this activity you will:
1. Observe the external anatomy of the fetal pig.
2. Observe the organs and organ systems of the abdominal cavity.

Materials

preserved fetal pig	dissecting tray
dissecting scissors	scalpel
probe	forceps
dissecting needles	dissecting pins
cord	microscope
slide	cover slip
metric ruler	latex gloves

Alternate Approach: Use a model of the fetal pig or a dissection guide to complete this lab activity. Ask your teacher about additional alternatives.

Procedures and Observations

PART I.   EXTERNAL ANATOMY OF THE FETAL PIG _____

Put on your gloves and wear them throughout this lab activity. Figure 1 shows the external anatomy of the fetal pig. Note that the back is the dorsal side and the belly is the ventral side. The head of the animal is anterior, while the tail end is posterior. Any reference to the right or left side refers to the pig's right or left side.

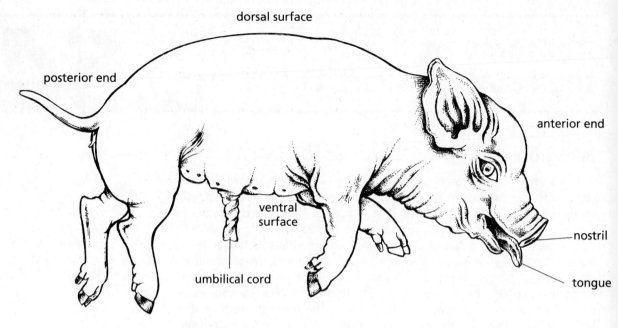

dorsal surface

posterior end

anterior end

ventral surface

nostril

umbilical cord

tongue

Figure 1

1. Pick up your pig and examine it. You can estimate the age of the pig from its length. Measure your pig from the tip of its snout to the base of its tail. Using the measurements given below, estimate the age of your pig.

   7 weeks: 28 mm   15 weeks: 220 mm

   8 weeks: 40 mm   17 weeks: 300 mm (length at birth)

   a. *What is the approximate age of your pig?*

The sex of a pig can be determined from the external structure. Both males and females have nipples on the ventral surface, so the presence of nipples cannot be used to determine sex. In both males and females the anus is located just beneath the tail. In males, the scrotal sac, which contains the testes, is located beneath the anus. The urogenital opening of the male is just posterior to the umbilical cord on the ventral surface. In females, the urogenital opening is beneath the anus, in a spikelike genital papilla.

2. Determine the sex of your pig.

   b. *Record the sex of your pig.*

---

3. Examine a pig of the opposite sex.

The umbilical cord contains blood vessels that connect the fetus to the placenta. In the pig, the umbilical cord extends from the midline of the ventral surface.

4. Examine the cut end of the umbilical cord. You should be able to see two arteries and a vein. The vein may be completely collapsed, which makes it difficult to find. If you cannot find the vein, use your scissors to make a fresh cut through the cord about 1 cm from the body wall, and examine the freshly cut end.

Anatomy of the Fetal Pig (Part 1)   (continued)   54

c. *In the box below, draw a cross section of the umbilical cord and label the blood vessels.*

[box]

5. Examine the feet of the pig.

  d. *How many toes does the pig have? How are the toes positioned?*

_____

PART II.   OPENING THE ABDOMINAL AND CHEST CAVITIES _____

1. Place the pig on its back in the dissecting tray. Tie a piece of cord around the "wrist" of one of the front legs. Run the cord under the width of the dissecting tray and tie it around the wrist of the other front leg. Pull the cord fairly tight so that the legs are spread apart. Secure the hind legs in the same manner.

2. Figure 2 shows where your incisions should be made. In making incisions use only the tip of your scalpel and do not press down hard. **CAUTION:** *Use the scalpel and dissection scissors with care throughout this lab activity.* Be particularly careful in the incision over the chest area. Begin the incision at the spot marked by the dot on line 1. Then make the incision shown by line 2, and so on.

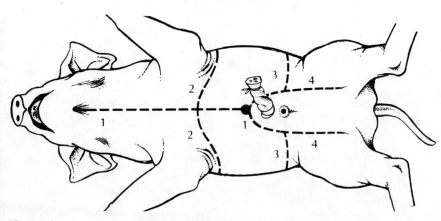

Figure 2

The ends of the diaphragm, the muscle that separates the abdominal and chest cavities, are attached to the body wall.

3. Gently pull apart the flaps of the body wall along the long incision between the front and hind legs. Do not lift the flap with the umbilical cord. As you separate the flaps under the front legs, use your scissors or scalpel to carefully cut the ends of the diaphragm at the body wall so that the flap can be pinned down.

4. Carefully pull up the flap with the umbilical cord a slight way. You will see the umbilical vein extending from the inside of the umbilical cord up through the liver, toward the head. In order to pull up this flap, use your scissors to cut the umbilical vein. Do not cut off the flap. After cutting the vein, just leave the flap extending backward between the hindlegs of the pig.

PART III.   THE ABDOMEN—DIGESTIVE SYSTEM

1. The organs of the abdominal cavity are covered by a membrane called the peritoneum. When you pulled apart the flaps of the body wall to expose the abdominal cavity, some of the peritoneum may have been pulled off. If not, carefully slit the peritoneum and then use your forceps to pull it off the organs of the abdomen.

2. Take your specimen and tray to the sink and rinse out the abdominal cavity.

Much of the upper part of the abdomen of the pig is filled by the red-brown liver, while the lower part is filled by the intestines. See Figure 3. The other organs of the abdomen can be seen by moving aside the liver and intestines.

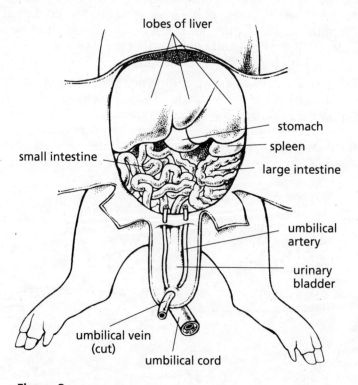

Figure 3

3. Examine the liver, both the upper and lower surfaces. Locate the gallbladder on the undersurface. Very carefully use your forceps to remove the peritoneum covering the gallbladder. Trace the duct that carries bile away from the gallbladder. Follow it until it enters the digestive tract.

   a. *How many lobes does the liver have?*

   _____

   b. *Describe the location and appearance of the gallbladder.*

   _____

   c. *Describe what happened to the duct from the gallbladder. Did it join other ducts? Where did the duct(s) end?*

   _____

   _____

   _____

4. When you have finished examining the liver, remove it. Identify the stomach. The long flattened, reddish organ that lies along the outer curve of the stomach is the spleen.

Find the junction of the stomach and the esophagus. Find where the stomach joins the small intestine. Cut open the upper surface of the stomach, beginning where it joins the esophagus and extending to the junction of the small intestine. Rinse out the stomach under running water and examine its inner surface, particularly where it joins the esophagus and small intestine.

   d. *Can you trace the esophagus very far from the stomach? Why not?*

   _____

   _____

   e. *Was the material that you found in the stomach food?*

   _____

   f. *The cardiac sphincter is found at the junction of the stomach and esophagus. Can you suggest its function?*

   _____

   g. *The pyloric sphincter is found at the junction of the stomach and small intestine. What is the function of this structure?*

   _____

5. Lift up the stomach and locate the pancreas. It is a whitish organ with a granular surface. The pancreatic duct extends from the end of the pancreas nearest the small intestine into the small intestine. However, it is very small and difficult to find.

6. Examine the small intestine, beginning at its junction with the stomach. Spread apart some of the coils of the intestine and note the mesentery, a membrane that holds the intestine in place. Blood vessels and nerves also run through the mesentery. Find the junction of the small and large intestines. Identify the caecum, a small pouch.

h. *Do the small and large intestine differ in external appearance? How?*

_____

7. Cut out a short section of the small intestine. Use a sharp scalpel to cut a very thin cross section of the small intestine. Put the section on a slide, then add a drop of water and a cover slip. Look at the slide under low power.

i. *What structural details can you see in the inner lining of the small intestine?*

_____

j. *Draw a cross section of the small intestine under low power.*

_____

PART IV.   THE ABDOMEN—UROGENITAL SYSTEM _____

1. If you have finished your study of the stomach and small intestine, very carefully remove them. Lift the stomach and, using scissors, cut it where it joins the esophagus. Then pull up the intestines and cut the large intestine, leaving a short section showing. Cut any attached blood vessels close to the intestinal walls. **Note:** *Be careful not to destroy the large blood vessels that lie beneath these organs.*

The large artery and vein that run along the midline of the dorsal surface of the abdomen are the aorta and the inferior vena cava. Branches from these vessels, the renal arteries and veins, serve the kidneys. Look at Figure 4 , the female pig, and Figure 5, the male, near the end of this lab activity.

2. Identify the abdominal aorta and the inferior vena cava.

3. Locate the kidneys, which are large, bean-shaped organs found against the dorsal body wall on either side of the abdomen. The kidneys are outside the peritoneum, so they will probably be covered by that membrane.

Anatomy of the Fetal Pig (Part 1) (continued) 54

Using your forceps, gently pull the peritoneum away from one kidney. Be particularly careful if your pig is a female because the small ovary is just below the kidney. Leave the kidney on the other side of the body intact.

4. On the side where the kidney is exposed, identify the renal artery and vein and the ureter, a large white tube that carries urine to the bladder. Examine the top, or head end, of the kidney.

   a. *What structure lies on top of the kidney?*

   _____

5. Trace the ureter from the kidney to the bladder, which is found in the flap of tissue containing the umbilical cord. Do not remove any structures that may be in the way. Just move them aside where necessary. Identify the urethra, which carries urine from the bladder to the outside of the body.

   b. *What blood vessels run on either side of the urinary bladder in the fetal pig?*

   _____

   c. *Describe the urinary bladder of the fetal pig.*

   _____

6. Use a sharp scalpel to cut through the kidney lengthwise midway between the front and the back. Remove the front half of the kidney.

   d. *Draw the cut section of the kidney. Show only the details that you can actually see. If you can see the three layers of the kidney, the* cortex, medulla, *and* pelvis, *draw them in and label them.*

7. Before starting your study of the reproductive system, you will have to open the pelvic region of the pig. Use your scalpel to make an incision, slightly to one side of the midline, through the flap containing the umbilical cord, toward the anus. See Figure 4. Pull back the skin, then carefully cut through the muscle and cartilage of the pelvis.

In the female pig, the small, kidney-shaped ovaries are found just below the kidneys. See Figure 4. Unlike the kidneys, however, the ovaries are inside the peritoneum. They are held in place by mesenteries. Eggs released from the ovaries enter the oviducts, which are twisting tubes that carry the eggs to the uterus. The uterus, which is small in the fetal pig, is found along the midline of the body. Extending from the uterus is the vagina. The vagina and the urethra share a single opening (the urogenital opening) to the outside of the body anterior to the anus.

8. If you have a female pig, locate an ovary. If you cannot find it on the side where you have studied and dissected the kidney, look on the other side. Remove any fat tissue that may be in the way, but be careful not to damage the oviduct and supporting membrane. From the ovary, follow the oviduct to the body of the uterus. Then trace the vagina toward the urogenital opening, and finally to the genital papilla on the body surface.

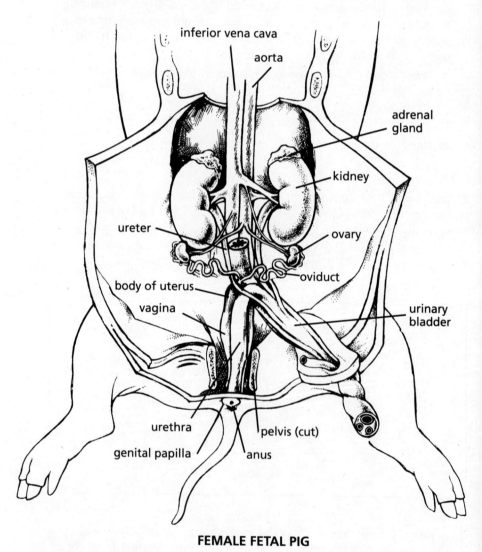

FEMALE FETAL PIG

Figure 4

In the fully developed male pig, the testes are located in the scrotum, a pouch found outside the body wall anterior to the anus. See Figure 5.

330

Anatomy of the Fetal Pig (Part 1) (continued)

54

The testes grow originally within the abdomen and descend into the scrotum as the fetus develops. The openings in the abdominal wall through which the testes pass are the inguinal canals. Sperm produced in the testes are stored in the epididymis, a small, coiled tube that lies next to each testis. The epididymis is continuous with the sperm duct. The sperm duct from each testis passes upward through an inguinal canal and enters the urethra. The urethra passes through the penis to the outside of the body.

9. If you have a male pig, carefully cut open one of the scrotal sacs and find one of the testes. (If the testes have not yet descended, they will be in the inguinal canals. Trace an inguinal canal either from the scrotum up or from the inside of the abdominal wall down, and locate the testes.) Identify the epididymis, which begins at the top, or head end, of the testis. Follow the epididymis around the testis, where it joins the sperm duct. Follow the sperm duct upward to where it enters the urethra.

Locate the penis, which is found in the strip of body wall that contains the urinary bladder. Both urine from the kidneys and sperm from the testes are released from the body through the penis.

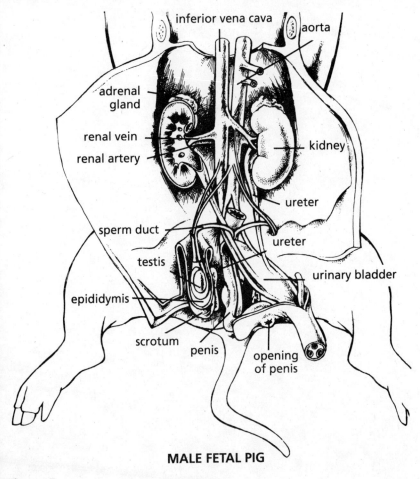

MALE FETAL PIG

Figure 5

Analysis and Interpretations

1. What is the function of the umbilical cord in the fetal pig?

_____

_____

2. What two body cavities are separated by the diaphragm?

_____

3. What is the name of the membrane that covers the organs of the abdomen?

_____

4. What small greenish sack is found on the underside of the liver?

_____

5. Would you expect to find food in the stomach of your fetal pig? Explain.

_____

_____

Anatomy of the Fetal Pig (Part 2)

Lab 55

Background

In this activity you will continue your study of the fetal pig. You will observe the organs of the thoracic, or chest, cavity as well as some of the structures of the mouth and the central nervous system.

Do your dissection slowly and carefully. Read each set of instructions completely before beginning work.

Objectives

In this activity you will:
1. Observe organs and organ systems of the chest cavity.
2. Observe structures of the mouth and of the central nervous system.

Materials

preserved fetal pig
dissecting scissors
probe
dissecting needles
cord

dissecting tray
scalpel
forceps
dissecting pins
latex gloves

Alternate Approach: Use a model of the fetal pig or a dissection guide to complete this lab activity. Ask your teacher about additional alternatives.

Procedures and Observations

PART I.   THE CHEST CAVITY—HEART AND LUNGS _____

Put on your gloves and wear them throughout this lab activity. The chest cavity, which contains the heart and lungs, is lined by membranes. The chest wall and the surface of the lungs are covered by the pleural membranes, while the heart is covered by the pericardium.

1. Gently pull apart the body wall of the chest along the incision made in Lab #54. Pin down the two flaps. See Figure 1 on the next page. Carefully remove any of the pleural membrane that has not been pulled away with the body wall. Note how the diaphragm forms a muscular floor for the chest cavity.

2. Examine the lungs.

   a. *How many lobes does the left lung have? the right lung?*

   _____

   b. *Are the lungs of the fetus functional?*

   _____

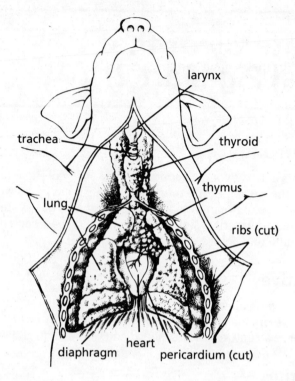

larynx

trachea

thyroid

thymus

lung

ribs (cut)

diaphragm

heart

pericardium (cut)

Figure 1

3. Lift the lungs out of the way and examine the heart, which is enclosed by the pericardium. See Figure 2. The upper, or head end, of the heart is partly covered by the thymus gland.

c. *Describe the relative size and location of the thymus gland.*

_____

_____

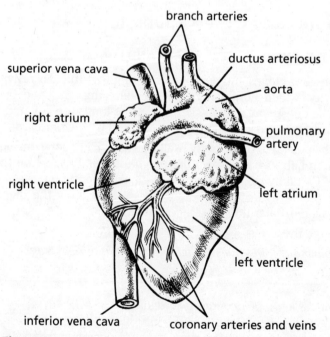

branch arteries

superior vena cava

ductus arteriosus

aorta

right atrium

pulmonary artery

right ventricle

left atrium

left ventricle

inferior vena cava

coronary arteries and veins

Figure 2

4. Remove the thymus and then cut away the pericardium around the heart.

   d. *Draw the heart in position in the chest. Label the* right *and* left atria *and* right *and* left ventricles. *In your drawing, put in any blood vessels that you see (without moving the heart).*

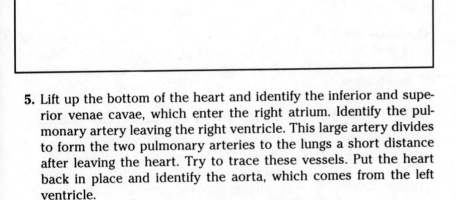

5. Lift up the bottom of the heart and identify the inferior and superior venae cavae, which enter the right atrium. Identify the pulmonary artery leaving the right ventricle. This large artery divides to form the two pulmonary arteries to the lungs a short distance after leaving the heart. Try to trace these vessels. Put the heart back in place and identify the aorta, which comes from the left ventricle.

In pigs (and in humans) there is a vessel called the *ductus arteriosus* that serves as a shunt between the pulmonary artery and the aorta prior to birth. In the fetus, where the lungs are not functioning in respiration, much of the blood bypasses the lungs. It passes from the right ventricle into the pulmonary artery and then through the ductus arteriosus to the aorta. At birth, the ductus arteriosus normally closes up, and all the blood from the right ventricle goes to the lungs.

6. Use scissors to very carefully cut the blood vessels around the heart. Do not cut them at the surface of the heart; cut at a short distance away. Leave enough of the vessels so that you can study their positions and relationships. **CAUTION:** *Use care in handling the dissection scissors and scalpel throughout this lab activity.*

7. Examine the back, or dorsal, side of the heart. Identify the ductus arteriosus.

 8. With a sharp scalpel cut through the heart lengthwise (the cut should be parallel to the front and back of the heart). You may not be able to see much detail of the internal structure of the heart.

e. *Describe as much of the internal structure of the heart as you can actually see from your dissection.*

_____

_____

9. With the heart removed, identify the trachea by its cartilage-ring structure. Find where it divides into the two bronchi, which enter the lungs. Identify the esophagus, which lies under (dorsal to) the trachea.

   f. *How do the esophagus and the trachea differ in structure and in appearance?*

   _____

   _____

The carotid arteries and jugular veins, which carry blood to and from the head, are found on either side of the trachea. Beneath, or dorsal to, them is the vagus nerve.

10. Identify the carotid artery, jugular vein, and vagus nerve.

    g. *Describe the vagus nerve.*

    _____

    _____

11. Follow the trachea upward toward the head. Locate the thyroid gland, which lies over, or ventral to, the trachea. It is reddish-brown and has two lobes. Find the larynx, which is at the top of the trachea.

PART II. THE HEAD

1. Examine the head of the pig. Open the mouth and examine the tongue, any teeth that are visible, and the back of the throat. If the teeth are not visible, you will probably be able to feel them in the gums. To view the epiglottis, glottis, and opening to the esophagus, use your scalpel to slit the corners of the mouth on both sides. See Figure 3. Also, note the hard and soft palates.

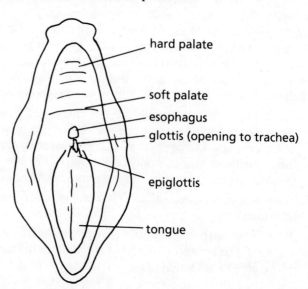

hard palate
soft palate
esophagus
glottis (opening to trachea)
epiglottis
tongue

Figure 3

Anatomy of the Fetal Pig (Part 2) (continued)

The pig has four pairs of salivary glands whose secretions are carried into the mouth by ducts. The largest of these is the parotid gland, which extends from the base of the ear to the shoulder and the jaw.

2. Using your scalpel, make an incision through the skin and facial muscles beginning at the base of the ear. See Figure 4. Be careful not to cut into the parotid gland, which lies beneath the muscle layer. Remove the skin and muscle layer and examine the parotid gland. Trace the duct from the gland as far as you can. Beneath the parotid gland is another salivary gland, the mandibular gland. Lift the parotid gland to see the mandibular gland.

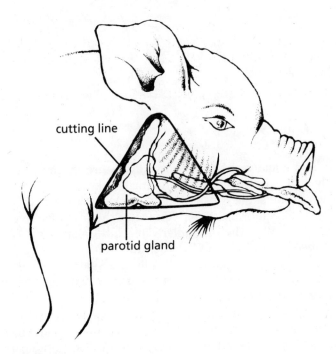

cutting line

parotid gland

Figure 4

a. *Describe the parotid and mandibular salivary glands.*

_____

_____

PART III.   THE NERVOUS SYSTEM _____

The nervous system of the pig is very similar to that of humans. There is the central nervous system consisting of the brain and spinal cord, and the peripheral nervous system consisting of cranial and spinal nerves and their branches.

1. Using your scalpel, make incisions through the skin of the head as shown in Figure 5. Peel off the skin. Look for lines in the skull, which indicate where the bones meet. Carefully insert the pointed end of your scissors between the bones. Then use the tips of your forceps to pull or break off pieces of the skull until you have opened up most of the skinned area.

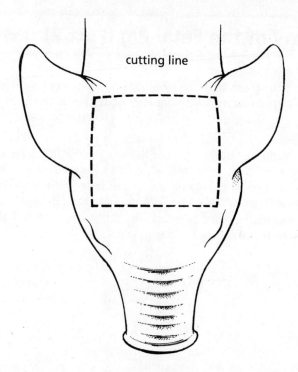

Figure 5

The brain and spinal cord are protected by three membranes known collectively as the meninges. The outermost of these membranes, which is just beneath the skull, is called the *dura mater*. It is the thickest and toughest of the membranes. The surface of the brain is covered by a thin membrane called the *pia mater*. The third membrane, called the *arachnoid membrane*, is found between the dura mater and pia mater. In living animals cerebrospinal fluid fills the space between the two inner membranes. In preserved specimens, the two inner membranes both adhere to the surface of the brain.

2. Cut through the dura mater, exposing the brain. See Figure 6. Identify the right and left cerebral hemispheres. Notice the deep longitudinal fissure between them. Identify the cerebellum, which is behind and beneath the cerebrum. Try to identify the medulla, which is behind and beneath the cerebellum. You may remove parts of the brain after you have identified them. In front of (anterior to) the cerebral hemispheres are the olfactory lobes, which are the brain centers for the sense of smell. Try to locate the olfactory lobes in your pig.

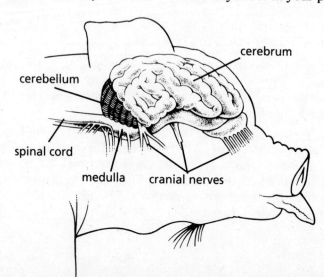

Figure 6

Anatomy of the Fetal Pig (Part 2) (continued) 55

    a. *Name the parts of the brain that you identified in your pig and describe the external appearance of each.*

_____

_____

The pig has 12 pairs of cranial nerves. These nerves mainly serve the sense organs of the head. The locations of the cranial nerves are shown in Figure 6.

3. Try to identify one or more of the cranial nerves.

The spinal cord is surrounded and protected by the vertebrae of the spinal column. In the fetal pig, the bones of the spinal column are not completely ossified (that is, developed from cartilage to bone), so they should not be difficult to cut.

4. Remove the skin from an area of the back so that about 8 to 9 centimeters of the spinal column are exposed. Use your forceps and carefully remove remaining tissues so that the spiny extensions of the vertebrae are completely exposed. You may notice thin white nerves that enter the back muscles. These are branches of spinal nerves.

5. Cut off the tops of the spiny extensions of the vertebrae with your scissors. This will expose the spinal cord and spinal nerves. The enlargements of the spinal nerves where they pass out of the vertebrae are the dorsal root ganglia.

Analysis and Interpretations

1. Arteries take blood away from the heart, while veins carry blood toward the heart. List the major arteries and veins you found around the fetal pig heart.

_____

_____

2. What is the function of the ductus arteriosus in unborn mammals?

_____

3. How does the ductus arteriosus improve the efficiency of fetal circulation?

_____

_____

4. Explain how the structure and function of the trachea differ from that of the esophagus.

_____

_____

_____

Identifying Adaptations in Birds

Lab 56

Background

Birds have many adaptations for flight. Hollow bones make birds light. Their feather-covered bodies are streamlined, which reduces air resistance. Strong flight muscles move the wings, and the wings provide aerodynamic lift.

Birds are also adapted to their food source and to their environment. Their beaks and tongues are shaped in ways that help in getting food. Their feet are modified to function in a particular environment.

The various sizes and shapes of beaks and tongues are adaptations for capturing, holding, and eating particular kinds of food. Tongues vary in length and shape. Some beaks are hooked or toothed for grasping and tearing; some are pointed for spearing food; some are long and thin, for probing flowers.

The legs and feet of birds are adapted for running, swimming, climbing, perching, seizing prey, and other activities. Toes on the feet may be long and slender, or short and stout. Many birds have a long toe that points backward. At the end of each toe is a nail, made of strong, hornlike material. Nails may be blunt or sharp. They may be long or short. The nails of birds of prey, such as hawks and owls, are called *talons*. These nails are very long, hooked, thick, and sharp.

Objectives

1. Observe adaptations of beaks of birds, and relate these to each bird's method of feeding.
2. Observe adaptations of legs and feet of birds, and relate these to each bird's environment.

Procedures and Observations

1. Examine the size and shape of the beak of each bird shown in Figure 1. Decide if each beak is long or short. A beak is *long* if it is the same size or longer than the bird's head. It is *short* if it is shorter than the bird's head.

   a. *Record these observations in Table 1 on page 346.*

2. You can determine the function of a bird's beak by examining its structure. The structure and function of various beaks are described in Table 2. Match these descriptions to the birds shown in Figure 1.

   b. *In Table 1, record the structure and function of each bird's beak.*

Pelican

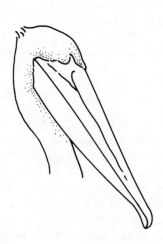

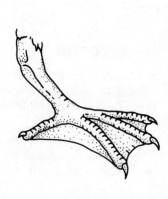

Heron

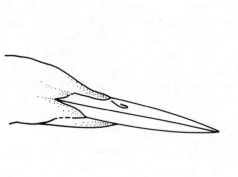

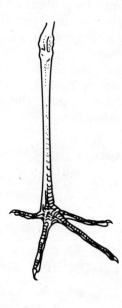

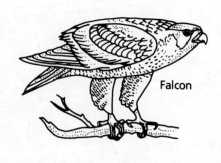

Falcon

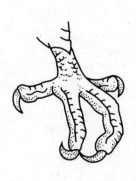

342

Identifying Adaptations in Birds (continued)

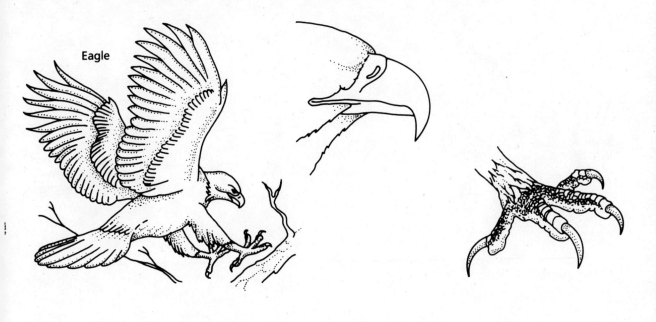

Eagle

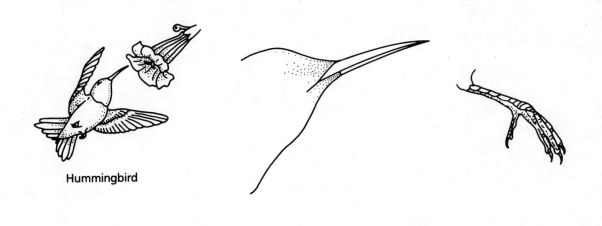

Hummingbird

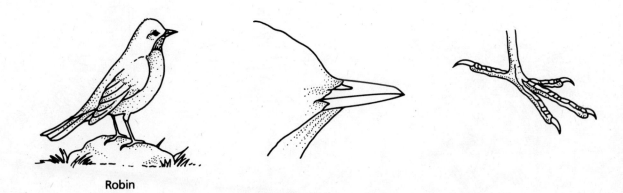

Robin

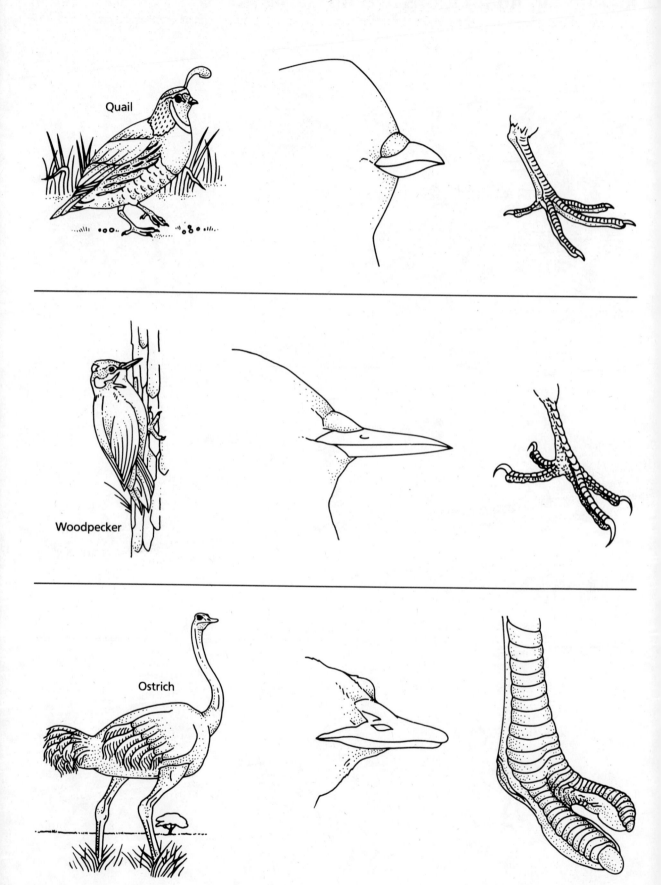

Quail

Woodpecker

Ostrich

Identifying Adaptations in Birds (continued)

Whippoorwill

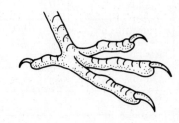

Jaçana

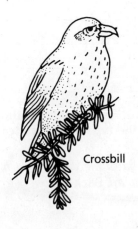

Crossbill

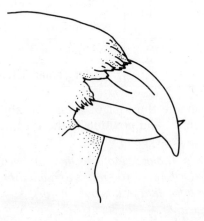

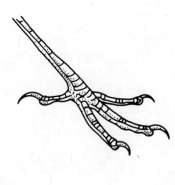

Table 1. Adaptations in Beaks of Birds

Bird	Length of beak	Structure of beak	Function of beak
Pelican			
Heron			
Falcon			
Eagle			
Hummingbird			
Robin			
Quail			
Woodpecker			
Ostrich			
Whippoorwill			
Jacana			
Crossbill			

Table 2. Sizes and Shapes of Beaks

Beak Structure	Function
short, hooked, thick	tearing flesh
short, very thick	cracking and crushing seeds
short, wide, with fringelike structures	trapping insects in the air
short, thick, hooked, with toothlike structure on each side of hook	capturing prey and tearing flesh
short, pointed	capturing worms and insects
short, with curved and crossed tips	prying open scales of pine cones
long, thin, pointed	probing into flowers to get nectar
long, straight, pointed	drilling into trees
long, thick, broad	capturing small animals, eating fruits, and picking up stones to mix with foods
long, with pouch	scooping fish
long, spear-shaped	spearing fish
long, straight, flattened slightly at tip	catching small fish and mollusks

3. Examine the foot of each bird shown in Figure 1. Notice that the number and position of the toes, as well as the type of nail, varies with the type of bird.

   c. *In Table 3, indicate the number and position of the toes for each bird.* Front toe *refers to a toe that points forward.* Back toe *refers to a toe that points backward.*

Identifying Adaptations in Birds (continued)

    d. *In Table 3, describe the type of nail of each bird.*

4. Use the descriptions given in Table 4 to determine the function of each bird's foot.

    e. *In Table 3, record the function of each bird's foot.*

Table 3. Adaptations in Feet of Birds

Bird	Toes		Nails	Function of foot
	front	back		
Pelican				
Heron				
Falcon				
Eagle				
Hummingbird				
Robin				
Quail				
Woodpecker				
Ostrich				
Whippoorwill				
Jacana				
Crossbill				

Table 4. Sizes and Shapes of Bird Feet

Foot Structure	Function
strong, thick toes; short, blunt nails	scratching
relatively long back toe, three front toes; short, sharp, curved nails	perching
webbing between toes; short nails	swimming
only two toes; short nails	running (on land)
very long legs and toes; short nails	wading
extremely long toes that are very widely spread; very long nails	running (over water plants)
two front toes, two back toes; nails are curved and pointed	climbing
stout toes; large, thick, very sharp, curved talons	grasping

Analysis and Interpretations

1. In the birds you studied, what was the most common function of the feet?

_____

2. What was the most common number and arrangement of toes on the birds that you studied?

_____

3. How are the beaks of the heron and pelican adapted for feeding on fish?

_____

_____

_____

4. How are the feet of a woodpecker adapted for the way the bird feeds?

_____

_____

_____

5. Some hummingbirds have longer beaks than others. How does this show that they are adapted for feeding on different flowers?

_____

_____

6. Imagine a bird with a certain habitat and feeding habits. What would this bird look like? What kind of beak and feet would it have? Describe the habitat and type of food that the bird would eat. Describe the physical characteristics of the bird

_____

For Further Investigation

1. Set up a bird feeder where you can see it from a window. Try putting out different kinds of bird food. Observe the birds that come to the feeder. Using binoculars, note the structure of the beaks of these birds, and try to determine the foods that different birds eat.

 2. Many bird watchers form clubs that go for bird-watching hikes. If such a group exists in your area, find out if you can accompany them on a hike. Be sure to get parental permission.

Investigating the Behavior of Ants

Lab 57

Background

At some time in your life you have seen a cat jump from the ground to a fence or a window sill. Even if you were at some distance from the cat, you knew it was a cat and not a dog. From your experience, you know that each animal has its own way of doing things, not only during one day, but all through its life. This special way of doing things is called an animal's **behavior.**

The biological study of animal behavior, which includes careful experiments carried out in the wild, *where the animal lives*, is called **ethology** (eh-*thahl*-uh-jee). In other kinds of behavioral studies, usually carried out in laboratories, people try to find out how animals change their behavior as a result of experience—how animals learn. Such studies are in the field of **animal psychology**. At the present time, ethologists and animal psychologists are combining their efforts to investigate how animals behave. From their knowledge about animal behavior, they hope to develop ways of controlling animals for their own benefit or for that of humans.

Keep in mind, however, that animals are *different* from human beings. They do not have human traits or feelings. Although we see animals do many things that people do, there are many things that we can do and they cannot do. Animals react only to signals of the present. Only humans have the ability to picture the future and plan for future needs.

In this activity you will investigate the behavior of ants, members of the phylum Arthropoda. In an ant community, all the individuals cooperate to support the colony. Each ant belongs to a caste, with a set role to play. In a colony there are at least two castes of females: worker females and the queen. Worker females are small, never develop wings, and perform most of the labor of the colony. These are the ants you are familiar with.

The queen is usually hidden within the nest. She bears wings until after her mating flight, usually in spring or summer. When she returns to the nest she loses her wings and crawls deep into the nest. There, in a special chamber she spends the remainder of her life laying eggs, constantly fed and cared for by the workers.

All females lay eggs, but only the fertile eggs laid by the queen develop into female ants. Males are hatched from unfertilized eggs laid by females other than the queen. The males develop wings at the time of the mating flight, in spring or summer. After the mating flight they do not return to the colony. During development, ants undergo the metamorphic stages typical of many insects: egg, larva, pupa, and adult. While in the larval stages, they are fed different kinds of foods by the workers. It is the different foods that cause them to become queens or worker females. The worker females are also fed different foods, so that they became either feeders, large soldiers, small soldiers, minor workers, or other specialized laborers, according to the characteristics of the species.

Objectives

In this activity you will:
1. Observe the behavior of one species of worker ants in an unfamiliar environment.
2. Answer questions about food-getting behavior and communicative behavior in ants in controlled settings.

Materials

ant colony: harvester ants *(Pogonomyrmex,* sp.)
    or mound-building ants *(Formica,* sp.)
large battery jar or other glass container
bits of sugar, cookie crumbs, or dry cereal crumbs
clean, sifted sandy soil   small watch glass
dark-colored paper   water-color brushes
honey or sugar syrup   small bits of carrot or potato
shallow glass baking dish,   small twigs
small blocks of wood,   small piece of sponge
green leaves   scissors
forceps   water

Procedures and Observations

PART I. MAINTAINING AN ANT COLONY _____

Obtain an ant colony. Your teacher will advise you about how to do this. Collecting ants requires knowledge of where to look for harmless species. Purchasing a colony is the safest and surest method of obtaining ants for study.

1. Place soil and ants (try to include a queen) in a large battery jar or other glass container. Watch the ants for a few minutes to see what they do.

   a. *What did you see the ants doing?*

   _____

   _____

   _____

   _____

   _____

   _____

2. Cover the container completely with dark paper and set in a dark cupboard for 48 hours. (Keep the container in the dark over weekends, also.)

3. Supply water every 2 days. Wet a small piece of sponge with water and place it in the container.

4. Supply food every 3–5 days. Only very small amounts are needed. Add bits of sugar to the soil. Or, add a few cookie crumbs, or crumbs of dry wheat breakfast food. Occasionally, add one drop of honey or sugar syrup to the soil, or place it on a dry leaf and set it on the soil. Small bits of carrot or potato may be added.

Investigating the Behavior of Ants (continued)

5. Watch all food for mold. Remove excess food to prevent mold, which may spread quickly through the soil and make the entire environment unfavorable for the ants.

6. After 48 hours, carefully remove the dark paper. Examine the contents of the container. Do not bump the container or disturb the ants.

   b. *What were the conditions in the container after 48 hours?*

_____

_____

_____

_____

_____

7. While maintaining the colony, watch the ants, and see how they live.

PART II. EXPERIMENTING WITH ANTS _____

While you observe ants, questions will probably come to mind as to how ants might behave under varying conditions. Experiments can be designed to try to answer these questions. A few words of caution: it is a mistake to try to predict the results of an experiment with the behavior of any animal. The purpose of the experiment is to *find out what the animal does* under certain conditions. Try not to confuse this idea with the thought that the animal is "supposed to behave in a certain way." In your observations, you can only record what you see the animal do. You should not be disappointed if the animal does not perform in some way that you expected. The answers to questions about behavior are not "right" or "wrong." They can be given only in terms of the behavior that you observe.

Since all animals search for food, or *forage*, the foraging behavior of ants can be studied within the container and outside of it. A sample question one might ask is: "Can ants vary their foraging behavior?" Another, related question is: "Will ants cross water to reach a food supply?"

Keep written records of the ants' activities as you carry out the following investigation.

1. Allow the ants to become hungry by not feeding them for an extra day beyond their usual feeding day. Place a few drops of honey, or a small amount of dry sugar on a small watch glass and set it in the container where food for the colony is usually placed. Record the time.

_____

2. At this point the entire class should agree on a time when Step 3 of the experiment (below) will end.

3. Observe the ants, making notes of their responses to the new conditions. If one ant finds the food first, record the time.

_____

a. *Describe an ant's behavior when it has found the food. Does it feed immediately? Does the ant seem to communicate in any way with other ants?*

_____

_____

_____

4. Work in teams of four. Arrange a shallow glass baking dish as shown in Figure 1. Pour water into the dish until the water is about 5 mm deep. A and B are small blocks of wood. They should be placed at least 2 cm from the sides and ends of the dish. They will remain in place if the water is not too deep. The blocks should not float. C is a small watch glass, which serves as a shallow container for food. To prepare this, dry the watch glass thoroughly and place several drops of honey, or a small amount of sugar, in it. With the forceps, carefully place the watch glass in the water in the position shown. The watch glass should not float.

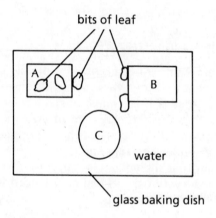

Figure 1

5. Prepare several bits of leaves by cutting green leaves into pieces large enough to support two or three ants. Place a few leaf bits in the water, as shown in Figure 1. Also, place a few bits on block A.

6. At this point, the entire class should agree at what time this part of the experiment will end.

7. On block B, place six to eight hungry ants, transferred from the colony in this manner: touch the end of a small twig to the soil directly in front of an ant, until the ant climbs the twig. Hold the twig in a vertical position as the ant climbs upward. Change hands before the ant reaches your fingers, and allow it to climb to the end of the twig. Quickly transfer the ant to block B, using the camel hair brush if necessary. With a little practice, you will learn how an ant moves, and you will be able to transfer one easily.

It is important to transfer at least six ants. Ants are social insects, and they normally function in groups. Observing a sample of only two or three ants would be a very poor indicator of the typical behavior of ant communities. Keep in mind, however, that the behavior of a small group of ants in any artificial situation such as this will not be entirely representative of normal behavior in larger, more natural ant colonies.

Investigating the Behavior of Ants (continued)

57

8. Record the time when all ants have been transferred.

9. Observe the ants' behavior. Perhaps each member of the team will follow the behavior of a certain ant. It may be possible to record the amount of time spent exploring, or the number of times each ant enters the water, if it does so. If you can differentiate the ants, you might want to assign them numbers or give them names. After you have accumulated some notes, you will be able to organize them to see what responses the ants have made.

b. *Record the activities of the ants, noting the time whenever possible.*

_____

_____

_____

_____

_____

10. Share your findings with other teams in class, either by recording on the blackboard or by means of a report given by one member of your team.

Analysis and Interpretations

1. In the study of animal behavior, how does the work of an ethologist differ from that of an animal psychologist?

_____

_____

_____

_____

_____

_____

_____

2. In addition to learning about animals, how can people hope to benefit from the findings of ethologists and animal psychologists?

_____

_____

_____

_____

_____

_____

3. If you perform studies of ants such as those in this activity, are you playing the role of an ethologist or of an animal psychologist? Give the reason for your answer.

_____

_____

_____

_____

_____

4. Describe any signs of communication between ants that you observed.

_____

_____

_____

_____

For Further Investigation

Get permission from your parents to study a colony of mound-building ants in their natural state. Find an ant mound in a sunny, grassy meadow, or on the southern slope of a hill. **CAUTION:** _Watch out for poison ivy and any other poisonous plants._ You will need a piece of string 10 meters long, a small watch glass, a small vial of honey, a small jar of white or yellow poster paint, a few toothpicks, a small notebook, a pencil, and a watch.

Use the string to measure a distance of 20 meters from the ant-mound. Set the watch glass with a few drops of honey at this distance. Keep the watch glass well shaded and out of direct sunlight. Using a twig, transfer six ants to the watch glass. After the ants have fed on the honey for a few minutes, use a toothpick to paint a tiny spot on the back of each of the six ants. Return the ants to the ant mound and record the time. Observe the watch glass and the ant mound. Record the movements of the ants at specific time intervals. Note whether any paint-marked ants return to the honey. Look for signs of communication among the ants.

Learning About Population Density

Lab 58

Background

Many populations of organisms interact in a biological community. An environment can successfully support a certain number of individuals of each population. The number of individuals in a population in a certain area is known as the *population density*. The largest population density that a certain environment can support is called its *carrying capacity*.

Biologists often attempt to measure the population densities of an area. Although fluctuations in population density are normal, large changes can indicate a serious problem—one that could harm the whole community. Human interference in the natural balance of biological communities has often resulted in unexpected and undesirable consequences.

Objectives

In this activity you will:
1. Practice one method of measuring population density.
2. Calculate the change in population density of one species.

Materials

meter stick
pencil
string

tongue depressors
notebook paper

Procedures and Observations

PART I.　MEASURING POPULATION DENSITY _____

One way to measure the population density of an area is to divide the area up into smaller areas called *quadrats*. The number of organisms in each quadrat is counted. The numbers are added up and then divided by the combined area of the quadrats to calculate the population density.

A biologist first decides on the area to be studied. The size of the quadrats is then determined—they can be large or small, depending on the organisms being studied. For example, the population density of raccoons in a forest could not easily be measured in quadrats of 1 square meter. Much larger quadrats would be used.

You will determine the population densities of three kinds of weeds in an area by studying a quadrat 1 meter square and pooling your results with those of your classmates.

1. Go to the location that your teacher assigns. Set up a quadrat of 1 square meter. Measuring carefully, place four stakes (tongue depressors) 1 m apart at the corners of the square. See Figure 1.

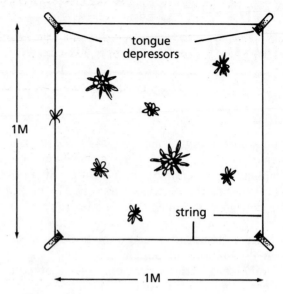

1M

tongue
depressors

string ——

1M

Figure 1

2. Then tie a piece of string around the perimeter of the quadrat.

   a. *Draw the quadrat to scale in the space provided. The box below has 10-cm sides, so your drawing will be on a scale of 1:10. Include in your diagram physical features (such as rocks, trees, and pavement) that happen to fall within your sample plot.*

Learning About Population Density (continued) 58

3. Study Figure 2 so that you can recognize dandelion, plantain, and clover plants.

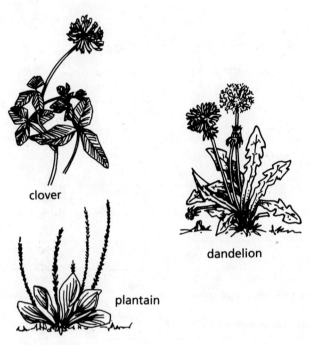

Figure 2

4. To count the plants in your quadrat accurately, you will have to divide the quadrat into smaller areas. Lay the meter stick along one side of the quadrat. See Figure 3. Lay a piece of string across the quadrat 10 cm from the boundary. Count the number of dandelion, plantain, and clover plants in section 1 of the quadrat.

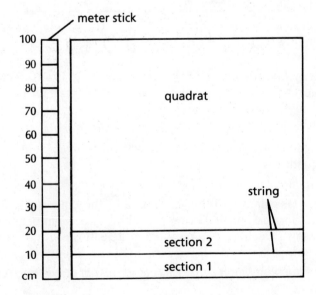

Figure 3

b. *In Table I, record the number of each of the three types of plants found in section 1.*

Table 1.   Numbers of Plants in a 1-m Quadrat

Section	Dandelion	Plantain	Clover
1			
2			
3			
4			
5			
6			
7			
8			
9			
10			
Total			

c. *Using the symbols shown in Figure 4, plot the approximate locations of the weeds on your quadrat drawing.*

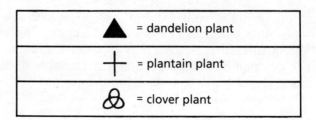

Figure 4

5. Repeat Step 4 until you have counted and mapped the 10 sections of your quadrat. Use the meter stick and string to mark off the section you are counting.

   d. *Complete Table 1 and the drawing of the quadrat.*

6. Total the numbers of dandelion, plantain, and clover plants counted in your quadrat.

   e. *Record the totals in Table 2 on the next page and on the board.*

7. Copy the class data in Table 2. Then add the columns to get the class totals for each plant. Divide each total by the number of groups in the class to calculate the population densities of the three types of plants/m^2.

   f. *Record the population densities (plants/m^2) of dandelion, plantain, and clover.*

Learning About Population Density (continued)

Table 2. Population Densities of Plants in a Community

Class Groups	Dandelion (total)	Plantain (total)	Clover (total)
Total			
Population density	/m^2	/m^2	/m^2

PART II. BALANCE OF POPULATION DENSITIES IN A COMMUNITY

The sizes of populations in a community are regulated in many ways. The story of the Kaibab deer shows how populations were balanced in one community and how humans upset this natural balance. In the early 1900s, the Kaibab plateau, north of the Grand Canyon in Arizona, supported a population of about 4000 deer on over 700,000 acres. Predators, such as coyotes, wolves, and pumas, helped to keep the deer population in check. It was estimated at that time that the plateau had a carrying capacity of about 30,000 deer, so that there seemed to be plenty of food for the population that existed.

Ranchers who moved into the area lost many sheep and cattle to the predators. In an effort to save livestock and increase the deer population the predators were hunted. With the successful removal of many of the natural predators, the deer herd increased dramatically in size. In 1924 there were 100,000 deer, as shown on the graph on page 360. This number was far in excess of the carrying capacity of the Kaibab plateau. As a result, 40,000 deer died in 1925 from starvation and disease. The population continued to decrease over the years and in 1940 returned to near its original level.

1. Examine the graph below.

   a. *Determine the approximate population density in deer/1000 acres for each year below.*

   Example for 1905: $\dfrac{4000\,\text{deer}}{700,000\,\text{acres}} = \dfrac{x\,\text{deer}}{1000\,\text{acres}}$ $x = 5.7$ deer/1000 acres

   1905 _____

   1915 _____

   1920 _____

   1925 _____

   1935 _____

Kaibab deer population 1905–1940 (In thousands)

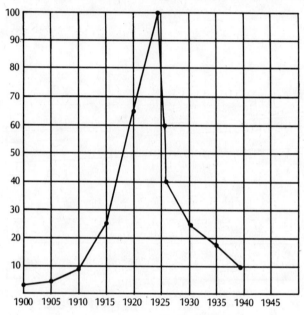

Analysis and Interpretations

1. Why is the class average a better measure of population density than an individual quadrat?

   _____

2. What environmental factors might affect the densities of the dandelion, plantain, and clover populations?

   _____

   _____

3. How would you measure the density of a mobile population, such as mice on a prairie or fish in a pond?

   _____

   _____

   _____

Learning About Population Density (continued)

4. What would be the population density of deer at the Kaibab plateau's carrying capacity (30,000 deer)?

_____

5. Explain the large increase in the deer population from 1905 to 1924.

_____

_____

6. Name some factors that contributed to the large change in the sizes of the deer population from 1925 to 1930.

_____

7. What role do predators play in biological communities? Why are they necessary for a balanced community?

_____

_____

_____

8. What happens if the population density of an organism increases beyond the limits of its food supply?

_____

9. What steps could have been taken to maintain the number of deer at the 1915 level?

_____

_____

_____

10. What changes in the community do you think occurred as the deer population increased?

_____

_____

Computer Activity

In Laboratory Experiment 58 you determined the population densities of several plants by counting how many of each there were in a square-meter area. The computer simulation *Oh, Deer!* requires you to manage a population of deer by *monitoring* the density of deer in an eight-square-mile area.

Field Study of a Terrestrial Community

Lab 59

Background

A terrestrial community is more than a collection of plants and animals. It involves complex interactions between the *biotic* (living) and *abiotic* (nonliving) factors of the environment.

A study of a terrestrial community consists of many separate investigations. The area is mapped; soil is analyzed; data on microclimates in several areas are collected; many organisms are tracked and identified; and population densities are determined. The outcome of such an investigation is a comprehensive record of a community.

Objectives

In this activity you will:
1. Investigate a terrestrial community.
2. Observe biotic and abiotic factors in a community

Materials

For outdoor work:

measuring tape	tongue depressors
string	meter stick
magnetic compass	notebook paper and pencil
graph paper	thermometer
light meter	sling psychrometer
relative humidity table	wind gauge
small shovel	plastic bags
keys to plants and animals	insect net
hand lens or magnifier	small collecting jars of ethyl alcohol

For work in lab:

graduated cylinder	slides and cover slips
methylene blue stain	microscope
ethyl alcohol	Berlese funnel apparatus
nutrient agar Petri dish	inoculating loop
soil sifter or screen	Bunsen burner
soil test kit	

Procedures and Observations

PART I.   MAPPING YOUR QUADRAT _____

1. Go to your assigned location and set up a quadrat of the size specified by your teacher. Use a measuring tape, compass, string, and tongue depressors to measure and mark your quadrat. **CAUTION:** *Watch out for biting or stinging insects and for poison ivy and other irritating plants. Tell your teacher of any serious allergies you may have.*

2. Prepare a map of your quadrat on graph paper. Use an appropriate scale; write the scale used in one corner of the map. On the map, indicate bushes, trees, grasses, ponds, paths, fences, and other features of the area on the map. Be able to locate your quadrat accurately on the larger community map in class.

PART II.   MICROCLIMATE DATA

1. Identify possible different microclimates in your quadrat.

   a. *Briefly describe the location of each microclimate in Table 1.*

2. At location 1, use a thermometer to measure the air temperature 1 m above the ground.

   b. *Record the air temperature in Table 1.*

3. At location 1, measure the soil temperature 5 cm below the surface of the ground.

   c. *Record the soil temperature in Table 1.*

4. Use a light meter to determine the light intensity at eye level.

   d. *Record the light intensity in Table 1.*

5. Use a sling psychrometer and relative humidity table to find the relative humidity of the air.

   e. *Record the relative humidity in Table 1.*

6. Use a wind gauge to determine wind direction and speed just above your head.

   f. *Record the wind direction and speed in Table 1.*

7. Repeat Steps 2 through 6 for each location you identified in Table 1.

Table 1.   Microclimate Data: Date: _____   Time: _____

Location of microclimate	Air temperature (°C)	Soil temperature (°C)	Light intensity	Relative humidity	Wind direction and speed

PART III.   SOIL TESTING

1. Choose a site in your quadrat to study the soil.

   a. *Describe the location.*

Field Study of a Terrestrial Community (continued) 59

2. Dig up a cube of soil 10 cm on a side. Immediately place the soil sample in a plastic bag and tie it closed. Further study will take place back in the lab.

A Berlese funnel may enable you to see any small organisms in your sample.

3. In the laboratory, place several cubic centimeters of your sample on the Berlese funnel grid, or screen. See Figure 1. Pour a few milliliters of ethyl alcohol into the collecting bottle. Turn on the light and leave overnight or until the sample is dry. When the sample is dry, examine the alcohol with a magnifier and then with a microscope.

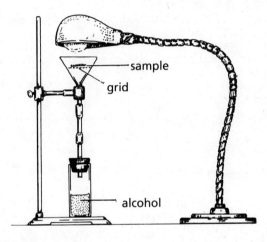

Figure 1

b. *In the space below, sketch what you found in the alcohol. Label each organism with its approximate size and estimate the number of each type of organism in the alcohol.*

Bacteria and molds that live in the soil can be grown on a Petri dish.

4. Sterilize an inoculating loop by holding it in a Bunsen burner flame until the loop glows red. Dip the sterile loop into the soil sample and streak the surface of the agar in a Petri dish. Cover the dish, tape it closed, and leave it in a warm place.

5. After a few days examine the agar for growth. **CAUTION:** *Do not open the Petri dish. It is possible that some of the bacteria on the agar could cause disease.*

   c. *How many different colonies can you see? Describe them.*

   _____

   _____

6. Sift the soil sample. Observe the color and relative moisture content (wet, damp, or dry). Note any living things in the sample.

   d. *Record your observations.*

   _____

   _____

7. After the contents settle, observe them. Note any layers of gravel, sand, or silt.

   e. *Record your observations.*

   _____

   _____

8. Following your teacher's instructions, use the soil test kit to determine the pH as well as the humus and phosphorus content. Perform any other available tests.

   f. *Record your observations.*

   _____

   _____

9. Place a small amount of the soil on a clean slide and observe it under the microscope. Use both low and high power.

   g. *Record your observations.*

   _____

   _____

10. Place a small amount of the soil in a drop of water on a clean slide. Add a drop of methylene blue stain and a cover slip. **CAUTION:** *Do not allow methylene blue to stain your hands or clothing.* Observe the soil under both low and high power.

    h. *Record your observations and sketch any organisms that you see.*

    _____

    _____

    _____

Field Study of a Terrestrial Community (continued) 59

PART IV.   POPULATION DENSITY OF PLANT GROUPS _____

For this activity, you can classify plants into four groups.
Trees: woody, usually with one main stem
Shrubs: woody with many stems
Herbs: nonwoody plants, grasses
Floor covering: mosses, lichens, algae, leaf litter, fungi

1. Observe the plants in your quadrat. Then classify them into the groups listed above and count the numbers of each.

   a. *Record the types of plants and their numbers in Table 2.*

2. For a rough estimate of the population density, divide the number of each type of plant by the area of the quadrat.

   b. *Record the population density of each group of plants in Table 2.*

Table 2.   Population Density of Plant Groups

Type of plant	Number	Population density

PART V.   ANIMAL IDENTIFICATION _____

1. Observe any animals, other than insects, in your quadrat. Watch for birds and small mammals in trees, and amphibians and reptiles at ground level. Note their approximate numbers.

   a. *Record your observations.*

_____

_____

2. Note any signs that indicate the presence of animals, such as tracks, hair, nests, droppings, or burrows.

b. *Record your observations.*

_____

_____

_____

3. Use any available reference books to identify the animals that you see.

c. *Record the names of any animals that you can identify.*

_____

_____

PART VI. INSECT IDENTIFICATION _____

1. Try to catch insects by sweeping an insect net through low vegetation. When you catch an insect, put it in a small jar of alcohol. As you collect, record the place where you found the specimen. Watch out for biting and stinging insects.

2. Check the leaves of bushes and small plants, as well as the ground surface for insects. Look under logs and rocks for crawling bugs. (Be sure to replace the logs or rocks.) Place the insects in a jar of alcohol and take them back to the laboratory. Record the place where you found each specimen.

3. In the laboratory, use an insect identification key to identify the insects that you caught. There may be many larvae that you will have trouble identifying. A hand lens or stereomicroscope may be helpful in making identifications.

a. *Record the kind, location in the community, and number of insects that you caught.*

_____

_____

_____

Analysis and Interpretations

1. How does your quadrat differ from other quadrats? Is there a feature of the area that you studied that is peculiar?

_____

_____

2. How is the microclimate related to the organisms living in your quadrat?

_____

_____

_____

Field Study of a Terrestrial Community (continued)

3. Compare the microclimate data of various groups. What are the major differences found in the data?

_____

_____

_____

4. What do the soil organisms do when the heat from the light bulb begins to dry out the soil in the Berlese funnel?

_____

_____

5. Compare soil data from various quadrats. Relate the moisture content, settling layers, and soil test results with the numbers of organisms found.

_____

6. What was the most common plant group of your quadrat? Does your observation agree with other groups?

_____

7. What was the most common insect in your quadrat? Did other groups have the same result?

_____

8. Examine the data collected by other groups in the class. Describe differences between your quadrat and the rest of the community.

_____

For Further Investigation

1. Dominant organisms provide habitats and set up conditions that are favorable for other types of organisms. Give an example of this in the community you studied.

2. Looking at class data, compare the number and variety of organisms found at each different site. How does environment seem to relate to the kind of organisms found?

3. What could be done to increase the number of soil organisms found? Design an experiment to test your hypothesis.

4. The niche of an organism is its role in the community and its position in the food web. Briefly describe the niche of one of the organisms that you observed in the community.

5. Make a partial food web using at least ten of the organisms found in the community.

Ecological Succession in a Microenvironment

Background

Ecological succession in an ecosystem is the gradual replacement of one community of organisms by another. Succession occurs because of changes in the biotic and abiotic characteristics of the environment. These changes often favor certain populations over others, so the new populations thrive while the old ones decline. Eventually, with time, a stable climax community that is resistant to change is established.

Most examples of succession must be studied over a period of many years. It takes a great deal of time for succession to occur in the environment. But a pond culture can be used as a small-scale example of succession and can show results in a relatively short period of time.

Objectives

In this activity you will:
1. Start a pond culture.
2. Observe ecological succession in the pond culture.

Materials

established pond culture	500-mL beaker
large jar with lid	hay, dried grass, or lettuce
hot plate	cold-water bath
medicine droppers	aged water
glass-marking pencil	thermometer
slides	cover slips
microscope	pH paper

Procedures and Observations

PART I.   STARTING THE POND CULTURE _____

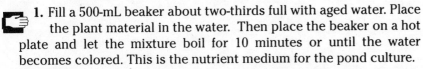

1. Fill a 500-mL beaker about two-thirds full with aged water. Place the plant material in the water. Then place the beaker on a hot plate and let the mixture boil for 10 minutes or until the water becomes colored. This is the nutrient medium for the pond culture.

2. Allow the beaker to cool. When the beaker is cool enough to touch, place it in a cold-water bath until it has cooled to room temperature. Then pour the liquid portion of the nutrient medium into a clean glass jar.

3. Add 2 or 3 medicine droppers of the established culture to the nutrient medium. Be sure to take the samples from different areas of the culture—top, middle, and bottom.

4. Using a glass-marking pencil, draw a line level with the liquid in the jar. Write your name on the jar. Then loosely place the lid on the jar and set it aside in a well-lighted area away from direct sunlight.

PART II.   OBSERVATION OF THE POND CULTURE _____

1. Observe the pond culture. If any water evaporates, add aged water to refill the jar to its original level. Note the color, cloudiness, odor, and any layers settling out.

   a. *Record the date and your observations in Table 1.*

2. Make three wet mounts of the pond water, taking one sample from each part of the culture—top, middle, and bottom.

3. Examine each slide under the microscope, first under low power, then high power. Use Figure 1 to help identify the organisms in your pond culture. Count the number of each kind of organism on each slide. Then average the numbers for each kind.

   b. *Record any organisms that you observe in Table 1.*

   c. *Record the average number of each organism in Table 1.*

4. Test the pH of the pond culture.

   d. *Record the pH in Table 1.*

5. Repeat Steps 1 to 4 daily, or as instructed by your teacher.

Table 1. Observations of Pond Culture

Date	Appearance of culture water	pH of culture water	Organisms in culture

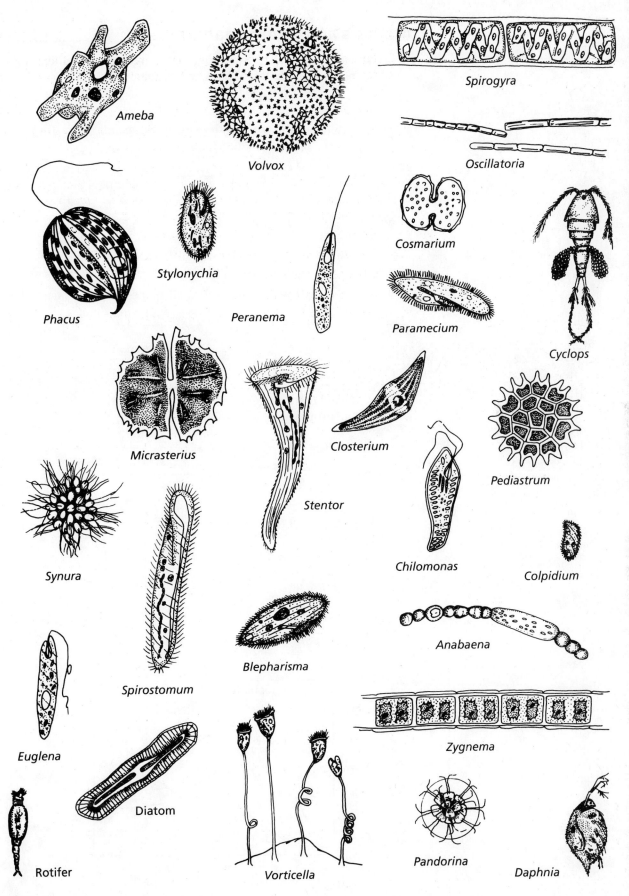

Figure 1

Analysis and Interpretations

1. Do you think that any living organisms remained in the nutrient medium after you boiled it? If so, what organisms?

_____

2. What happened to the pond culture organisms after they were added to the nutrient medium?

_____

_____

3. What organisms were the first to become abundant in your pond culture?

_____

4. Did you see any evidence of ecological succession? If so, describe it.

_____

_____

_____

5. What caused the changes in the biotic and abiotic parts of the pond culture environment?

_____

_____

_____

6. Explain Figure 2 in terms of ecological succession.

_____

_____

_____

_____

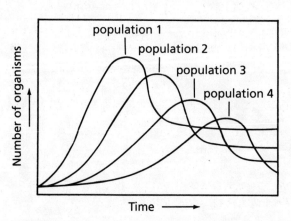

Figure 2

Climates and Biomes
_____ Lab 61

Background

A biome is defined as a large geographic region that has a particular type of climax community. Biomes are identified by the characteristic plants that dominate the landscape (such as grasslands) or by physical features and climate (such as deserts or tundra). While you are probably familiar with many of the biomes of the world, you may not know what causes biomes to exist. The kinds of plants and animals that coexist and survive in a particular area are determined by the soil, topography, and climate in that area. Biomes take many years to establish. Keep in mind that their boundaries are not as distinct as we would like to think of them, and actually blend into each other.

Objectives

In this lab you will:
1. Investigate some of the physical processes that determine climate.
2. Graph climate data from different places.
3. Classify climate graphs into general biome categories.
4. Use your graphs to compare various biomes.

Materials

graph paper   ruler
colored pencils   political/relief maps of
calculator   North America

Procedures and Observations

PART I.   LATITUDE AND RADIANT ENERGY _____

Because the earth is shaped like a sphere, the sun's rays strike the earth at different angles. Look at Figure 1 on the next page. Although the amount of energy striking points A, B, and C is equal, the amount that is absorbed depends on the angle of the sun's rays.

1. Consider the effect that latitude has on radiant energy (heat) absorption.

   a. *Why is more radiant energy absorbed at A than at B or C?*

   _____

   _____

   b. *What immediate effect would the amount of radiant energy striking a part of the earth have on that place?*

   _____

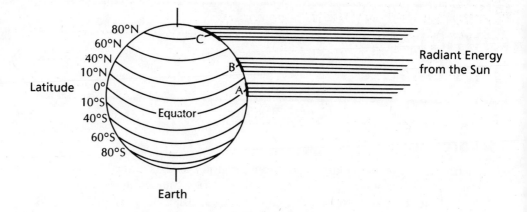

Latitude

Radiant Energy from the Sun

Earth

Figure 1. Latitude and Radiant Energy

c. *In general, what happens to temperature as one moves north or south of the equator?*

_____

PART II. EFFECT OF LARGE BODIES OF WATER _____

Land warms and cools quickly. Places near the middle of a continent will experience temperature extremes—hot summers and cold winters. Water, however, warms and cools more slowly than land. In fact, ocean temperatures in a given region do not vary much during the year. This causes the temperatures in coastal areas (where the wind blows off the water) and on islands to be consistent throughout the year.

Large lakes and oceans also add humidity to the air and increase precipitation. "Lake effect" snow results from cold air blowing across a large lake, gathering moisture and then, upon further cooling, dropping moisture in the form of snow on the shoreline and slightly inland.

a. *In which of the cities shown in Figure 2 would the most consistent temperatures be found?*

_____

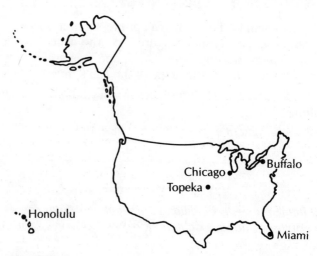

Figure 2

Climates and Biomes (continued)

b. *Where would extremes in temperature be expected?*

_____

c. *Where would the most precipitation be expected?*

_____

d. *Where would precipitation likely fall as "Lake Effect" snow?*

_____

PART III.   MOUNTAIN EFFECTS _____

The most obvious mountain effect on climate is the elevation effect. As elevation increases, average temperature decreases.

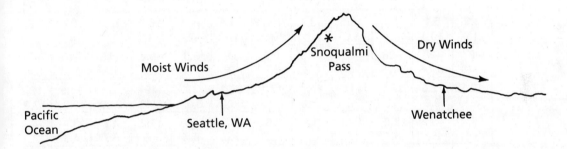

Figure 3. Effects of Mountains on Climate

a. *Would you expect Seattle or Snoqualmi Pass to have a higher annual average temperature?*

_____

_____

b. *How is altitude on a mountain similar to the effect of latitude in Part I?*

_____

_____

_____

When moist air from over the ocean is blown inland toward a mountainous area, the air is pushed up by the mountain and cooled. Cooling causes condensation and so rain or snow falls on the mountainside close to the ocean. By the time the air moves over the top of the mountain, it has lost its moisture. Moving down the other side of the mountain, the air is warmed. It becomes a warm, dry wind.

c. *Which place shown in Figure 3 would have the greatest annual precipitation?*

_____

d. *Which place would have the lowest annual precipitation ?*

_____

e. *Which place would have the most snowfall?*

_____

PART IV.   GRAPHING CLIMATE DATA _____

Scientists often put data into graphic form for analysis. This makes the information easier to interpret and understand.

1. Study the data in Table 1, which was collected from the National Oceanic and Atmospheric Administration (NOAA).

Table 1

City	Month												Temperature (°C) (boldface top number) Rainfall/Precipitation (cm) (bottom number)
	J	**F**	**M**	**A**	**M**	**J**	**J**	**A**	**S**	**O**	**N**	**D**	
Portland, OR	**3.3** 15	**6.1** 10.4	**7.8** 9.1	**10.5** 5.6	**13.9** 5.3	**16.7** 4	**19.4** 1.3	**19.4** 2	**16.7** 4	**12.2** 9.1	**7.2** 14.2	**5** 15.2	
Pt. Barrow, AK	**−27** 0.48	**−28** 0.44	**−26** 0.28	**−18** 0.28	**−7.5** 0.3	**0.6** 0.9	**3.9** 2	**3.3** 2.3	**−0.8** 1.6	**−8.5** 1.3	**−18** 0.58	**−24** 0.43	
Santa Monica, CA	**12.1** 8.1	**12.3** 8.6	**12.9** 5.3	**14.5** 3.2	**15.8** 0.28	**17.1** 0.15	**19.1** 0.02	**19** 0.05	**19** 0.43	**16.5** 0.99	**14.5** 2.9	**12.7** 7.2	
Des Moines, IA	**−5.2** 3.1	**−3.2** 2.8	**2.2** 3.1	**10.4** 6.3	**17** 10.2	**23** 12.3	**25.2** 7.6	**24** 9.7	**19.2** 7.6	**13** 5.7	**3.8** 4.3	**−2.4** 2.8	
Minneapolis, MN	**−10.9** 1.8	**−9** 2	**−2.4** 3.8	**6.8** 4.7	**14** 8.1	**19.2** 10.2	**22.4** 8.3	**21.1** 8.1	**15.7** 6.1	**9.4** 4	**−0.4** 3.6	**−7.7** 2.2	
Wichita, KS	**0** 2.5	**3** 2.5	**7.5** 4.3	**13.5** 8.9	**18.2** 9.7	**24** 12.5	**27.1** 8.6	**26.7** 7.3	**22** 8.1	**15.6** 5.4	**7.3** 4.3	**1.9** 2.8	
Phoenix, AZ	**10.5** 1.8	**12.8** 1.5	**15.5** 2	**20** 0.76	**24.5** 0.25	**29.4** 0.25	**32.8** 2	**31.7** 3	**28.9** 1.8	**22.2** 1.3	**15.5** 1.3	**11.6** 2	
Nashville, TN	**3.3** 12.2	**5** 11.2	**9.4** 12.7	**15.5** 10.4	**20.5** 10.4	**25** 8.6	**26.7** 9.7	**26.1** 8.1	**22.2** 7.9	**16.1** 5.6	**8.8** 8.9	**4.4** 11.4	
Winnipeg, Manitoba	**−19** 2.1	**−16** 1.8	**−8** 2.3	**3** 3.9	**11** 6.6	**17** 8	**20** 7.6	**18** 7.5	**12** 5.3	**6** 3.1	**−5** 2.5	**−14** 1.9	
Fairbanks, AK	**−24** 2.3	**−19** 1.3	**−13** 1	**−1.4** 0.6	**8.4** 1.8	**14.6** 3.6	**15.3** 4.7	**12.4** 5.6	**6.3** 2.8	**−3.2** 2.2	**−15.6** 1.5	**−22** 1.4	
New Orleans, LA	**11.6** 11.4	**13.3** 12.2	**16.1** 13.9	**20.5** **10.7**	**23.9** 10.7	**26.7** 12	**27.7** 17	**27.7** 13.5	**25.5** 14.2	**21.1** 5.8	**15.5** 9.9	**12.8** 13	
Pittsburgh, PA	**0** 7.1	**0.5** 5.8	**4.5** 8.8	**11.2** 8.6	**16.9** 9.6	**21.8** 10.1	**23.8** 9.1	**22.8** 8.8	**18.9** 6.8	**12.3** 6.4	**5.9** 5.9	**0.6** 6.3	

a. *Use the data in Table 1 to make graphs of average temperature and average precipitation versus month of the year for each city. A sample graph for Portland, Oregon, is shown on the next page. Label each graph with the city whose weather data is plotted.*

Climates and Biomes (continued)

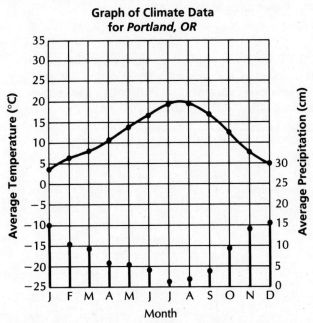

Graph of Climate Data for *Portland, OR*

Use your graphs to classify each city in a biome. Consider the range of temperatures and the total amount of precipitation.

b. *Complete Table 2 by filling in the column marked "Examples" with the name of the cities which fit in each biome.*

Table 2

Name	Yearly Average Rainfall/ Precipitation	Yearly Temperature Range (winter lows and summer highs)	Examples
Tundra	1–12 cm/yr.	Very Cold Winters (−28°C) Summers (3–12°C)	
Taiga	Far north (8 cm) West (40 cm) Central (50 cm)	Cold Winters (−25°C) Short Summers (20°C)	
Temperate Deciduous Forest	60–150 cm/yr.	Cold Winters (−10°C) Warm Summers (26°C)	
Temperate Grassland Prairie	25–75 cm/yr.	Cold Winters (−5°C) Warm Summers (28°C)	
Mid-Latitude Rain Forest	90–200 cm/yr.	Small Year-Round Variance Winters (2°C) Summers (20°C)	
Chaparral	Dry Summers (0.3 cm) Wet Winters (3.5 cm)	Cool Winters (12°C) Warm Summers (20°C)	
Desert	Less Than 25 cm/yr.	Winters (8°C) Summers (39°C) Large Daily Variation	

Analysis and Interpretations

1. Look at the graphs of Pt. Barrow, Fairbanks, Winnipeg, and Minneapolis. Locate them on a map. Explain how the temperature and precipitation change with latitude.

_____

2. Graph the data given below for Walla Walla, Washington. Then compare this graph carefully with the Portland graph on page 379. Locate these two cities on a map. Explain the differences in yearly temperature range and precipitation.

_____

_____

_____

	Temp. (°C)	Precip. (cm)
J	0.6	4.8
F	3.5	3.8
M	7.8	3.9
A	12	3.6
M	16	3.8
J	19.5	3
J	24.5	0.5
A	23.2	0.75
S	18.9	1.9
O	12.8	3.8
N	5.7	4.3
D	3.2	4.7

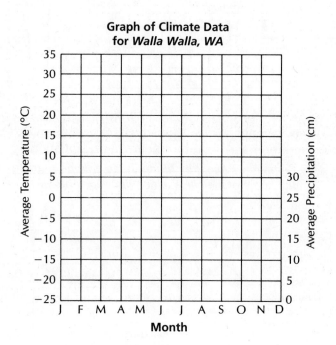

Graph of Climate Data for *Walla Walla, WA*

3. Which of the locations was difficult to place into a biome? Why?

_____

_____

_____

4. What seems to be the difference between the graphs of Des Moines and Nashville? Is this enough to separate the two places into separate biomes?

_____

_____

_____

Climates and Biomes (continued)

5. Graph the following data given below for Chicago, IL. In what biome might Chicago be classified?

_____

_____

	Temp. (°C)	Precip. (cm)
J	−4.4	4.8
F	−2.7	4
M	2.8	6.9
A	10	9.6
M	15.5	8.6
J	21.7	10.1
J	23.9	10.4
A	23.3	7.8
S	18.9	7.6
O	12.8	6.6
N	4.4	5.6
D	−1.6	5.3

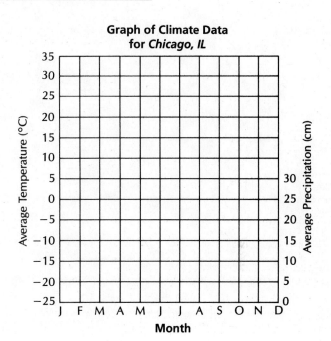

Graph of Climate Data for *Chicago, IL*

Water Pollution

Lab 62

Background

Water is one of our most precious resources. In nature, water is kept pure by the actions of certain microorganisms, by being filtered through soil and rocks, by its continual evaporation in the water cycle, and by other processes. In many places, sewage and industrial wastes have been dumped in such large quantities into the waterways that the water cannot be purified by natural processes. By contaminating the water, humans affect not only the quality of the water they themselves use, but also the environment of many necessary and desirable water organisms.

Objective

In this activity you will observe some samples of polluted river water, pond water, and relatively pure stream water.

Materials

stock solutions of polluted river water, pond water, and stream water

50- and 250-mL beakers	25-mL graduated cylinders
pH paper	test tubes
test tube stoppers	funnels
glass stirring rods	filter paper
bulb pipettes	metric ruler
glass-marking pencil	slides
cover slips	microscope

Procedures and Observations

CAUTION: *Treat each water sample as if it contained disease-causing organisms. Do not get samples on your clothes or body. Wash hands thoroughly after handling samples.*

1. Stir the stock solution of polluted river water. Then pour some into a 250-mL beaker until it is about two-thirds filled. Label the beaker. Do the same with the pond water and pure stream water stock solutions. Be sure to use a clean stirring rod for each solution.

2. Observe the appearance of each water sample. Look for any traces of oil in each.

   a. *Record your observations of the appearance of each water sample in Table 1.*

3. Cautiously sniff each water sample to detect any odors.

   b. *Record the odor of each water sample in Table 1.*

Table 1. Observations of River, Pond and Stream Water

Condition	River Water (polluted)	Pond Water (polluted)	Stream Water
General appearance			
Odor			
pH			
Foaming ability			
Appearance of filtered water and filter paper			
Microorganisms			

4. Using a bulb pipette, place 1 drop of the polluted river water sample on a strip of pH paper. Compare the resulting color with the chart on the dispenser to determine the pH of the sample. Then repeat the procedure for the other two water samples, using clean pipettes and new pH strips each time.

   c. *Record the pH of each water sample in Table 1.*

5. Pour some polluted river water into a test tube until it is about one-third filled. Stopper the tube. Then shake it vigorously for 10 seconds to determine if any detergents are present in it. Watch for the appearance of foam. If there is foam, measure its height in mm, and time how long it takes for the foam to disappear. Repeat the procedure for the other two water samples, using clean test tubes and stoppers each time.

   d. *Record your observations in Table 1 about the presence of foam in each water sample, its height, and how long it took to disappear.*

6. Fold a piece of filter paper so that it fits snugly into a funnel. Stir your sample of polluted river water, and measure 25 mL of it into a graduated cylinder. Pour the sample through the funnel into a 50-mL beaker. Note the appearance of the filter paper and the filtered water. Repeat the procedure for the other water samples. Use clean filter paper and glassware each time.

   e. *Record your observations of the appearance of the filtered water and the filter paper for each water sample in Table 1.*

7. Make several wet mounts of each water sample. Take them from the bottom, surface, and middle of the samples. Then observe them under the microscope, first under low power, then high power. Note any organisms that you see.

   f. *Record in Table 1 your observations about the presence of organisms in each water sample.*

8. Clean your equipment and wash your hands thoroughly before leaving the lab.

Analysis and Interpretations

1. Why did you stir the stock water solutions before taking samples of them?

Water Pollution (continued)

62

2. What conclusions can you draw about each water sample in terms of pH and presence of detergents and suspended matter? Give answers based on your data.

_____

_____

_____

3. Try to think of some ways that pollutants could be removed from the river water sample.

_____

_____

_____

_____

_____

4. Sometimes clean-looking water can be very dangerous. Explain why the quality of drinking water must continually be tested.

_____

_____

For Further Investigation

1. You have probably heard of many different pollutants—phosphates, nitrates, DDT, PCB, etc. Investigate some of these substances. What substances could have been in the water samples but were not tested or detected in your observations?

 2. Visit a nearby waterway and list or take photographs of evidence of pollution. Try to determine the source of the pollution. Take water samples and test them as you did in this activity.

Computer Activity

In Laboratory Experiment 62 you examined several samples of water for odor, pH, presence of microorganisms, foaming, and general appearance, in order to determine the water's degree of pollution. The computer program *Water Pollution* allows the user to simulate a variety of water environments of varying purity. The user sets the amount and type of waste flowing into the water, type of waste treatment, water temperature, and whether or not the water is in a pond, lake, or stream. The resultant levels of dissolved oxygen and waste—two factors important to fish survival—are displayed by the computer and monitored by you to determine what measures to take in managing the water resource.

Air Pollution

Lab 63

Background

Everyone is affected by polluted air. Air pollution is a mixture of particles, gases, and hazes. The particles in air pollution may come from windblown dirt and pollen, machinery, burning material, and the brake linings and tires of automobiles. Polluting gases are usually products of burning. Hydrocarbons and oxides of sulfur, nitrogen, and carbon are common examples. Haze is made up of liquid droplets suspended in air. Fog is an example of a haze of water droplets suspended in the air.

An increasingly serious result of air pollution is acid rain. When some of the sulfur and nitrogen oxides in the air combine with rainwater, they form acids, which fall to the ground. This acid rain can damage crops and buildings and may even kill all the organisms in a lake.

Objectives

In this activity you will:
1. Conduct simple tests for air pollutants.
2. Relate weather conditions to air pollution.

Materials

Petri dish	scissors
double-stick tape	beaker
glass-marking pencil	funnel
filter paper	pH paper
microscope	

Procedures and Observations

PART I. ACID PRECIPITATION _____

1. Collect rainwater or snow in a plastic container.

2. Use pH paper to measure the acidity or alkalinity of the liquid.

   a. *Record the pH of the precipitation.*

_____

3. Save your sample for Part II.

PART II. TRAPPING PARTICLES _____

1. Line a funnel with filter paper and filter your sample. Examine the filter paper carefully for any particles.

   a. *Record your observations of the filter paper.*

_____

2. Place three squares of double-stick tape in the bottom half of a Petri dish, as shown in Figure 1. Put the lid on the dish.

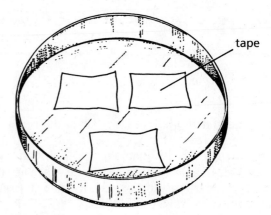

tape

Figure 1

3. Go to the location suggested by your teacher and expose the tapes to the air for at least 15 minutes. After the exposure, cover the dish and write the location on the lid.

4. When you have returned to the laboratory, place the bottom half of the Petri dish on the stage of your microscope. Then choose at random one microscopic field of view on each piece of tape and count the particles that you see under low power.

> **b.** *In the space below, record the number of particles seen on each piece of tape. Then average the numbers.*
>
> Tape #1: _____ Tape #2: _____ Tape #3: _____
>
> Average number: _____
>
> **c.** *On the board, record the location where you tested for air pollution and the average number of particles you found on the tapes. In Table 1, copy your data and the data collected by other students.*

Table 1. Observation of Air Pollution Particles in Various Locations

Location	Average number of particles

Air Pollution (continued)

63

PART III.   AIR POLLUTION AND THE WEATHER _____

Daily newspapers often print pollution reports with daily weather maps and forecasts.

1. Collect five consecutive days of pollution reports from your local newspaper. Include a newspaper for the day you trapped particles in the Petri dish.

2. Compare the level of pollution and the type of weather on each of the five days. Look for any relationship between them.

   a. *Record your observations of pollution levels and the weather.*

   _____

   _____

   _____

Analysis and Interpretations

1. Which location investigated by your class had the most pollution in the air? What do you think caused the pollution?

   _____

   _____

   _____

2. Which location investigated by your class had the cleanest air? Why do you think this is so?

   _____

   _____

3. Rain and other forms of precipitation clean the air of particles and water-soluble gases. Did you find any evidence of this in your data? If so, describe the evidence.

   _____

   _____

4. In what type of weather would you expect to find the worst air pollution? Explain.

   _____

   _____

5. What are some things that you can do to help reduce the air pollution in your community?

   _____

   _____

For Further Investigation

Use the particle trapping method from this lab to determine the locations of the cleanest and dirtiest air in your community.

Computer Activity

In Laboratory Experiment 63 your class measured pH and observed airborne particles as a relative measure of air pollution. The computer simulation *Air Pollution* allows you to measure carbon monoxide levels as another parameter of pollution. Measurements are taken for a hypothetical city under a variety of conditions, including varying wind speed, number of buses, and average traffic speed.

Review of Laboratory Skills

In the course of your laboratory work in biology, you have had an opportunity to acquire a number of skills. These skills can be described by the following list:

A. Analytical Skills

1. Formulate a question or define a problem, and develop a hypothesis to be tested in an investigation.
2. Given a laboratory problem, select suitable lab materials, safety equipment, and appropriate observation methods.
3. Distinguish between controls and variables in an experiment.
4. Collect, organize, and graph data.
5. Make inferences and predictions based upon data collected and observed.
6. Formulate generalizations or conclusions of the investigation.
7. Assess the limitations and assumptions of the experiment.
8. Determine the accuracy and repeatability of the experimental data and observations.

B. Technical Skills

9. Identify parts of a light microscope and their functions, and focus in low and high power.
10. Determine the size of microscopic specimens in micrometers.
11. Prepare wet mounts of plant and animal cells, and apply staining techniques using iodine or methylene blue.
12. Identify cell parts under the compound microscope, such as the nucleus, cytoplasm, chloroplasts, and cell wall.
13. Use and interpret indicators such as pH paper, Benedict's (Fehling's) solution, iodine (Lugol's) solution, and bromthymol blue.
14. Use and read measurement instruments, such as metric rulers, Celsius (centigrade) thermometers, and graduated cylinders.
15. Dissect plant and animal specimens for the purpose of exposing major structures for suitable examination.

16. Demonstrate safety skills involved in heating materials in test tubes or beakers, use of chemicals, and handling of dissection instruments.

These skills can be grouped into three basic categories:

(1) Skills relating to the planning of an investigation before it is carried out. Analytical skills 1, 2, and 3 are in this group.
(2) Post-lab skills related to the interpretation of the results of an investigation. Analytical skills 4 through 8 are in this group.
(3) Skills that are related to the performance of a laboratory investigation. Technical skills 9 through 16 are in this group.

The purpose of this section of the book is to review the essentials of these skills and to provide questions that test your understanding of and proficiency in each.

Analytical skills used in planning an investigation and then in interpreting its results are discussed in Part 1. Discussion of the technical skills employed in the performance of a laboratory investigation follows in Part 2.

PART 1. ANALYTICAL SKILLS

The analytical or investigative skills of the biologist relate, first, to the planning of an investigation and, second, to the interpretation of the results (Skills 1–3, 5–8). Since these two sides of every investigation are closely related, we treat these skills together. Discussion of Skill 4 on collecting, organizing, and graphing data appears separately at the end of this section.

SKILL 1: Formulate a question or define a problem, and develop a hypothesis to be tested in an investigation.

SKILL 2: Given a laboratory problem, select suitable lab materials, safety equipment, and appropriate observation methods.

SKILL 3: Distinguish between controls and variables in an experiment.

SKILL 5: Make inferences and predictions based upon data collected and observed.

SKILL 6: Formulate generalizations or conclusions of the investigation.

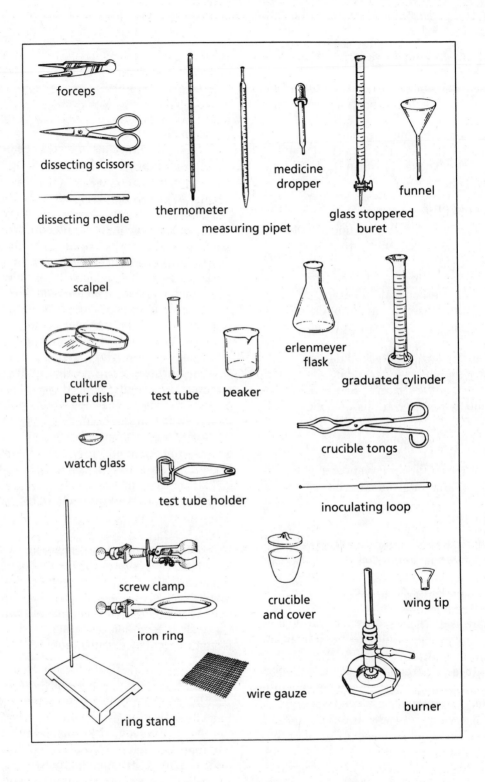

Figure 1. Some common laboratory apparatus

Review of Laboratory Skills (continued)

SKILL 7: Assess the limitations and assumptions of the experiment.

SKILL 8: Determine the accuracy and repeatability of the experimental data and observations.

As part of your study of biology, you have carried out many scientific investigations in the laboratory. Most of these were experiments that have been performed many times before. Your purpose in doing these experiments was not to make a startling discovery, but rather to gain an understanding of how new knowledge is obtained in science. You have found that there are certain general approaches or steps that are used in most scientific investigations. These steps are sometimes called the *scientific method*.

Some Steps in the Scientific Method

Defining the problem. When at work, the practicing scientist is usually trying to answer a specific question. The question may have come up in the scientist's previous work, or it may have come out of another scientist's observations. The scientist may be attacking the problem independently or as a member of a team. In any case the question to be answered has been clearly stated. No serious scientific investigation can be carried out without a clear statement of what is being sought.

Questions in science can often be stated very simply. Consider the question, Why are leaves green? This is a question that might have occurred to anyone who noticed that among thousands of plants that differ in many ways, the leaves are all similar in color.

Observations. The example of a scientific question given in the preceding section is the result of observation. In fact, it is the result of many observations in which a *pattern* or *regularity* was discovered. In the course of scientific investigation, careful and continued observation frequently serves to identify such patterns in nature. Scientists ultimately seek to explain why patterns and regularities exist.

Careful observation is an essential part of all science. Some observations, like those of the color of leaves, can be made by the unaided senses. Most observations in modern science, however, are made with the aid of instruments.

The hypothesis. Faced with a scientific question, the scientist will try to think of a possible answer. Such a possible answer to a question is called a *hypothesis*. In ordinary language we would call it a guess. In the case of our question about why leaves are green, one hypothesis might be that all leaves contain a certain chemical substance that is green.

Note that this is not the only possible hypothesis. There may be several different substances that account for the green color of plants. Another possibility is that the color is not caused by a substance at all. It could be the result of the way light is reflected from the leaf surface. The colors of some butterfly wings, for example, are produced this way. In any event, whether we have one hypothesis or many, each must be tested to determine whether it is true.

Testing the hypothesis. A hypothesis is usually tested by an experiment—or more often, by a series of experiments. A scientific experiment may be thought of as a way of making nature furnish observations that would not occur naturally. In our example, we want to test the hypothesis that there is a particular substance in leaves that makes them green. To do this, we can perform chemical experiments to determine what compounds are present in leaf tissues. If we find the same green substance in all green leaves, our hypothesis will have received strong support. If we can't find such a substance, our hypothesis will become doubtful. We would probably then test some other hypothesis.

As it happens, experiments show that there is a kind of green substance called chlorophyll that can be found in all green leaves. We can therefore answer the original question: Leaves are green because they contain chlorophyll.

The Controlled Experiment

An important type of experiment in biological investigations is the *controlled experiment*. In a controlled experiment, the same experiment is performed twice. All conditions in the two experiments are made as alike as possible, but one of the conditions or factors is changed in one experiment and not in the other. If the results of the two experiments are different, we can conclude that the difference was due to the one change that was made.

A condition or factor that is deliberately changed in a set of experiments is called a *variable*. Many experiments are conducted to study the effect of the changed variable. Some typical variables in biological experiments are temperature, amount of light, amount of water, amount of food, and kind of food. It is important that *only one* variable be allowed to change in any experiment. If more than one condition varies, no conclusion can be drawn about which change was responsible for observed results. The experimental setup in which no change is made is called the *control*. In a controlled experiment, the controls are the conditions that remain the same.

Let us continue with the study of leaves to illustrate a controlled experiment. We begin with the knowledge (gained from earlier experiments) that green leaves carry on photosynthesis. This is a process in which a carbohydrate such as starch is made from carbon dioxide and water in the presence of light. Since green leaves carry on photosynthesis, and we now know that green leaves contain chlorophyll, we can form the following hypothesis: Chlorophyll is necessary for photosynthesis.

How can we test this hypothesis? What we need is a controlled experiment in which all conditions are alike except that in one case chlorophyll is present and in the other it is not. To perform such an experiment, we can use an assortment of plants, some of which are completely green, and some of which have variegated leaves. In a variegated leaf, one region is green (contains chlorophyll) and another is some other color, for example, white (does not contain chlorophyll). We expose all the plants to light so that photosynthesis can occur. We then test leaves from all the plants for the presence of stored starch. We find that the all-green leaves have starch throughout. In the variegated leaves, only the green regions have starch.(See Lab 23.)

In this experiment, the variable is the presence or absence of chlorophyll in different regions of the variegated leaves. The controls are the all-green leaves. The results tend to confirm the hypothesis that chlorophyll is necessary for photosynthesis.

Scientific Reasoning

Inferences. A conclusion or belief that is based on the evidence from an experiment is called an *inference*. In the experiments with variegated leaves, the conclusion that chlorophyll is necessary for photosynthesis is an inference.

Let us look at another example. A number of rats are divided into two groups. One group is fed a normal diet. The other group is fed the same diet, but with one particular mineral omitted. The animals in the second group gradually grow weaker. The ones receiving a complete diet remain healthy. We can draw the inference that the missing mineral in the second diet is necessary for the health of these rats.

Predictions. Like a hypothesis, every inference in science needs to be tested and confirmed by further experiments. One way to test an inference is to make a prediction based upon it. If the prediction turns out to be true, this is strong evidence that the inference is correct. For example, in the experiment with the rats, we inferred that the missing mineral in the diet is necessary for the health of the rats. If this is true, we can predict that if we add the mineral back to the diet of the weakened rats, they will regain their health. If we carry out this experiment and the rats do regain their health, this is strong evidence that the original inference was correct.

Sufficient Samples. Every experiment must contain a sufficient number of samples to make it a valid test. For example, a researcher wanted to determine whether bean plants would grow better in green light than in white light. He took two bean plants and grew one in green light and one in white. He treated both plants the same in every other way. After two weeks, the plant in white light grew 4 centimeters taller than the one in green light. He concluded that bean plants grow better in white light than in green. The obvious flaw in his experiment is the sample size. The more plants available for the experiment the better! This is because individual plants may possess adaptations or characteristics that may mislead the researcher. The plant grown in white light might have grown 4 centimeters taller than the other even if they had been grown under the same light. These "individual differences" have a reduced effect when large numbers of plants are used and average results are tabulated. In the rat experiment, many rats would be used in each group.

Generalizations. If an experiment is repeated many times under a variety of conditions, and similar results are always obtained, the scientist can then formulate a *generalization*. A generalization in science is a statement that is true for a broad range of situations. For example, the experiment with the rats and the missing mineral can be repeated with other kinds of mammals. If the results are always the same, we can state the generalization that the mineral is necessary for the health of mammals.

Review of Laboratory Skills (continued)

Limitations and assumptions of an experiment. The scientific investigator must be careful not to draw inferences or conclusions beyond the limitations of the experiment. In experiments on rats, conclusions cannot automatically be applied to other animals, or even to other rats. The conclusions are limited to these particular rats until they are extended to other animals by further experiments.

It is also important to recognize the assumptions that are being made in an experiment. An *assumption* is something we accept as being true. Usually the assumptions of an experiment are things that have been demonstrated by past experiments and that are generally accepted by scientists. In the experiment with the variegated leaves, an important assumption is that starch appears where photosynthesis has occurred. This assumption may not be true. For example, starch may not always accumulate where photosynthesis is occurring. Starch may be converted to glucose and transported from one part of a plant to another. Careful investigators make sure of their assumptions before drawing inferences and making predictions based on their experiments.

Questions on Analytical Skills (Skills 1–3 and 5–8)

_____ 1. Spirogyra is an alga characterized by a single, spiral chloroplast. Which of the following tools would be most useful in observing the development of the chloroplast following cell division?
   (1) ultracentrifuge
   (2) compound microscope
   (3) microtome
   (4) chromatography

_____ 2. Certain migratory salmon hatch in the headwaters of streams, spend several years in the ocean, and then return to the stream they were hatched in to spawn. A biologist has formed a hypothesis that an organ called an olfactory sac enables a salmon to recognize the water of its home stream. Which of the following experiments should be performed to test this hypothesis? (Assume that all fish in each experiment are marked so that they can be recognized at a later time.)
   (1) Mark two young fish, and remove the olfactory sac from one of them. At the proper time, watch to see whether either fish returns to the stream.
   (2) Mark a thousand or more young fish, and remove the olfactory sacs from all of them. Determine whether any of the marked fish return to the stream.
   (3) Transplant the olfactory organs from fish from one stream into fish from another stream. Determine which stream the recipients of the transplants return to.
   (4) Mark a large number of fish from the same stream, and remove the olfactory sacs from half of them. Determine how many from each group are later observed returning to the stream.

_____ 3. A necessary assumption of the experiments in Question 2 is that:
   (1) Removal of the olfactory sacs does not reduce the chance of survival of the fish.
   (2) Olfactory sacs are glands that secrete hormones.
   (3) Spawning salmon recognize the opposite sex by odor or taste.
   (4) Nearly all the fish hatched in any given year eventually return to spawn.

_____ **4.** A scientist has formed a hypothesis that females of a certain insect species produce a chemical substance that attracts males to them for mating. Which of the following experimental procedures will best demonstrate the presence of such a chemical attractant?
(1) Take a combination of laboratory chemicals that have odors and see if male insects are attracted to them.
(2) Make an extract of substances from the bodies of female insects who are ready to mate and see if males are attracted to the extract.
(3) Place female insects in a strong magnetic field and see whether males are attracted to them.
(4) Place female insects who are ready to mate in a screened enclosure and see whether males are attracted to the enclosure.

_____ **5.** Population studies in a certain woodland community show that an increase in the population of owls is followed by a decrease in the population of rabbits. To determine whether there is a direct cause-and-effect relation in this observation, a reasonable step would be to determine:
(1) the type of habitat occupied by owls
(2) the food that rabbits eat
(3) the food that owls eat
(4) the producer organisms of the community

_____ **6.** A biologist wants to study the group behavior of monkeys in a specific region of Africa. In order to make meaningful observations, the scientist should select for observation:
(1) a group containing a small number of monkeys
(2) a group containing a large number of monkeys
(3) several groups of monkeys of various numbers
(4) a group in the middle of the region where the monkeys are found

Base your answers to questions 7 through 9 on the following information:

The apparatus below is to be used in an experiment to show that exhaled air contains more carbon dioxide than inhaled air. (Bromthymol blue turns yellow when carbon dioxide is bubbled through it.)

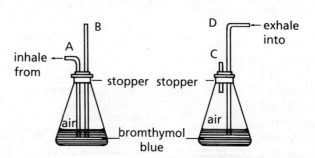

_____ **7.** Which error was made in setting up the apparatus?
(1) Tube A should not extend into the bromthymol blue.
(2) Tube B should not extend into the bromthymol blue.
(3) Tube C should extend into the bromthymol blue.
(4) Tube D should not extend into the bromthymol blue.

_____ **8.** If the error in question 7 is corrected and the apparatus is used in an experiment the bromthymol blue will:
(1) turn yellow in the inhale flask only
(2) turn yellow in the exhale flask only
(3) turn yellow in both flasks
(4) remain blue in both flasks

396

Review of Laboratory Skills (continued)

_____ **9.** Which liquid could be substituted for bromthymol blue?
  (1) iodine solution
  (2) limewater
  (3) ammonium hydroxide
  (4) Benedict's solution

Base your answers to questions 10 through 12 on the activities described in the paragraph below and on your knowledge of biology.

A tomato plant was placed under a sealed bell jar and exposed to light. Carbon dioxide containing radioactive carbon was introduced into the bell jar as shown in the diagram.

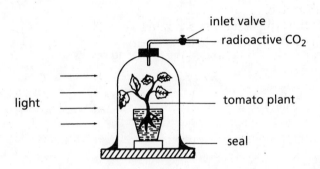

After an hour the inlet valve was closed. Later the entire plant was removed from the soil and cleaned by rinsing in water. A Geiger counter indicated radioactivity in the roots. These roots were then dried and chopped into very small pieces. They were sprinkled into an aquarium containing a hungry goldfish which was not radioactive. Four days later, the fish was removed from the aquarium and a tissue section from the fish was tested with a Geiger counter. The counter indicated an above-normal count.

_____ **10.** Which cycle is primarily being studied by means of this investigation?
  (1) oxygen
  (2) carbon
  (3) nitrogen
  (4) water

_____ **11.** A control setup for this investigation would be identical to the one described except for the replacement of the:
  (1) tomato plant with a geranium plant
  (2) goldfish with a tadpole
  (3) radioactive CO_2 with atmospheric CO_2
  (4) soil with distilled water

_____ **12.** This investigation suggests that when plants are eaten by animals, some plant materials may be:
  (1) changed to animal tissue
  (2) separated into molecules before being digested
  (3) eliminated by the animal in a form that allows the plants to grow again
  (4) used in regulating the animal's digestive processes

_____ **13.** A rock containing fossils is dated by radioactivity to be older than any previously discovered fossil-bearing rock. Which of the following conclusions is supported by this observation?

(1) Fossils are still being formed in rocks today.
(2) Life was present on the earth at the time the rock was being formed.
(3) Life appeared on the earth as soon as the first rocks formed.
(4) Radioactive dating is becoming more accurate.

Questions 14 through 17 are based upon the following experiments:

Thin pieces of mica were inserted into the growing tips of two oat seedlings as shown in the diagram, and a third tip was left alone. All three tips were then exposed to light from the right.

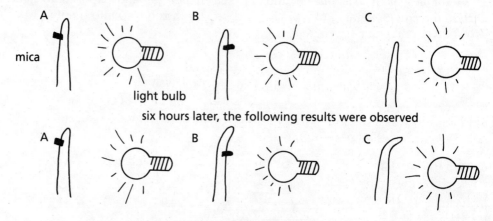

14. If bending results from a substance being made in the tip and being transported downward, then the above experiment shows that the substance is:

(1) unequally distributed because of gravity
(2) transported down the dark side and stimulates growth
(3) transported down the light side and inhibits growth
(4) transported laterally from the light side to the dark side and stimulates growth

_____ **15.** An assumption made in this experiment is that:

(1) the light from the bulb is the same as sunlight
(2) six hours is a sufficient amount of time for the experiment
(3) the mica does not allow substances to pass through it
(4) the mica kills the cells through which it is inserted

_____ **16.** The purpose of plant C is to act as a(n):

(1) control
(2) variable
(3) indicator
(4) assumption

_____ **17.** The variable in this experiment is the:

(1) viability of the seeds
(2) temperature
(3) amount of light
(4) location of the mica

Base your answers to questions 18 through 20 on the experiment described below:

Fifty clover seeds are surface-sterilized in an antiseptic solution. Half are planted in sterile soil in pot A; the other half are first mixed with *Rhizobium* nitrogen-fixing bacteria and then planted in sterilized soil in pot B.

Review of Laboratory Skills (continued)

_____ **18.** The plants in pot A are:
  (1) experimental
  (2) controls
  (3) variables
  (4) hypotheses

_____ **19.** The variable in this experiment is:
  (1) the seeds in pot A
  (2) the seeds in pot B
  (3) the availability of nitrogen
  (4) sterility

_____ **20.** An assumption of this experiment is that:
  (1) all the seeds will germinate
  (2) sterilization kills seeds
  (3) nitrogen is needed for plant growth
  (4) seeds will germinate in sterilized soil

Base your answers to questions 21 through 23 on the following information and on your knowledge of biology.

If heavy rains occur while apple orchards are in bloom, the apple crop the following fall is usually much smaller (fewer apples) than would normally be expected.

_____ **21.** The information given above is best described as:
  (1) an inference
  (2) a hypothesis
  (3) a prediction
  (4) an observation

_____ **22.** A likely reason for the small crop after heavy rains during the flowering season is that:
  (1) heavy rains reduce the normal activity of most insects
  (2) water that collects in the ovules prevents fertilization
  (3) sunlight is necessary for photosynthesis
  (4) wet weather results in the growth of harmful molds

_____ **23.** The completed statement in question 22 is best described as:
  (1) an observation
  (2) a hypothesis
  (3) a conclusion
  (4) an assumption

_____ **24.** Tomato seeds will not germinate in the ripe fruit. This seems to indicate that something in the fruit prevents germination. An experiment to check this would be to moisten seeds with tomato juice. The best control for this experiment would be to moisten:
  (1) other kinds of seeds with water
  (2) other kinds of seeds with tomato juice
  (3) tomato seeds with water
  (4) tomato seeds with hormones

Technical skills, such as those that will be discussed in Part 2, are important for obtaining useful results from an experiment or investigation. However, the purpose of a laboratory investigation goes beyond the mere carrying out of a procedure. A laboratory technician can do that, but it is the scientist who actually sets a goal for an investigation and plans a procedure for reaching that goal. A scientist also must interpret the results, draw inferences and conclusions, and discover new questions that need further investigation.

One of the important steps in scientific investigation is to organize and present observations so that they can be easily analyzed and interpreted. This is a skill that is partly technical, partly analytical. It is therefore treated separately from the other skills.

SKILL 4: Collect, organize, and graph data.

Recording Data

Every laboratory investigation involves observations that must be recorded for later study and interpretation. The recorded observations of an investigation are called *data*. Data are very often recorded in a *data table*, which is a form that has been specially set up to make it easy to record the observations in a systematic way. A data table usually has labeled columns and rows for the various items of data that the investigation is expected to produce. Figure 2 shows a data table for recording the results of a blood-typing investigation like that in Lab 15. Samples of blood were tested for the presence of A and B antigens by adding anti-A and anti-B antibody preparations and noting whether agglutination occurred. This data table also provides a column for entering blood type inferred from the observations.

Blood sample	Effect of		Blood type
	Anti-A serum	Anti-B serum	
1	+	–	A
2	+	+	AB
3	–	–	O

Figure 2. Data table for a blood-typing investigation

Data in a scientific investigation often consist of numerical results or measurements. When mea-

surements are to be recorded, the data table must state the unit of measurement, such as cm, mL, or °C. Figure 3 shows a data table for an experiment in which the growth of seedlings was observed. Note the unit of measurement in the heading.

Time (days)	Length (cm)
1	–
2	0.5
3	1.5
4	3.5
5	7.0
6	9.8
7	10.8

Figure 3. Growth of radish seedlings

Graphing Data

Figure 4 shows the data table for an investigation of the effect of temperature on the breathing rate of a particular species of fish, as indicated by movement of the gill covers. There are two variables in this investigation: temperature and breathing rate. One of these, the temperature, is under the control of the experimenter and can be set at any value. This is called the *independent variable*. The other variable, the breathing rate of the fish, depends upon the temperature. As the temperature changes, the breathing rate changes. The breathing rate is called the *dependent variable*, because it is dependent upon the independent variable, the temperature.

In experiments involving a dependent and an independent variable, the investigator is usually looking for a relationship between them. It is difficult to see a relationship among numbers in a data table. However, if the data are plotted on a graph, the relationship often becomes evident at a glance.

The type of graph that best shows the relationship between two variables is the *line graph*. Figure 5 shows a line graph for the experiment with the fish. Values of the independent variable have been marked off along the horizontal axis of the graph. This is usually called the x-axis. Values of the dependent variable are marked off along the vertical axis, or y-axis. For each value of temperature in the data table, there is a certain value of the breathing rate. These two pieces of data locate a point on the graph. The figure shows how the point for a temperature of 15° C and breathing rate of 25 per minute was "plotted" on the graph.

Temperature (°C)	Breathing rate (per minute)
10	15
15	25
18	30
20	38
23	60
25	57
27	25

Figure 4. Temperature and breathing rate of freshwater sunfish

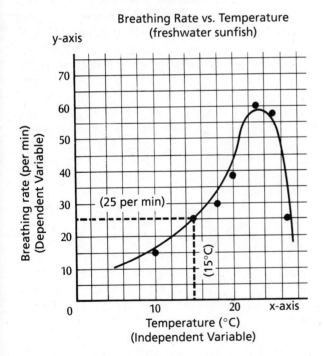

Figure 5. Line graph of data in Figure 4

When all the data points have been plotted, a smooth curve is drawn through them. The basic assumption in drawing such a curve is that the dependent variable changes smoothly as the independent variable changes. Even though we do not actually make observations at all possible

values of the independent variable, the graph is assumed to tell us what the observations would have been for any value. For example, the graph tells us that for a temperature of 12° C, the breathing rate is probably 18 per minute. This kind of information is almost impossible to obtain just from the observations in a data table.

A line graph shows whether the dependent variable increases or decreases as the independent variable increases, and how rapidly the dependent variable changes over any particular range. A steep curve indicates a rapid rate of change. A flat (nearly horizontal) curve indicates very slow change. The graph for the fish breathing rate shows that as the temperature rises from a low value, the breathing rate at first increases at a fairly uniform rate. As the temperature rises further, the breathing rate increases sharply, then suddenly falls off. The investigator may wonder why this happens, may formulate a hypothesis to explain it, and may perform new experiments to test the hypothesis. Graphing is an important tool both for interpreting data and for raising new questions to be investigated.

Constructing a Line Graph

When plotting data on a line graph, you must decide which of the variables is independent and which is dependent and label the axes of your graph accordingly. Then you must decide on the scale of each axis, that is, how much each unit along the axis will represent. Scales should be chosen to make the graph as large as possible within the limits of the paper and still include the largest item of data. If the scale unit is made too large, your graph will be cramped into a small area and will be hard to read and interpret. If the scale unit is too small, the graph will run off the paper. Scale units should also be selected for ease of locating points on the graph. Multiples of 1, 2, 5, or 10 are easiest to work with.

Other Types of Graphs

The line graph is most useful for showing relationships between variables that change continuously over a range of values. Sometimes, however, we simply want to compare data. A *bar graph* is an effective way to show comparisons. Figure 6, on the next page, compares average annual precipitation in six major terrestrial biomes. In this graph, precipitation is marked off along the vertical axis, and the height of each bar corresponds to a particular amount of precipitation. There is no scale along the horizontal axis. The bars are simply spaced apart by any convenient amount. The bars of a bar graph can also be drawn horizontally and arranged one below the other rather than side by side. The horizontal arrangement is often easier to read when the bar labels are long words or phrases.

A *circle graph* (sometimes called a "pie chart") is a convenient way to show the relative size of the parts that together form a whole body of data. Figure 7 is a series of circle graphs showing the components of a sample of soil. The first graph (A) shows the division of the soil into mineral (inorganic) matter and organic material. The second graph (B) shows the division of the organic material into dead matter, plant roots, and living organisms. The third graph (C) shows the proportions of different types of organisms in the soil. Note that in each case the segments of the graph add to 100%.

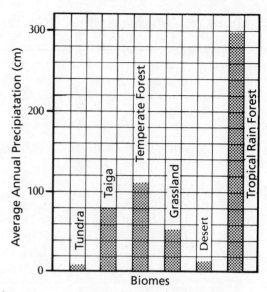

Figure 6. Example of a bar graph

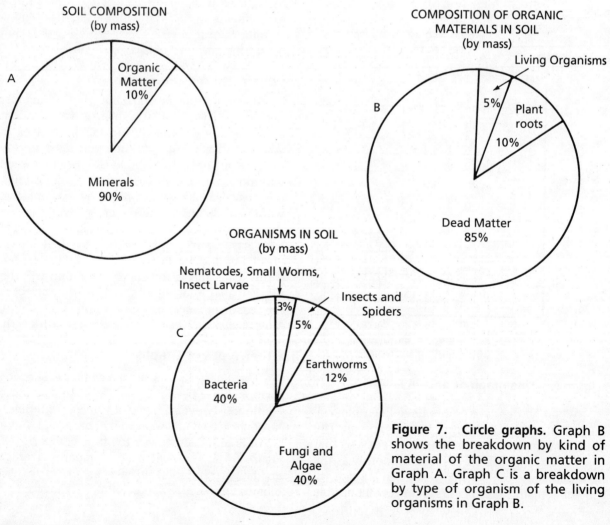

Figure 7. Circle graphs. Graph B shows the breakdown by kind of material of the organic matter in Graph A. Graph C is a breakdown by type of organism of the living organisms in Graph B.

Review of Laboratory Skills (continued)

Questions on Organizing and Graphing Data (Skill 4)

A laboratory investigation was performed to determine the length of time necessary to digest protein (egg white). Five grams of egg white taken from a hard-boiled egg, 15 milliliters of pepsin solution, and 2 milliliters of hydrochloric acid were added to a test tube. The percentage of protein digested was recorded over a 24-hour period, as shown in the data table below.

Using the grid and data table provided on the next page, construct a graph according to the directions below.

1. Give the graph a title.
2. Label each axis.
3. Mark an appropriate scale on each axis.
4. Plot the data and connect the points.

DATA TABLE

Time (in hours)	Percentage of Protein Digested
0	0
4	5
8	15
12	50
16	75
20	85
24	90

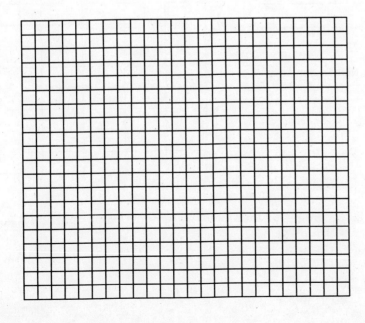

_____ 5. According to the data, during which four-hour time period did the greatest amount of protein digestion occur?
(1) 0–4 hours
(2) 4–8 hours
(3) 8–12 hours
(4) 20–24 hours

Base your answers to questions 6 through 8 on the information below and on your knowledge of biology.

A student was working on an investigation to measure the relative activity of an enzyme at various pH values. He collected the following data:

pH 2, enzyme activity 10; pH 8, enzyme activity 50;
pH 12, enzyme activity 10; pH 4, enzyme activity 20;
pH 6, enzyme activity 40; pH 10, enzyme activity 40.

6. Organize the data above by filling in the Data Table below, following these directions:
(a) label each column with an appropriate heading
(b) complete the two columns in the data table so that the pH values are increasing

7. Using the information in the data table you prepared and the grid below, construct a graph, following the directions below:
(a) title the graph, then label and make an appropriate scale on each axis
(b) plot the data and connect the points

DATA TABLE

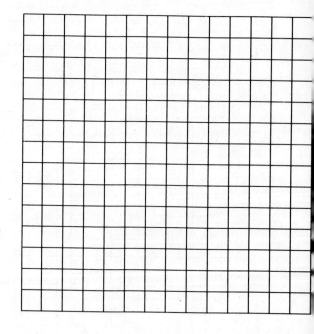

_____ 8. According to the data, this enzyme would probably work best at which pH values?
(1) 7 and 8
(2) 2 and 12
(3) 6 and 7
(4) 4 and 10

404

Review of Laboratory Skills (continued)

Use the following information for questions 9 through 12.

In an experiment, 100 frogs *(Rana pipiens)* were separated into four equal groups, A, B, C, and D. Each group was maintained in a separate enclosure at a different constant temperature. Data was collected for the average heartbeat rate and the average breathing rate for each group. The data table below gives the results of these observations.

DATA TABLE

Group	Temperature (°C)	Average Heartbeat Rate (per minute)	Average Breathing Rate (per minute)
A	5	10	7
B	10	20	14
C	15	30	20
D	20	40	22

9. In this experiment, the independent variable was:
   (1) frog species
   (2) temperature
   (3) heartbeat rate
   (4) heartbeat rate and breathing rate

10. Construct line graphs that will best show the relationships in this data.

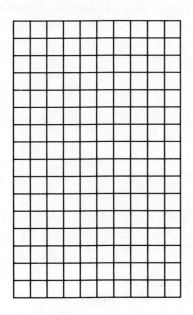 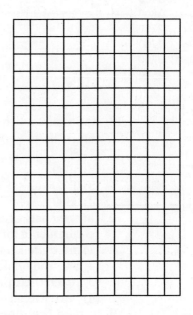

11. According to the data of this experiment, as the temperature increases:
    (1) heartbeat increases and breathing rate decreases
    (2) heartbeat decreases and breathing rate increases
    (3) both rates increase
    (4) both rates decrease

_____ **12.** Compared to the increase in heartbeat rate, the breathing rate:
(1) increases more rapidly
(2) increases less rapidly
(3) increases at the same rate
(4) increases, then decreases

The data table below shows the average daily calorie requirements of boys and girls at various ages. Construct line graphs from this information. Place age in years on the x-axis and calories on the y-axis. Use a solid line for boys and a dashed line for girls. Answer questions 13 through 15 on the basis of your completed graphs.

DATA TABLE

Age in Years	Calorie Requirements	
	Boys	Girls
1	1000	800
2	1200	1000
3	1400	1200
4	1500	1300
5	1700	1400
6	1800	1500
7	2000	1700
8	2200	1900
9	2300	2000
10	2400	2200
11	2500	2300
12	3000	2500
13	3400	3100
14	3500	2800
15	3600	2700
16	3700	2700
17	3800	2700
18	3000	2500

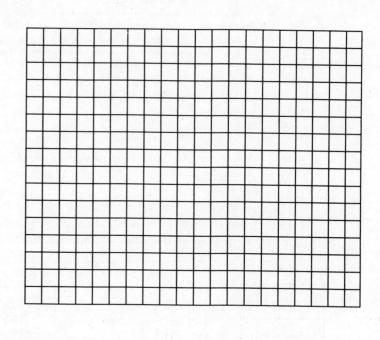

_____ **13.** Approximately how many more calories per day are required by boys than girls at age 17?
(1) 800
(2) 1000
(3) 2500
(4) 3500

_____ **14.** On the basis of the graph it may be assumed that, in general, calorie requirements for boys and girls:
(1) are quite similar until age 17
(2) are wholly dissimilar
(3) reach their peak at about the same age
(4) have a similar rate of increase until after age 12 to 13

_____ **15.** If there is a direct relationship between physical growth and calorie intake, the graph indicates that most girls will have completed their physical growth about:
(1) the same time as boys
(2) 1 to 2 years sooner than boys
(3) 4 years sooner than boys
(4) 6 years sooner than boys

Review of Laboratory Skills (continued)

PART 2. TECHNICAL SKILLS

SKILL 9: Identify parts of a light microscope and their functions, and focus in low and high power.

You were introduced to the use of the microscope in Lab 1, and you have used it many times in the biology laboratory. The following is a review of basic rules and procedures in the use of this instrument.

Handling the Microscope

1. When carrying a microscope, keep the instrument in an upright position by holding the arm with one hand and using the palm of your other hand to support the base. See Figure 8.

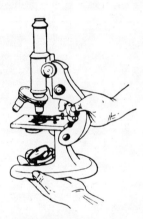

Figure 8. The proper way to carry the microscope

2. Gently place the microscope at your work station. Remove the dust cover, unwind the illuminator cord (if any), and plug it into the nearest socket. Make sure that the cord is not dangling or lying where it may be accidentally pulled or tripped, as this could pull the microscope off the table.
3. Use only soft lens paper to clean the lenses and mirror.
4. Before putting the microscope away, move the nosepiece so that the low-power objective is in line with the tube. Using the coarse adjustment, lower the tube as far as it will go. Neatly wind up the power cord, and place the dust cover over the microscope. Using two hands, carry the microscope by arm and base to its storage place.

How to Focus a Microscope

1. Place the prepared slide on the stage with the specimen in the center of the stage opening.
2. Set the diaphragm at its maximum opening.
3. Turn the nosepiece until the shorter, lower power objective is in direct line with the tube. You will hear a click when the position is correct.
4. Turn on the substage light. If there is none, face the mirror toward a light source. Look through the eyepiece and move the mirror around until you get the brightest light possible. Use a light source in the classroom. Do NOT use direct sunlight. The rays could damage your eyes.
5. While looking at the microscope from the side, turn the coarse adjustment downward until the objective is very close to the slide. Do not let the objective touch the slide.
6. Now look through the eyepiece and turn the coarse adjustment upward until the specimen on the slide can be clearly seen. Adjust the diaphragm to produce the sharpest image.
7. If you go too far in one direction, reverse the adjustment to bring the specimen back into focus. Use the fine adjustment to obtain the sharpest possible image of the portion of the specimen you wish to examine.
8. If you now wish to examine the specimen under high power, turn the nosepiece until the high-power objective clicks into position. Most microscopes are parfocal, which means that the object will still be approximately in focus when you switch from low to high power. Use the fine adjustment only to bring the image into sharp focus. Never use the coarse adjustment with the high-power objective. Always begin the examination of a specimen under low power.
9. You will notice that the brightness of the field is reduced when you switch from low to high power. You may want to adjust the diaphragm for better illumination.
10. You can sometimes get better resolution and a clearer image by using a smaller diaphragm opening, even though this reduces the overall brightness. Try different settings of the diaphragm to find the best viewing conditions.

Questions on the Parts and Use of the Microscope (Skill 9)

Base your answers to questions 1 through 3 on the information and the sketches below and on your knowledge of biology.

The illustrations numbered 1 through 4 below are sketches of plant tissue that were viewed through a microscope. The position of the specimen slide remained unchanged while various adjustments were made on the microscope in between sketches.

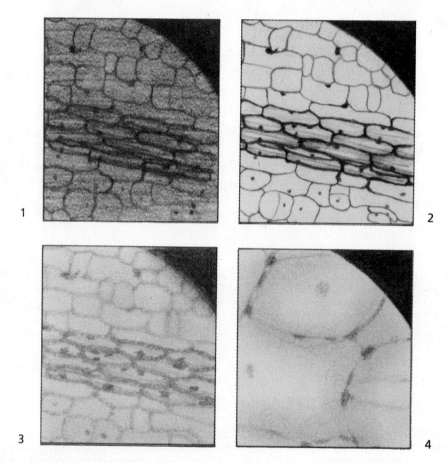

1

2

3

4

1. Describe one adjustment that could have been made to the microscope after sketch 1 was drawn in order to obtain sketch 2.

_____

_____

_____

2. Describe one adjustment that could have been made to the microscope after sketch 2 was drawn in order to obtain sketch 3.

_____

3. Describe one adjustment that could have been made to the microscope after sketch 3 was drawn in order to obtain sketch 4.

_____

_____

Review of Laboratory Skills (continued)

_____ 4. During the observation of a prepared microscope slide, a sharp crack is heard as the objective presses against the slide and breaks it. Which of the following actions might have caused this result?
(1) changing the diaphragm opening under high power
(2) using the fine adjustment to focus under low power
(3) using the coarse adjustment to focus under high power
(4) switching back to low power after focusing under high power

_____ 5. A student prepares a slide of the letter "e" and positions the slide on the stage of a compound microscope so that the letter is in a normal reading position. What will be the appearance of the letter when viewed through the microscope?
(1) **e**   (2) **ǝ**   (3) **ә**   (4) **ɓ**

_____ 6. A student observed a paramecium under the low–power objective of a microscope (100X) and then under high power (400X). The image of the paramecium under low power, compared to the image of the same paramecium under high power, would be:
(1) smaller and in a darker field of view
(2) smaller and in a brighter field of view
(3) larger and in a darker field of view
(4) larger and in a brighter field of view

SKILL 10: Determine the size of microscopic specimens in micrometers.

Lab 4 deals with techniques for using the microscope to find the actual size of observed specimens. You will recall that to do this, we first determine the diameter of the field of the low-power or high-power objective. We then compare the size of the specimen with the diameter of the field. The low-power objective is used for specimens that are too large for the high-power field. The high-power objective is used for smaller subjects.

Measurement with the Low-Power Objective

1. Switch the low-power objective into position. Adjust the mirror or switch on the light and open the diaphragm to its maximum setting.
2. Place a transparent plastic metric ruler on the stage of your microscope. Focus on the lines of the millimeter scale.
3. Move the ruler until the edge bisects the field of view. The millimeter scale should now be seen in the lower half of the field as shown in Figure 9.
4. Adjust the ruler so that one mark is at the left edge of the field. A millimeter is measured from the middle of one mark to the middle of the next.
5. Measure the diameter of the field. Since there

may be a fraction of a millimeter space left over, estimate the remaining distance to the nearest tenth of a millimeter (0.1 mm).

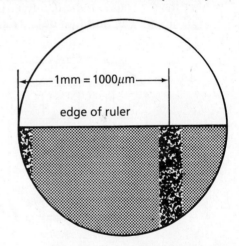

Figure 9. **Measuring the diameter of the low-power field.** The diameter of this field is about 1.2 mm or 1200 μm.

6. Change the millimeter measurement to micrometers. For example, suppose your microscope has a field diameter of 1.2 millimeters. Since 1 millimeter is equal to 1000 micrometers, the diameter in micrometers is 1200:

1.2 millimeters x 1000 micrometers/millimeter = 1200 micrometers

7. Knowing the field diameter, you can now estimate the size of objects. If, for example, a specimen is approximately 1/3 the diameter of the low-power field, its length may be calculated as approximately 1/3 of 1200 micrometers = 400 micrometers.

Measurement with the High-Power Objective

The high-power field is only a fraction of a millimeter in diameter. Its diameter cannot be measured directly with a millimeter ruler. However, the diameter can be calculated by using the ratio between the low-power and high-power magnifications. For example, if the low-power magnification is 100X and the high-power is 400X, the ratio between them is:

$$\frac{100X}{400X} = \frac{1}{4}$$

The diameter of the high-power field is then 1/4 the diameter of the low-power field. If we know the diameter of the low-power field, we simply take 1/4 of it (divide by 4) to find the high-power field. If the diameter of the low-power field is 1200 micrometers, that of the high-power field is 300 micrometers.

Once we have calculated the diameter of the high-power field, we can measure objects in that field by comparing them with the diameter of the field. (See example below.)

Remember that if the diameter of the high-power field is 1/4 that of the low-power field, its area is only 1/16 that of the low-power field. This means that if 16 cells of uniform size fill the low-power field, just one cell will fill the high-power field. See Figure 10.

Metric Units of Length

You should be familiar with the following relationships in the SI system of measurement.

$$
\begin{aligned}
1 \text{ meter (m)} &= 100 \text{ centimeters (cm)}\\
1 \text{ m} &= 1000 \text{ millimeters (mm)}\\
1 \text{ m} &= 1,000,000 \text{ micrometers } (\mu m)\\
1 \text{ mm} &= 1000 \text{ } \mu m\\
1 \text{ inch} &= 2.54 \text{ cm} = 25.4 \text{ mm}
\end{aligned}
$$

Example: Under high power, you estimate that the length of an object is 0.7 times the diameter of the field.

The low-power (100X) field =
    1200 micrometers
The high-power (400X) field =
    1/4 X 1200 micrometers =
    300 micrometers
The size of the object is
    0.7 X 300 micrometers = 210 micrometers

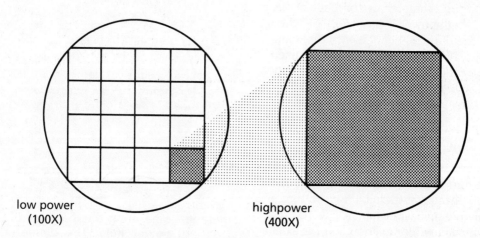

low power
(100X)

highpower
(400X)

Figure 10. Under low power, 16 squares can be seen in the field. Under high power, the side of each square is magnified 4 times more. As a result, a single square fills the high-power field.

Review of Laboratory Skills (continued)

Questions on Measuring Microscopic Specimens (Skill 10)

_____ 1. Bacteria observed under the microscope are measured as being 10 micrometers long. How many of these bacteria could be placed end to end in a space of 1 millimeter?
(1) 10
(2) 100
(3) 500
(4) 1000

_____ 2. In a compound microscope, which combination of eyepiece and objective will give the largest field of vision?
(1) 5X eyepiece, 10X objective
(2) 5X eyepiece, 44X objective
(3) 6X eyepiece, 10X objective
(4) 6X eyepiece, 40X objective

_____ 3. In question 2, which combination will give the largest image of a specimen?

_____ 4. A microscope has a 10X eyepiece and a 10X and a 40X objective. The measured diameter of its low-power field is 1200 micrometers. The diameter of its high-power field is:
(1) 120 micrometers
(2) 12,000 micrometers
(3) 300 micrometers
(4) 400 micrometers

_____ 5. The accompanying diagram represents the field of view of a microscope under high power. The diameter of the field is 0.5 millimeter. What is the approximate diameter of each circle shown within the field?
(1) 1000 micrometers
(2) 800 micrometers
(3) 250 micrometers
(4) 25 micrometers

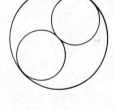

_____ 6. The diagram represents a field of view through a compound light microscope. What is the approximate length of the organism in the field of view?
(1) 60 micrometers
(2) 120 micrometers
(3) 600 micrometers
(4) 1000 micrometers

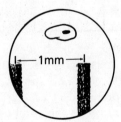

_____ 7. The diagram represents the field of vision of a microscope. What is the approximate diameter of the cell shown in this field?
(1) 50 micrometers
(2) 500 micrometers
(3) 1000 micrometers
(4) 2000 micrometers

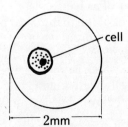

Base your answers to questions 8 and 9 on the diagram and information below and on your knowledge of biology.

A measuring device has been placed across the middle of the field of view of a microscope. When using the low-power objective (10X) with a 10X eyepiece, one can see a row of cells as shown in the diagram.

_____ 8. What is the average cell length?
(1) 100 micrometers
(2) 200 micrometers
(3) 400 micrometers
(4) 1000 micrometers

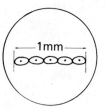

_____ 9. Approximately how many cells could be seen if the high-power objective (40X) were used?
(1) 1
(2) 0
(3) 5
(4) 10

_____ 10. A microscope has a 10X low-power objective and a 40X high-power objective with a 10X ocular (eyepiece). A slide showing evenly distributed red blood cells is examined under low power and 320 cells are observed. If you turn the nosepiece to high power, you should be able to observe approximately:
(1) 20 cells
(2) 320 cells
(3) 640 cells
(4) 1280 cells

SKILL 11: Prepare wet mounts of plant and animal cells, and apply staining techniques using iodine or methylene blue.

SKILL 12: Identify cell parts under the compound microscope, such as the nucleus, cytoplasm, chloroplasts, and cell wall.

The basic technique of preparing a wet mount is covered in Lab 1 (Part II). Labs 6 and 7 include techniques for mounting, staining, and observing several kinds of cells.

Preparation of a Wet Mount

One of the best ways to examine plant and animal cells with the microscope is by making temporary slides called *wet mounts*. In this type of slide the specimen is prepared in water. The following is a procedure for preparing a wet mount.
1. With a medicine dropper, place a drop of water in the center of a clean slide.
2. Place a tiny amount of the material to be studied in the center of the drop of water.
3. Place one edge of a clean cover slip against the edge of the drop of water. Support the opposite edge of the cover slip with a dissecting needle or your fingers and slowly lower it until it lies

flat (Figure 11). This technique minimizes the number of air bubbles in the wet mount. If air bubbles are present, push them out by gently pressing on the cover slip with the back of the dissecting needle or with an eraser. Any water on the top of the cover slip can be absorbed with pieces of paper toweling.
4. Place the slide on the stage of the microscope and examine it under low power. Then carefully observe it under high power. Do not tilt the stage of your microscope as the cover slip might then slide off the mount.
5. Because the water in the wet mount evaporates, it must be periodically replenished. This is accomplished by adding, with a medicine dropper, a drop or two of water to the edge of the cover slip.

Staining a Wet Mount

Although living protozoa, plant cells, and animal cells may be examined in wet mounts in the natural state, stains such as Lugol's iodine solution and methylene blue help us to see more specific details of cell structure. To stain a wet mount, place a small drop of stain at one edge of

Review of Laboratory Skills (continued)

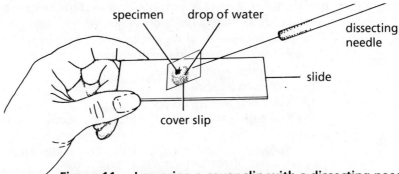

Figure 11. Lowering a cover slip with a dissecting needle

the cover slip. Then draw the stain under the cover slip by touching a piece of paper towel to the opposite edge.

Most dyes, such as Lugol's iodine solution, kill the cells they stain almost immediately. On the other hand, *vital stains*, such as dilute methylene blue, bring out structural details without killing the cells. Even after a vital stain is absorbed, the cells continue to carry on their life activities.

Typical Wet Mounts

Onion epidermis. Using forceps or your fingernail, peel off the thin membrane that lines the inside of the leaves of an onion. Place a small piece of this membrane in a drop of water on a slide and apply a cover slip. Without stain, little else but the cell wall, the rectangular shape of the cells, and possibly the nucleus can be seen in the colorless cells (Figure 12-A). By drawing a drop of stain, such as Lugol's iodine solution, under the cover slip, the following structures can be clearly seen in each cell: nucleus, nucleoli, vacuole, cytoplasm, and cell wall (Figure 12-B).

A) UNSTAINED

B) STAINED

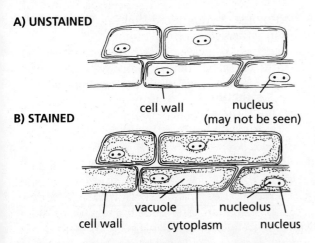

cell wall   nucleus
                   (may not be seen)

vacuole   nucleolus
cell wall   cytoplasm   nucleus

Figure 12. Structures visible in onion cells before staining and after staining

Elodea (leaf cells). Elodea, a water plant, is commonly used in aquariums. Its thin leaves usually are two cell layers thick. If a wet mount made of a young leaf taken from near the growing tip is examined under the microscope, the cell wall, cytoplasm, and chloroplasts can be identified in the unstained cells. Sometimes in the living, unstained cells the chloroplasts can be seen moving in the flowing cytoplasm. If a stain, such as Lugol's iodine, is added to the wet mount, the nucleus, nucleoli, and vacuoles can clearly be identified in the dead cells. See Figure 13.

nucleus
nucleolus   vacuole

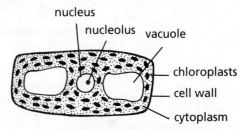

chloroplasts
cell wall
cytoplasm

Figure 13. Structures visible in an elodea cell after staining

Cork cells. When dead cork cells are examined in a wet mount, only the cell walls can be seen.

Cheek (epithelial) cells. Epithelial cells can be observed in scrapings obtained with a toothpick from the inside of the cheek. The scrapings are spread in a drop of stain (Lugol's iodine solution or methylene blue stain) on a slide. Under the microscope the nucleus, granular cytoplasm, and cell membrane of these flat cells can be seen. See Figure 14.

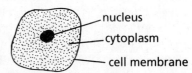

nucleus
cytoplasm
cell membrane

Figure 14. Stained epithelial cell from human cheek

Questions on Preparing Wet Mounts and Staining and Identifying Cell Structures (Skills 11 and 12)

_____ 1. You are observing a wet mount of a paramecium culture under low power of a compound microscope. After a time you notice that the range of movement of the organisms is shrinking toward the center of the mount. What should you do to restore the activity of the organisms?
(1) Add a drop of vital stain.
(2) Switch to high power.
(3) Use a brighter light source.
(4) Add a drop of water to the edge of the cover slip.

_____ 2. To stain onion skin cells for observation in a wet mount, you should:
(1) apply stain to the edge of the cover slip and draw it in with a paper towel touched to the opposite edge.
(2) dip the onion skin in the stain before mounting it
(3) wash the slide with stain before making the mount
(4) lift the cover slip with a dissecting needle and drop some stain on the onion skin after mounting it.

_____ 3. A student makes a wet mount of onion epidermis cells. When the cells are viewed under the microscope, little cellular detail can be seen. To make more cellular detail visible, the student should add to the slide a drop of:
(1) methylene blue
(2) bromthymol blue
(3) litmus
(4) Benedict's solution

4. The diagram shows the structures that can be observed in stained onion epidermis cells with a light microscope.

(a) List and identify the numbered structures that can also be seen in the unstained cells.

(b) List and identify the numbered structures that are made visible by the stain.

(a) _____

(b) _____

5. The following is a list of cell structures:

(1) cell membrane	(4) nucleoli	(7) chloroplasts
(2) cell wall	(5) cytoplasm	(8) mitochondria
(3) nucleus	(6) large vacuoles	(9) ribosomes

For each of the following specimens, list the numbers of the cell structures that can be seen with a light microscope.

(a) Stained cheek cells _____

(b) Unstained elodea cells _____

(c) Stained elodea cells _____

(d) Cork cells _____

Review of Laboratory Skills (continued)

SKILL 13: Use and interpret indicators such as pH paper, Benedict's (Fehling's) solution, iodine (Lugol's) solution, and bromthymol blue.

Indicators are valuable to the biologist because they demonstrate the presence, absence, or concentration of a substance by means of a characteristic color change. Biologists commonly use pH indicators for acids and bases, and indicators or tests for such biologically important compounds as simple sugars, starch, and proteins.

The following section summarizes several indicators and testing techniques with which you should be familiar.

pH Indicators

Generally speaking, a pH indicator is a substance that has one color in an acidic solution and another in a basic solution. Actually, the color change does not occur suddenly as the pH passes through 7 (neutrality). The color changes gradually over a particular pH range, which may be mostly on the acidic side of 7, mostly on the basic side, or spread equally on both sides of the neutral point. The choice of an indicator for a particular investigation may depend on its pH range.

Litmus paper is a very common pH indicator that is red in acidic solutions and blue in basic solutions. Its pH range is rather broad—from about 5 to about 8. It is not very useful for detecting slight degrees of acidity or alkalinity. It is, however, simple to use and very handy for quickly determining whether a solution is acidic or basic.

Bromthymol blue is yellow in acidic solutions and blue in basic solutions. The color change occurs in a fairly narrow range, from 6.0 on the acidic side to 7.6 on the basic side. It is very useful for detecting a slightly acidic solution, such as the carbonic acid formed when carbon dioxide dissolves in water. Bromthymol blue is therefore often used to indicate the presence or absence of carbon dioxide in a solution.

When one exhales through a straw into a bromthymol blue solution, the carbon dioxide in the exhaled air causes the indicator to turn yellow. If an elodea plant is placed in a tube of this yellow bromthymol blue solution and the tube is exposed to light, the indicator will gradually turn blue. This color change is evidence that the elodea plant used the carbon dioxide for photo-synthesis. Bromthymol blue is often used in experiments to demonstrate the consumption of carbon dioxide by plants during photosynthesis and the production of carbon dioxide by plants and animals during respiration.

Although litmus paper and bromthymol blue tell us whether a solution is acidic or basic, they do not tell us the actual pH of a solution. To determine pH values, pH paper or a pH meter can be used.

Hydrion paper or **pH paper** is often used in the laboratory to measure the pH of a solution. At each pH value, pH paper turns a different color. To find the pH of a solution, a drop of the substance is placed on the pH paper. Then the color of the pH paper is compared with the colors on a printed chart to find the pH value it indicates.

Indicators for Biologically Important Compounds

A frequent problem in biological investigations is that of determining what chemical compounds are present in a particular tissue, material, or solution. A number of tests have been developed for indicating the presence of certain classes of compounds. The biology student should be familiar with the tests for the major nutrients—simple sugars, starch, proteins, and fats and oils.

Test for simple sugars. To test for a simple sugar, such as glucose or fructose, add *Benedict's* (or *Fehling's*) *solution* to the sample and heat to boiling in a water bath for a few minutes. A simple sugar is present if the blue solution changes to a green, yellow, orange, or brick red color. If the blue color of the Benedict's solution remains, then the substance being tested does not contain a simple sugar.

Test for starch. To test for the presence of starch, add a few drops of an iodine solution (*e.g., Lugol's solution*) to the sample. The appearance of the blue-black color in the sample indicates the presence of starch. No color change indicates that starch is not present in the substance being tested.

Tests for proteins. *Xanthoproteic test.* To test for the presence of protein, place the substance being tested in concentrated *nitric acid*. If proteins are present, a yellow color develops on the substance. *Biuret Test.* To test for the presence of protein, mix the sample with colorless

415

biuret reagent. The appearance of a pink or purple color in the biuret solution indicates the presence of protein.

Test for fats and oils. To test for fats or oils, rub the sample on brown paper from a paper bag. Allow the paper to dry in a warm place. Hold the paper to the light. The presence of a translucent spot through which light can pass indicates the presence of fats or oils. *Note:* Any spots that are caused by water will dry in a short time and disappear.

The chemical substance called Sudan III can be used as a test for oil. A small quantity of the powder placed in oil will dissolve.

Questions on Indicators and Chemical Tests (Skill 13)

_____ 1. An acid-base indicator that is easy to use, but relatively insensitive, is:
(1) methylene blue
(2) bromthymol blue
(3) Lugol's solution
(4) litmus

_____ 2. When a person exhales into a solution of bromthymol blue, the solution changes color because:
(1) bromthymol blue reacts with oxygen
(2) the carbon dioxide in the exhaled air produces a slightly acid solution
(3) exhaled air is warm and moist
(4) the hydrogen ion concentration in the solution decreases

Base your answers to questions 3 through 5 on the following experimental procedure and on your knowledge of biology.

Step 1. A student exhales into a solution of bromthymol blue.
Step 2. A small plant is placed in the solution and exposed to light for several hours.

_____ 3. As the result of Step 1, the color of the solution:
(1) changes from blue to yellow
(2) changes from yellow to blue
(3) changes from blue to yellow and then back to blue
(4) does not change

_____ 4. As the result of Step 2, the color of the solution:
(1) changes from blue to yellow
(2) changes from yellow to blue
(3) changes from blue to yellow and then back to blue
(4) does not change

_____ 5. A conclusion that may reasonably be drawn from the results of this experiment is that during Step 2 the plant:
(1) absorbed bromthymol blue
(2) absorbed oxygen
(3) absorbed carbon dioxide
(4) did not carry on respiration

For questions 6 through 9, select the number of the item in the following list that best completes the statement.

(1) Benedict's solution
(2) Lugol's solution
(3) biuret solution
(4) none of the above

Review of Laboratory Skills (continued)

_____ 6. To identify starch in a leaf, use _____ .

_____ 7. To see if a solution contains carbon dioxide, use _____ .

_____ 8. To determine the presence of glucose in a solution, use _____ .

_____ 9. To test for the presence of protein in a food, use _____ .

_____ 10. A sample of food is placed in Benedict's solution and the mixture is heated to boiling. After boiling for a time, the solution is blue. It can be concluded that:
(1) starch is present
(2) starch is not present
(3) a simple sugar is present
(4) a simple sugar is not present

SKILL 14: Use and read measurement instruments, such as metric rulers, Celsius (centigrade) thermometers, and graduated cylinders.

Measuring instruments are used often in the biology laboratory. Here are some basic facts that you should know about the use of these instruments.

The Metric Ruler

On a metric ruler, the numbered scale markings are centimeter marks. Each centimeter is usually divided into millimeters, with the fifth millimeter mark somewhat longer than the others. Remember that there are 10 millimeters in 1 centimeter and 100 centimeters in 1 meter. A meter stick is a metric ruler that is 1 meter, or 100 centimeters, long. Smaller rules, 15 cm or 30 cm long, are more convenient for the most common measurements in the laboratory.

Measurements with a metric ruler are made to the nearest millimeter. It is not practical to try to estimate fractions of a millimeter with the naked eye. The length of the object in Figure 15 would be reported as 6.7 cm.

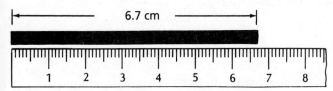

Figure 15. **Using a centimeter ruler.** Each small division is 1mm. The length of the object is 6.7cm or 67mm.

On some rulers, the left edge is the zero mark. It is often difficult to line up the zero of such a ruler with the end of an object being measured. The ruler may also be worn or rounded at the corners, adding to the difficulty of making an accurate measurement. In such cases, greater accuracy can be obtained by measuring from one of the numbered centimeter marks, instead of from the zero end. You must of course remember to subtract the starting point from the reading of the scale. Figure 16 shows a metric ruler being used in this way.

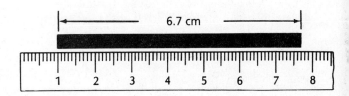

Figure 16. **Measuring from the 1-cm mark.** The length of the object is 7.7 − 1.0 = 6.7cm

The Celsius Thermometer

The unit of measurement of temperature in the SI system is the Celsius degree, formerly called the centigrade degree. On the Celsius scale, 0° C is the freezing point of water and 100° C is the boiling point of water. There are 100 degrees between the freezing point and the boiling point of water on the Celsius scale. The Celsius thermometer commonly used in the laboratory has a temperature range of −20° C to 100° C. The smallest division or mark represents a single degree. Starting from 0° C, every tenth degree mark is longer and is numbered in tens, for example, 10° C, 20° C, 30° C. Those divisions

417

below 0° C are read as negative (*e.g.*, −8° C) and those divisions above 0° C are read as positive (*e.g.*, +25° C). Usually the plus symbol is understood and is omitted. Measurements to the nearest degree are usually precise enough for biological experiments. See Figure 17.

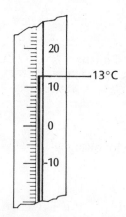

Figure 17.   Portion of Celsius thermometer. The temperature reading is 13° C.

Graduated Cylinders

The unit of volume in the SI system is the liter (symbol, l or L). In the biology laboratory the most commonly used unit of volume is the milliliter (symbol ml or mL). One milliliter is equal to 1/1000 liter, that is, 1000 mL equals one liter.

One of the commonly used instruments for measuring the volume of a liquid in the laboratory is the graduated cylinder. Graduated cylinders come in a variety of sizes. It is best to use a size that is appropriate for the volume of liquid to be measured. You can measure a volume of 6 mL much more precisely in a 10-mL graduated cylinder than in a 100-mL or 500-mL cylinder.

When water, or liquids like water that "wet" glass, are placed in a graduated cylinder, the liquid rises up along the sides of the cylinder (Figure 18). The curved surface of the liquid is called a *meniscus*. When reading the scale, read the bottom of the meniscus. (In the case of mercury and other liquids that do not wet glass, the meniscus curves the other way. You then read the top of the meniscus.) When making readings, it is important that the eye be at the proper level. Figure 18 shows the correct line of sight for viewing a meniscus. The bottom of the meniscus is also read when reading the volume of liquid in a pipette or burette.

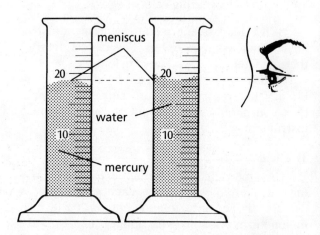

Figure 18.   Reading a graduated cylinder. The volume in each case is 19 mL.

Questions on Measurement Instruments (Skill 14)

_____ **1.** The diagram below represents a centimeter ruler. What is the length of the line?
(1) 4.2 mm
(2) 42 mm
(3) 420 mm
(4) 42 cm

_____ **2.** The diagram at left represents a portion of a 10-mL graduated cylinder. What is the volume of the liquid in the cylinder?
(1) 3.4 mL
(2) 3.3 mL
(3) 3.2 mL
(4) 2.8 mL

_____ **3.** The diagram at right represents a portion of a Celsius thermometer. What is the temperature indicated on the thermometer?
(1) 66° C
(2) 59° C
(3) 54° C
(4) 50° C

Review of Laboratory Skills (continued)

SKILL 15: Dissect plant and animal specimens for the purpose of exposing major structures for suitable examination.

It is not possible to summarize in a few paragraphs the procedures and observations of the many dissections that you may have performed. You should review them now. Labs 33, 46–50, and 52–55 are the main dissection labs in this book.

SKILL 16: Demonstrate safety skills involved in heating materials in test tubes or beakers, use of chemicals, and handling of dissection instruments.

General safety precautions and techniques are described on pages v and vi. Specific safety measures are highlighted wherever necessary in the individual labs. The following questions will test your awareness of some of these important principles of safety in the laboratory.

Questions on Safety (Skill 16)

_____ 1. When heating a test tube containing a liquid, which of the following is a dangerous procedure?
(1) wearing safety goggles
(2) using a metal test tube holder
(3) wearing a laboratory apron
(4) watching through the open end of the test tube for any possible chemical reaction

_____ 2. In the laboratory, which of the following is NOT recommended?
(1) wearing loose clothing
(2) having your setup checked by the teacher before starting a procedure
(3) reading the instructions through to the end before starting an investigation
(4) being familiar with the location and use of emergency equipment

_____ 3. If you should accidentally spill an acid on the table, the first thing you should do is:
(1) report the spill to the teacher or lab assistant
(2) pour water over it
(3) allow it to evaporate
(4) put on your safety goggles

_____ 4. Which of the following is least likely to be dangerous?
(1) using an open flame near a flammable liquid
(2) touching the preservative in which a dissection specimen is stored
(3) playing "practical jokes" in the laboratory
(4) using dissection instruments